J. M. MACSWEEN

Warfare in the
Ancient World

WARFARE IN THE
ANCIENT WORLD

Richard Humble

Book Club Associates London

For my family

First published in 1980 by Guild Publishing
the Original Publications Department of
Book Club Associates

Designed by Graham Keen

Set in 12/12 Garamond 156
and printed by W & J Mackay Limited, Chatham

Whilst every reasonable effort has been made to find the copyright
owners of the illustrations in this book the publishers apologize to any
that they have been unable to trace and will insert an acknowledgment
in future editions upon notification of the fact

FRONTISPIECE: *Alexander at the Battle of Issus. (Sonia Halliday)*
ENDPAPERS: *Phoenicians bringing tribute.* (British Museum)

Contents

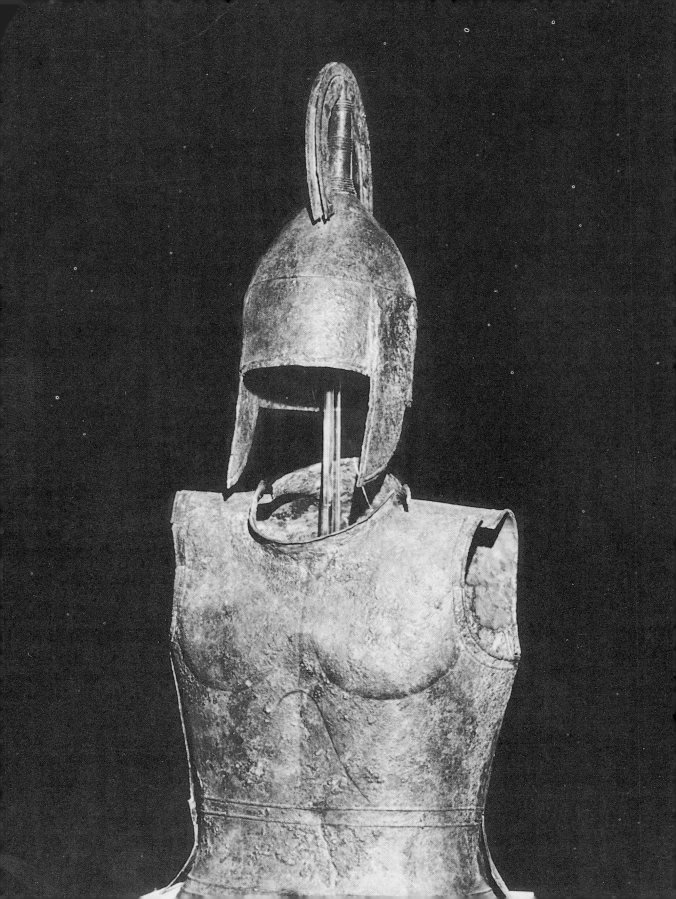

INTRODUCTION

The Ancient Art of War

For the purposes of this book, the 'ancient' period is defined as the period between the earliest dominant civilizations of the third millennium BC and the collapse of the western Roman Empire in the fifth century AD. This tremendous span of some 3,500 years is constantly being pushed further and further back into what was once prehistory by archaeological discoveries, but it is still possible to make a start with the first known *armies* – in Mesopotamia and Egypt – of the third millennium BC. Concentrating as it does on warfare, this book cannot pretend to be anything more than a specialized introduction to the ancient world.

Apologies are due to oriental readers: the military histories of India, South East Asia, China, Korea, and Japan have been omitted only for the sake of brevity, certainly not because they are lacking in interest. Also for the sake of brevity (because of the extensive arguments involved on each side), this book follows the 'traditional' time-structure of ancient history which accepts Manetho's outline of Egyptian chronology (Old, Middle, and New Kingdoms, thirty dynasties in all, c. 3100–343 BC).

For nearly half the ancient period, the surviving written military information is depressingly slim. Almost in passing, terse chronicles refer to such amazing feats as the great Hittite march on Babylon (see p. 57) without ever providing such details as the number of troops involved, difficulties in planning and executing the operation, or casualties suffered. Even when the first real historians appear on the scene in the fifth century BC, their invaluable testimony is often questionable on points of military detail. A good example is Herodotus, the Greek 'Father of History'. His indispensable coverage of the rise and defeat of the Persian Empire is full of vivid stories which have entertained his readers down the ages. But Herodotus was no soldier, nor was he writing military history. He could talk of a Persian army of over a million strong without realizing that his troop strengths were surely wildly inflated. Even those classic military memoirs, Julius Caesar's *Commentaries*, must be read with a pinch of salt. When Caesar composed his memoirs he was thinking acutely of his political image and was quite ready to 'remember with advantages' if it suited him.

Yet despite the formidable gaps in our knowledge of the ancient world, clear-cut milestones have survived as far as the evolution of

OPPOSITE: Along with mobility and hitting-power, armoured protection was established as one of the three essential ingredients of military supremacy in the ancient world. This bronze helmet and flared or 'bell' cuirass, from the museum at Argos in southern Greece, is the oldest discovered suit of armour worn by the élite armoured infantry of the Greek city states: the hoplites

7

ancient warfare is concerned. We know what Sumerian and Egyptian soldiers looked like in the middle of the third millennium; we can point to the different ways in which Egyptians, Hittites, and Assyrians fought from chariots 1,000 years later; we have at least one specimen of armour from about the time of the Trojan War; and so on. Fragments of memorials, wall paintings and carvings, pottery decorations – even, in a few instances, models of soldiers – are invaluable supplements to the surviving weapons, armour, and written records when following the early story of warfare.

And what a story it is – far removed from the popular misconception that warfare in the age of the spear and sword was somehow more romantic than the modern age of the battle tank, flamethrower, and stand-off bomb. The Assyrians were a byword for calculated ferocity. Hannibal and his Roman victor Scipio used tactics as deadly as a nuclear strike. The Israelite invaders of Canaan practised cold-blooded genocide on their captives. And the Roman capture of Jerusalem in AD 70 was attended by scenes of horror surpassing the Nazi destruction of the Warsaw Ghetto in 1943. The ancients knew all about 'total war'.

Their great captains set standards of achievement against which military commanders have never ceased to match themselves, usually in vain. Sargon 'The Great' was the first recorded commoner to make himself king in a *coup d'état* and set out to build a world empire on military conquest. Cyrus of Persia, waging war with the delicacy of a surgeon, founded the mighty Persian Empire with the minimum of destruction. Themistocles of Athens, leading his countrymen against the invading Persians on land and sea, encouraged his people to win through to victory when all had seemed lost – the Churchill of the fifth century BC. Philip of Macedon built a military machine against which no other power could stand, and under the inspired leadership of his son Alexander it rolled unchecked from the Dardanelles to India. And in the long death-struggle between Rome and Carthage the careers of Hannibal and Scipio eerily anticipated the confrontation between Napoleon and Wellington.

The efforts made to capture objectives were often prodigious. Both Alexander the Great's causeway at Tyre (see p. 178) and Flavius Silva's mighty siege ramp at Masada (p. 231) are still there. The Persians and Romans built thousands of miles of roads for speeding the movements of armies, anticipating Hitler's *autobahnen* by 2,000 years. Ancient warfare developed the art of the close blockade and siege-craft, siege and field artillery, incendiary missiles (including a primitive flamethrower – see p. 150), and field engineering of the highest order. The Greeks became masters of amphibious warfare. After the Assyrians had pioneered the art of fighting on horseback, succeeding military supremacies learned the deadly effect of cavalry operating independently, yet in overall harmony with the efforts of the foot soldiers – the essence of the armour/infantry collaboration of modern warfare. And just as modern-day scientists have their brain-power pressed into service to support the efforts of the fighting men, so the ingenuity of the philosopher Archimedes helped keep the Romans out of Syracuse during the long siege of 214–211 BC.

To the victor, the spoils — in this case the sacred emblems from the Temple in Jerusalem, looted by the Romans in AD 70 after a murderous siege, and depicted on the Arch of Titus in Rome

The enormous time-span of the ancient period can be daunting. But it helps to point out the long-term causes of the rise and fall of kingdoms and empires. One common factor is that none of those vanished supremacies came or went by peaceful means. They were all the products or the victims of war. And their story is well provided with lessons for a world still armed to the teeth, though shrinking from the horrors of a nuclear war. No peoples who have ever looked for soft options to military preparedness — both in the will to survive and the provision of up-to-date weaponry — have held out for long against the ambitions of militant neighbours. The glib claim of the modern age that 'violence never settles anything' would surely provoke the most bitter mirth among the ghosts of ancient Babylon, Nineveh, Mycenae, Troy, Carthage, and Rome.

War, organized war, is not a human instinct. It is a highly planned and co-operative form of theft. And that form of theft began ten thousand years ago when the harvesters of wheat accumulated a surplus, and the nomads rose out of the desert to rob them of what they themselves could not provide.

So argues Dr Bronowski in *The Ascent of Man*, but it seems a little hard. After all, lacking horns, tusks, fangs, claws, or a tough protective hide, the ability to burrow out of danger, fly, or outpace the fastest predator, primitive man was naturally thrown back on artificial aids. He learned to pick up rocks and throw them accurately, and to smite with clubs; he moved on to fashion spears and bows and arrows. Whether hunting for food or defending himself against predatory beasts, he also learned that teamwork in stalking and ambushing yielded much better results than individual action. In short, organization and weapons gave him, to use the lofty language of *Genesis*, 'dominion over the fish of the sea, and over the birds of the air, and over the cattle, and over all the earth, and over every creeping thing that creeps upon the earth'. But there was one setback: it also applied to his fellow man. When the first prehistoric tribe discovered that organization and weapons could eliminate danger from rival tribes — that, surely, was when war was born.

After thousands of years of recurrent conflict, 'civilized' man emerged with his mind programmed for war. The retreat of the ice, the coming of warmer climates, a growing dependence on agriculture as well as hunting, all failed to erase the programme. Now indeed the prize was the best pasture and ploughland, drawing hungry nomads like a magnet. When not directly menaced by hostile 'have-not' aliens, the growing city-civilizations which grew up in the fertile plains bickered and fought each other over their conflicting spheres of influence.

Such is the story told by the earliest written records, dating from the third millennium BC and relating to the cities of Sumer, between the lower reaches of the Rivers Tigris and Euphrates — the Biblical 'land of Shinar'.

PART ONE

From Sargon the Great to Cyrus

CHAPTER ONE

Mesopotamia and Assyria

THE EARLIEST SUMERIAN RECORDS from Mesopotamia include a wealth of myth and legend, honouring gods and heroes, ordeal and triumph, great feats of strength when the world was young. And they also show that it was already a world in which war was an accepted part of human existence. Ninurta was the god of war, Ishtar was the goddess of war, and prowess in arms was an essential attribute for any leader of men on earth. Foremost among the stories of this heroic age is the epic of Gilgamesh, 'two-thirds god and one-third man', King of the Sumerian city of Uruk ('Erech' in the Old Testament).

A remote and legendary figure from the very dawn of history, Gilgamesh and his deeds seem disturbingly familiar. Gilgamesh, in fact, is the archetypal hero, the blueprint for Hercules, Jason, Aeneas, Romulus, Siegfried, and a host of other worthies extending without any real break down the ages to the Christian Beowulf and the Viking era. Among his other virtues Gilgamesh is, of course, a mighty warrior; and passages from the epic in praise of his military skills bear startling witness to the sophistication achieved in warfare and weaponry by about 2500 BC.

Enkidu, friend and companion of Gilgamesh, hails his hero as warlord:

The father of the gods has given you kingship, such is your destiny, everlasting life is not your destiny . . . He has given you unexampled supremacy over the people, victory in battle from which no fugitive returns, in forays and assaults from which there is no going back.

One obvious answer to the formidable mud-brick walls of Sumerian cities had already been developed:

It is not an equal struggle when one fights with Humbaba; he is a great warrior, a battering-ram.

The axe, the sword and the bow were familiar weapons of war, custom-built to the requirements of major warriors:

He went to the forge and said 'I will give orders to the armourers; they shall cast

13

us our weapons while we watch them'. So they gave orders to the armourers and the craftsmen sat down in conference. They went into the groves of the plain and cut willow and box-wood; they cast for them axes of nine score pounds, and great swords they cast with blades of six score pounds each one, with pommels and hilts of thirty pounds. They cast for Gilgamesh the axe 'Might of Heroes' and the bow of Anshan; and Gilgamesh was armed and Enkidu; and the weight of the arms they carried was thirty score pounds.

They brought to them the weapons, they put in their hands the great swords in their golden scabbards, and the bow and the quiver. Gilgamesh took the axe, he slung the quiver from his shoulder, and the bow of Anshan, and buckled the sword to his belt; and so they were armed and ready for the journey.

The age-old struggle between weapons and protection was already well advanced and body armour was part of a Sumerian hero's war gear:

Gilgamesh heard him; he put on his breastplate, 'The Voice of Heroes', of thirty shekels' weight; he put it on as though it had been a light garment that he carried, and it covered him altogether.

A description of Gilgamesh in action shows that Sumerian warriors often fought with a weapon in each hand — rapier-and-dagger style — and, as a bonus, it adds the throwing-spear or javelin to the Sumerian armoury:

He took his axe in his hand, and his dagger from his belt. He crept forward and he fell on them like a javelin.

The demand for mobility on the battlefield had brought forth the war chariot, which was drawn by mules, while other mounted warriors bestrode 'the stallion magnificent in battle'. Trying in vain to seduce Gilgamesh, the war goddess Ishtar offers this bribe:

I will harness for you a chariot of lapis lazuli and of gold, with wheels of gold and horns of copper; and you shall have mighty demons of the storm for your draft-mules . . . Kings, rulers, and princes will bow down before you, they shall bring you tribute from the mountains and the plain.

And when Gilgamesh laments the death of the faithful Enkidu he does not omit Enkidu's military virtues:

O Enkidu, my brother,
You were the axe at my side,
My hand's strength, the sword in my belt,
The shield before me . . .
The warriors of strong-walled Uruk
Weep for you.

The Gilgamesh epic therefore provides a comprehensive survey of the weapons familiar to Sumerians by the middle of the third millennium BC. The *axe*, a light, one-handed weapon, was normally carried in the

PREVIOUS PAGES: The Assyrians, heirs to the earlier empires of Sumer, Akkad, and Babylon, introduced a new technique for keeping conquered peoples subdued. This was the mass deportation of civilian populations, here carried out under the watchful eyes of Assyrian officials

Where myth and history blend; the exploits of Gilgamesh, the warrior-hero of Uruk in Sumer, were preserved for centuries by the Akkadian and Babylonian conquerors of Sumer. Here Gilgamesh is shown fighting a lion and crossing the waters of death – two scenes from the hero's life, depicted on a cylinder-seal dating from the time of Sargon the Great

belt. The *dagger*, also carried in the belt, was used for in-fighting, often as an adjunct to the axe carried in the other hand. The *sword* was clearly of the long or broadsword type, suitable for thrusting or cutting, with the weight of the blade counterbalanced by a heavy pommel. Given the craftsmanship required for casting and balancing, the sword was clearly a weapon reserved for kings and heroes. (The casting of Gilgamesh's sword is a vivid anticipation of the weapons made for the Greek heroes, described in equal detail by Homer.)

The status of the *bow* in the Gilgamesh epic is particularly interesting. This, too, was a specialist weapon, fit for heroes – a highly significant beginning to the strange, erratic story of the use of the bow in war. Reserved for the ruling *élite*, the bow was never to become the dominant weapon of Sumerian armies. The *war chariot* was also reserved for the great, though Gilgamesh is always described as fighting on foot. References to chariots in the epic invest the vehicle with the role of the victor's triumphal car. The only form of *armour* mentioned is the *breastplate* – like the bow, a custom-built heirloom dignified with a resounding name. The *shield* is not mentioned as part of the hero's war-gear, but the reference to Enkidu as 'the shield before me' establishes its existence and suggests that warriors of high rank went into action accompanied by a shield-bearer.

The Gilgamesh epic therefore paints a dim background of the wars between the cities of the Mesopotamian plain – wars in which the city's ultimate defence was its walls, and in which the ultimate menace to the walls was the *battering-ram*. Against this shadowy background the exploits of the heroes stand out in sharp relief, exactly like those of the Greek and Trojan heroes in Homer's *Iliad* (see pp. 100–104).

FROM LEGEND TO REALITY: THE WARS OF SUMER

The Sumerians seem to have begun as 'have-not' invaders who came down from Persia into lower Mesopotamia in the fourth millennium BC. The mud of the river plains provided the material for the inscribed writing which they perfected and the bricks for the cities which they raised: the 'strong-walled Uruk' of Gilgamesh, Kish, Shuruppak, Ur, Lagash, Larsa, and Umma – the precursors and eventual subjects of Babylon.

The narrow orbits of the city-states were in constant collision for predominantly economic reasons: the Mesopotamian plain harboured neither common metals nor hard timber, let alone gold or jewels. These had to be fought for. Gilgamesh himself, as hero-king of Uruk, had made an expedition to the cedar mountain of Humbaba, destroyed its guardian, and felled the cedars — and he had embarked on this exploit, as the epic makes quite clear, as much for glory as for material profit. 'I have not established my name stamped on bricks as my destiny decreed; therefore I will go to the country where the cedar is felled', vows the hero.

The *lugal* (king) or *patesi* (governor) of a Sumerian city owed his elevation to proven military ability: he was the father of his people and their defender in times of crisis. When not actually fighting off the menace of outright conquest, he knew that his rivals would edge him out of the trade in all vital raw materials if he let them. Conversely, if he could subdue enough rivals in battle he would be able to secure all the imports he needed: cedar and ebony down the great rivers, and copper, tin and bullion overland from the wild lands to the west, north and east. With these material prizes at stake and military glory accepted as one of the most important trappings of power, no Sumerian city could live at peace for long.

By around 2500 BC the heroic life and times of Gilgamesh were deeply embedded in legend, and the wars of the city-states were throwing up a rapid succession of short-lived supremacies: first Kish, then Ur, then Lagash, then Umma. Two splendid archaeological finds provide a vivid glimpse of what Sumerian armies of the time looked like. These are the colourful mosaic known as the 'Standard', from Ur; and the fragmentary war memorial known as the 'Stele of the Vultures', from Lagash. Both do full justice to the men who never qualified for a detailed mention in the Gilgamesh epic: the rank-and-file infantry of the Sumerian armies.

The 'Standard of Ur' shows an army of helmeted spearmen in battle formation accompanied by spearmen in heavy war chariots, advancing to victory over the bodies of the slain and finally leading off a column of prisoners. The helmets are close-fitting 'pixie-caps', secured by chin-straps, and the main weapon is obviously a thrusting-spear. If any secondary weapons are carried in the belt, these are concealed by the calf-length cloaks worn by the troops, fastened at the neck but falling open to give the arms full play. The tunic worn under the cloaks ends at thigh-level in a fringe of 'tails', which may have been stiffened to afford protection for the groin.

These simple infantrymen are holding a close formation, though not shoulder-to-shoulder, and advance with spears levelled, held in both hands to present a bristling hedge. The long cloaks clearly give their wearers considerable protection, but the troops are barefoot. The spearmen of the battle line are in marked contrast to the group of guardsmen surrounding the king at the top of the 'Standard'. These wear the same helmets and fringed tunics as the spearmen, but instead of the cloak they wear what appears to be an ornate 'plaid' draped over the left shoulder. The guardsmen stand at 'attention' with the butts of their spears on the ground, and they carry light axes in the right hand.

The Ur 'Standard', one of the earliest-known depictions of an army in battle array: light spearmen, chariot troops, and elite guards flanking the king

The war chariots shown on the Ur 'Standard' are massive, 'boxy' affairs running on four wheels, the wheels being made of two jointed semicircles of solid wood. Jutting forward from the front of the chariot is an angled receptacle holding a sheaf of spears or javelins. The chariot crews consist of a driver and a spearman, both helmeted and wearing the plaid over the left shoulder; the chariot spearmen are shown with spears brandished for throwing. The teams consist of four mules harnessed abreast; the artist has emphasized their ears and tails as if to stress that they *are* mules.

The obvious tactic for such an army would be a concerted attack by the chariots, raining down spears on the enemy infantry and sending in the main formation of spearmen to deliver the *coup de grâce*. The chariots could then take up the running to pursue the retreating enemy, as shown at the bottom of the 'Standard'. Infantry of the type shown on the Ur 'Standard' would have no protection against such an attack; but the 'second generation' of Sumerian infantry, as shown on the 'Stele of the Vultures' depicting the army of Lagash, tells a very different story.

The 'Stele of the Vultures' is a victory monument in honour of a war between Lagash and its nearest rival, Umma. The Stele shows Eannatum, the *patesi* or governor of Lagash, leading his troops into battle over a carpet of enemy dead and finally riding in triumph in his chariot, with his soldiers marching in column behind. Like the troops on the Ur 'Standard', these are spearmen – but spearmen of a very advanced type. Their spears are much longer and they advance in tight formation, packed shoulder to shoulder behind a wall of deep rectangular shields. The troops wear the same close-fitting helmet as the spearmen of Ur, but no cloak; the big shields cover the whole of the body and are studded with rows of broad discs. Unlike the helmets, which may have been leather, these shield-discs were almost certainly of bronze, and would have had a dual purpose. They must have given the shield-wall a most menacing appearance, making it glitter in the sun like a huge reptile's scales; and, if convex, they would have helped to throw off enemy weapons. As shown in the bottom section of the Stele, 'battledress' consisted of a calf-length kilt of fleece or hide, with the plaid slung over the left shoulder.

To judge from the prominence given it in Eannatum's monument, this spear-and-shield wall – the first appearance of the *phalanx* of heavy infantry which the Macedonians were to bring to perfection 2,000 years later – was a Sumerian army's trump card, the product of much drill and a fearsome weapon against shaky enemy forces. When the shield-walls of two rival armies clashed, the effect must have been very like a scrum in Rugby football. The side which kept the closest formation and shoved hardest would win; the side which had just a few front-rank soldiers toppled off balance would fall apart like a row of dominoes.

Unlike the Ur 'Standard', the 'Stele of the Vultures' is an incomplete fragment and we do not know what the full battle array of Eannatum's army looked like. There is every chance that as well as chariots, it included light infantry of the Ur type. A hedge of pikes or long spears was certainly formidable, but not impregnable: it lacked flexibility. Fast-moving attackers, able to dodge in between the spear-points and thrust themselves down between the shafts, could wreak havoc by stabbing over the tops of the shields, or hacking with the Sumerian light axe. Such attacks could only be fought off by breaking up the shield-wall's close formation – precisely the idea of the attack. Light infantry with the nerve to press home attacks in this way could certainly break an enemy shield-wall's cohesion, or thin it out enough to make a charge by their own heavy infantry decisive. Such light infantry tactics seem to have been ideally suited to the Sumerian lust for glory through personal feats of arms; they are suggested by more than one passage in the Gilgamesh epic.

Apart from the troops, the 'Stele of the Vultures' also shows us what a Sumerian king looked like when equipped for battle. In the upper section Eannatum is shown carrying an axe in his right hand. He carries no shield, but it seems probable that the missing section of the carving would have shown a shield-bearer advancing close beside the person of his monarch. It has never been part of a commander-in-chief's duty to get himself killed unnecessarily, at the head of his troops. Good for promotion it may well be, but it usually has terrible effects on the men's morale. If Eannatum had not been a highly successful general the 'Stele of the Vultures' would never have been carved! (Eannatum was in fact killed in battle in a later war, when Umma rebelled against the rule of Lagash.)

Apart from the same kilt-and-plaid battledress worn by the troops, Eannatum wears the distinctive helmet of Sumerian royalty. This was a wig-like design with a prominent 'bun' at the back. Sir Leonard Woolley's excavations at Ur in the 1920s yielded a magnificent gold specimen of the type: a wrap-around helmet enclosing the ears in chased cavities, with overall chasing reproducing the hair-style in wonderfully fine detail. Beautiful though it is, the Ur helmet was surely for ceremonial wear only, chased gold having no more protective qualities than cardboard. Battle helmets worn by fighting royalty were most likely to be identical in pattern but of gilded bronze.

Although Eannatum carries an axe when leading his troops on foot, he is shown brandishing a long spear when riding in his chariot in the victory parade. Only the top half of the chariot has survived, but it is clearly of the massive type shown on the Ur 'Standard'. There is one provoking enigma: the sheaf of missiles carried in the chariot. These are most carefully depicted and are certainly not the long spears carried by the infantry, or of the type in Eannatum's hand. Although they are most likely to be javelins, they *could* be long arrows, though too little of the chariot has survived to show whether or not a bow was included in Eannatum's war-gear. But the surviving representation confirms the role which the war chariot was never to lose: a vehicle for spearmen or archers, a medium for mobile fire-power on the battlefield.

FROM EANNATUM TO SARGON (C.2460–2305 BC)

Light infantry spearmen; heavy infantry phalanx spearmen; war chariots – such were the basic troops of the third millennium BC in the Sumerian wars. Eannatum's triumph over Umma was short-lived; under Lugalzaggisi, Umma staged a comeback and went on to conquer not only

A Sumerian warlord leads his army into battle: Eannatum of Lagash at the head of his close-packed shield wall, spears levelled for the charge. This is the first appearance of the heavy infantry phalanx, destined to remain a dominant infantry formation until the perfection of the Roman legion

OPPOSITE: Sargon of Akkad, 'The Great', first 'world emperor' of western Asia. Note the similarity in shape between his ornate helmet and that of his Sumerian predecessor, Eannatum, which can be seen above

Lagash but Uruk as well. But Lugalzaggisi himself did not last long, for all the cities of Sumer were rapidly swallowed by a new power from the north – the Akkadian Empire of Sargon 'The Great'.

The story of Sargon's rise to power has a familiar ring. He was no ambitious princeling, but a commoner who started his career in the service of Ur-ilbaba of Kish and reached the eminence of royal cupbearer. The details of Sargon's *coup d'état* are lost; maybe he had risen further to become commander of the royal guard. If this was the case, and if Sargon owed his early prominence to the support of the troops, it would certainly help to explain the remarkable military adventures which followed. Sargon founded a new capital at Agade, or Akkad, in upper Mesopotamia and started by subduing all the cities of the northern plains before turning south to reduce the cities of Sumer. But he did not stop there. Under his leadership, for the first time, armies from the Mesopotamian plains attempted to take and hold the surrounding highlands.

Such a venture has always been a tricky military proposition. No matter how great the strength of the invaders, or their supremacy on the flat, moving into the hills means entering an alien environment. (For a modern equivalent, the advance of the 8th Army after Alamein, from

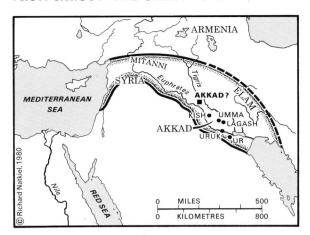

© Richard Natkiel, 1980

LEFT: The probable extent of the empire of Sargon, connecting the Mediterranean with the Persian Gulf

RIGHT: The Naramsin stele

the desert terrain of Egypt and Libya into the hill country of Tunisia, gives a good idea of the problem.) Close infantry formations are hard to maintain in broken terrain and mountain country, and no shield-wall could have been of much use against an elusive enemy who chose to rely on ambushes and hit-and-run tactics. The invader's best chance of finishing a hill campaign fairly quickly has always been to lure the hillsmen into a series of set-piece fights and kill as many of their warriors as possible each time. This guarantees the invaders a period of peace until the next generation of hostile warriors has grown up.

This is what Sargon seems to have achieved. He conquered the mountain lands of Elam in western Persia, and pushed north into Armenia and west into Syria. By the time he died in c. 2305 BC, Sargon was ruling an empire stretching from the Persian Gulf to the Mediterranean. He had carved out the world's first-known multi-national empire to be conquered by force of arms and ruled by a central government. And he had made a thorough job of it: his conquests did not melt away on his death. Little or no military activity is associated with the reigns of Sargon's sons, Rimush (c. 2304–2296 BC) and Manishtushu (c. 2295–2281 BC) – a quarter-century of peace free from military crises. Sargon's grandson Naramsin (c. 2280–2244 BC) was the loftiest of the Akkadian emperor-kings after Sargon himself. Naramsin claimed divine status and styled himself ruler of the world's 'four quarters' – but he had to fight to live up to such an ambitious title. And a commemorative carving known as the 'Stele of Naramsin' shows that under his rule Mesopotamian tactics had come a long way from the time of Eannatum and the early Sumerian spearmen-armies.

The Naramsin stele is a triangular fragment, showing the king mowing down his enemies among the mountains. There is no mistaking the prime weapon here: this is a triumph for the bow. Naramsin dominates, the archer-king reaching for a new shaft while a dying enemy writhes at his feet, clutching at a long arrow in his throat. There are no heavy infantrymen in close formation, peering menacingly over the tops of their shields; Naramsin is accompanied by light infantry armed with spears, their free hands resting on weapons slung from their belts. These could be either axes or long knives – the sandstone is too eroded to tell for sure. Troops like this would have been well suited to the fluid tactics of a mountain campaign, being sufficiently lightly equipped to move fast in rocky terrain and catch a fleeing enemy. But the dominant message of the Naramsin stele is the deadly fire-power of the bow.

The bow evolved in two forms: the *stave bow* and the *composite bow*. As its name implies, the former was a long wooden stave relying on the natural whippiness of the wood to drive the arrow. But the composite bow was a deeply-curved sandwich of substances of varying elasticity: wood, horn, and sinew. Sometimes only half the length of a stave bow, it demanded far greater strength to be drawn for a shot, but its compound strength gave the arrow tremendous punch and range. Naramsin's deeply-curved bow is clearly of the composite type. The prominence it is given suggests the possibility that his army included sharp-shooting archers, with the King himself a famed practitioner of the bow.

THE AKKADIAN WAR MACHINE

The Akkadian kings were the first recorded warlords to make systematic use of all available weapons and tactics, and they flourished mightily in consequence. By equipping specialized units with the right tools for the job, they built up an army which could fight and win in mountain country as well as lowland plains. The Akkadians improved mightily on the first Sumerian armies, giving the heavy infantry phalanx the assistance of light infantry, making use of light mountain troops and possibly, as suggested above, making the first use in Mesopotamia of the bow for trained marksmen. And Sargon's conquest of the cities of Sumer suggests that he had mastered the basics of siege assault tactics with the battering ram.

The most obvious weakness of the Akkadian army was its almost complete reliance on infantry. Lacking the mobility which only cavalry could provide, it never stood a chance of defending the immensely long frontiers of the empire. Naramsin's successor Sharkalisharri (c.2243–2219 BC) struggled unavailingly to beat off waves of invaders from the north, west, and east. The prime enemies were the Gutians of the Zagros mountains, blood foes of Akkad and out for revenge after their humiliation by Naramsin. By 2180 BC Akkad itself had fallen to the Gutians, and Sargon's empire had dissolved into its component city-states.

For Mesopotamia, nearly 900 years separated the Akkadian and Assyrian empires — a long interlude studded with city-state wars, rising and falling supremacies, and recurrent 'break-ins' by barbarous desert and mountain tribes. During this interlude Ur enjoyed a last great flourishing (the 'Third Dynasty' of Ur, c.2060–1950 BC) which united the cities of Sumer for the last time before Sumer went under to Amorite nomads from the west and north, and Elamites from the mountains of the east, around 2000 BC. The Amorite settlement of Mesopotamia did not destroy the country's urban structure, but took over at the top. Between about 2000–1750 BC, the new Amorite supremacy in upper and lower Mesopotamia had taken the form of five main concentrations. These were the kingdom of Assyria between the upper waters of the

Sumerians at war

Constantly at war with each other, the city states of Sumer in lower Mesopotamia developed several fundamental military techniques which were used throughout ancient history. These included the central shock formation or phalanx of heavy infantry, protected by large shields and bristling with spears; light infantry ideal for skirmishing and rapid flank attacks; and the first primitive use of chariots to attain mobility — switching troops about the battlefield at speed to where they were most needed

ABOVE LEFT: The ornate helmet of Mes-kalam-dug from Ur, showing the intricate reproduction of the hair-style. Note the similarity with Eannatum's helmet on the 'Stele of the Vultures' (p. 19). ABOVE: Detail from the Ur 'Standard', showing a four-mule chariot rolling forward over enemy dead.

LEFT: Reconstruction of Sumerian troops going into action, with phalanx spearmen at left, light infantryman at centre, and a general in his chariot at right

Tigris and Euphrates, the kingdom of Mari on the middle Euphrates, the kingdom of Eshunna east of the Tigris, the kingdom of Babylon in the north of ancient Sumer, and the kingdom of Larsa in the far south.

Under Hammurabi (c. 1728–1686 BC) all the Amorite kingdoms of southern Mesopotamia were conquered by the troops of Babylon; but nothing like the Ur 'Standard' or the 'Stele of the Vultures', showing the Babylonian army of the second millennium in battle array, has yet been discovered. Some pointers to the military establishments kept by the Amorite kings have been provided by the haul of about 13,000 archive tablets unearthed at Mari in 1936. The king of Mari maintained a standing army of about 10,000 men, kept up to strength by compulsory military service. The main function of these troops was police action against nomadic bandit raids from the desert on the settled lands. Diplomatic exchanges with neighbouring kings have been deciphered, telling of troops being lent to a friendly neighbour with trouble on his borders – and one protest that the troops had not been sent back to Mari once the trouble had been cleared up. We also know that Mari was particularly noted for the excellence of its chariots, before it was conquered and sacked by Hammurabi around 1697 BC.

Hammurabi created the first Babylonian empire and he did it by armed conquest, but the military details of his era are virtually non-existent. He is best remembered for his extensive code of laws, and for making Babylon the dominant city of southern Mesopotamia – a tradition which endured for nearly 1,400 years until the conquest of Alexander the Great. As a military power, Hammurabi's empire certainly seems to have been much less formidable than the earlier Akkadian empire of Sargon the Great and Naramsin. It did not include Syria, and it began to break up soon after Hammurabi's death. Despite the enormous prestige of Babylon by the middle of the second millennium, its military strength was brittle; and the impotence of Babylon was trumpeted to the world by the great Hittite raid of 1531 BC (see p. 57). When the Hittites marched 500 miles down the Euphrates to sack and destroy Babylon it was not an attempt at conquest but a demonstration of a new military power taking shape to the north and west of Mesopotamia.

This new power was represented by the growth of the Hittite kingdom in Asia Minor and northern Syria, and the Hurrian kingdom of Mitanni east of the upper Euphrates. In their ascendancy these kingdoms adopted the horse for military purposes and introduced iron weapons – a twin revolution in ancient warfare which was the prelude to the rise of Assyria as the dominant military power. In its longevity, the military supremacy of the Assyrians was not to be surpassed until the rise of Rome to world empire.

THE SUPREMACY OF THE ASSYRIANS

Down to about 1360 BC, Assyria was the south-eastern province or vassal state of the kingdom of Mitanni, which at its height straddled the upper reaches of the Tigris and Euphrates. But Hittite pressure on Mitanni out of Asia Minor enabled Assyria to cut loose as a military power in its own right, overrunning Babylonia to the Persian Gulf,

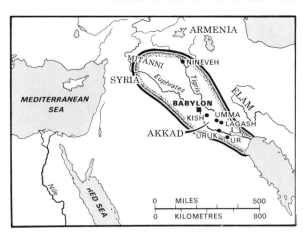

LEFT: Hammurabi of Babylon. His empire (RIGHT), though considerable, never approached that of Sargon at its widest extent. Its military establishment proved quite unable to prevent the sack of Babylon by the Hittites in 1531

swallowing its former overlord, Mitanni, and reducing Syria to become the first sea-to-sea empire since that of the Akkadians. Further conquests followed in Palestine and Egypt. With various ups and downs, expansions and contractions, the supremacy of the Assyrians endured over 700 years. Tough, resilient and highly organized, they owed their tremendous run of military victories to the method which they brought to the waging of war.

The Assyrians are the first known military power to have tested, refined, and improved every established type of soldier and weapon, and to have made important contributions of their own. Sargon of Akkad may have done the same; Hammurabi of Babylon almost certainly did not. Both of these conquerors undoubtedly made extensive use of the military systems and weaponry which they found ready to hand. But the Assyrians transformed the role of the infantry by the widespread introduction of the bow, which gave their infantry long-range hitting power. They put great stress on protection, in the form of body armour and the use of specialized shield-bearers. They mounted archers in fast horsed chariots, and used the horse to create first mounted infantry, then specialized cavalry units. With their elaborate siege engines and the use of mining, they raised siege warfare to a deadly art. And they made intelligent use of their communications, together with the polyglot military contingents provided on demand by Assyria's client and subject rulers.

The Assyrian story falls into two phases. The *Middle Empire*, dating from the middle fourteenth century to the eleventh century BC, was marked by the reigns of powerful warrior-kings such as Assuruballit I (1366–1331 BC), Adadnirari I (1305–1276 BC), Shalmaneser I (1275–1246 BC), Tukultininurta I (1245–1209 BC) – the first Assyrian ruler to claim the kingship of Babylonia – and Tiglathpileser I (1116–1078), who extended the empire from sea to sea. Then came a century and a half of temporary eclipse, caused by a flood of Aramean and Chaldean invasions out of Arabia, before Assyrian might was re-established and spread still further to form the *New Empire*. Assyrian warrior-kings of the New Empire included Shalmaneser III (859–825 BC), Tiglathpileser III (745–728 BC), Sargon II (722–706 BC),

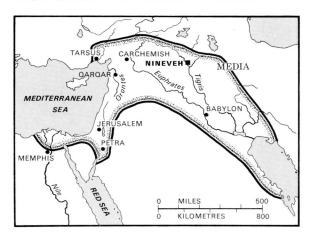

Sennacherib (705–682 BC), and Assurbanipal (669–c.627 BC).

The Assyrian war machine was brought to peak efficiency by the kings of the New Empire. Before the reign of Tiglathpileser III there was, for instance, no standing army, and the Assyrians relied on a national call-up directed by the provincial governors, who led their contingents on campaign. This yielded an army of regional formations each armed and equipped for its particular speciality: heavy or light troops, spearmen or archers.

The breakdown of Assyrian army units was on a decimal basis, the lowest element being a squad of ten. Ascending units of 50 and 100 men made up the basic tactical unit or *kisri*, the equivalent of a twentieth-century rifle company – around 200 men, but varying in size according to the strengths of the local contingents. The *kisri* were massed in provincial divisions of about 15,000 which, together with allied co-belligerent forces, could yield a total field strength of between 100–200,000 men. Few nations have ever produced such a sequence of able warrior-kings as the Assyrians, but not all Assyrian kings com-

ABOVE LEFT: The Assyrian empire at its zenith.

ABOVE: Assyrian archer protected by shield-bearer, carrying a sword for close combat

BELOW: Mobility and hitting-power combined – Assyrian lancer and mounted archers

manded their armies in person. Supreme field command could be assumed by a senior general or *turtan*, the equivalent of a modern field-marshal. His civilian equivalent was the *Rabshakeh* or 'chief of the princes', and the Old Testament describes both *turtan* and *rabshakeh* demanding the surrender of Jerusalem in the name of Sennacherib (*2 Kings* 18:17–25). In the early years of the Assyrian empire there were two of these *turtans*, who sat on either side of the king and outranked all civilian officials and courtiers.

Sifting the many references to the composition of Assyrian armies, and allowing for exaggeration in numbers, a distinct pattern emerges. Despite the stress put on the Assyrian horsemen and chariotry the Assyrian army was not exclusively horsed, any more than Hitler's *Wehrmacht* was exclusively a tank army: it just looked that way to the defeated side. In fact the Assyrians relied on their *infantry* to clinch a victory. The chariots and cavalry softened up the enemy beforehand and completed his rout after the infantry had done their work. Expressed in figures, the breakdown of an Assyrian host was probably in the region of 1,000 infantry: 100 cavalry: 1 chariot.

Often in considerable detail, Assyrian monuments and bas-reliefs show a wide variety of troop types. Their *infantry* seems to have been graded into heavy, medium, and light troops, and divided into *missile units* (archers, equipped with the composite bow, plus slingers), and *shock units* (spearmen with shields and swords).

The heavy archer is shown clad in a calf-length tunic of scale armour made up of overlapping scales, his head protected by an armoured 'balaclava helmet' of scale armour and topped with a pointed helmet. Armed with a composite bow, he also carries a sword and is shown attended by a shield-bearer. The latter also carried a sword, together with the archer's quiver. His main job was to carry the tall, free-standing wicker shield or *gerrhon*. Medium archers only wore a scale-armour corselet over their calf-length tunic, but they, too, were attended by shield-bearers. The light archers were equipped for speed and agility, with no armour or helmet – but careful protection was given to the slingers, who wore both helmet and corselet.

The heavy spearmen carried both sword and long shield; they formed the central shock force or phalanx, and wore both helmet and corselet. Light spearmen wore helmets but no corselet. Assyrian recruiting zones were so widespread that there were many variants on these basic types. Some regions, for instance, supplied light archers who carried conical shields for the better deflection of enemy missiles. The Babylonian infantry looked like a throwback to the Sumerian wars of the third millennium, armed with bows but still carrying axe and dagger. Officers are shown carrying maces. The essential point was that the multi-national contingents of the Assyrian host were intelligently grouped in homogeneous units for maximum efficiency.

The use of horsed chariots in mass was one of the most feared of the Assyrians' tactics, and the chariot has always been one of the most misunderstood weapons of ancient warfare. To the twentieth-century mind the chariot, as the first successful vehicle, is instinctively associated with the tank: the first battlefield juggernaut, full of clatter and

BELOW: Infantry missile-power – Assyrian slingers at the siege of Lachish. Note helmets and body-armour, plus swords to give even these auxiliary troops maximum combat value

dash and towering menace. But the tank was developed to roll clean over the enemy and crush him in his positions while the chariot was never a shock weapon, using its momentum to bowl over enemy troops where they stood. On the contrary, any chariot crew which tried to charge into steady troops holding their ground would have had a very short life expectancy indeed.

As perfected by the Assyrians and Egyptians, chariots seem to have been much more of a psychological weapon, a sort of military devil-mask. When used in mass, their purpose was to make the enemy lose his nerve and break formation. Unlike the clumsy four-wheeled vehicles shown on the Ur 'Standard', Assyrian and Egyptian chariots featured a rear-slung axle and only two wheels. This feature enabled them, if the enemy stood his ground, to wheel sharply out of range and retire — perhaps to make a massed feint attack on one end of the enemy line, where the bulk of the enemy troops would not be able to see what was going on. And if that tactic failed the chariots could start a series of 'nuisance attacks' in small groups, rattling in from dozens of different angles, loosing off arrows and javelins before retiring to repeat the performance. As in the days of the lumbering, four-wheeled Sumerian chariots, the faster two-wheeled horsed chariot remained a platform for mobile fire-power, whether the latter was delivered by an archer or a javelin-thrower.

Troops faced with chariots knew that they would have nothing to worry about as long as they kept formation; yet, at the same time, no sizeable chariot force could be ignored. If the chariots went into a prolonged spate of nuisance attacks, the defenders would have had to put up with a steady trickle of casualties which, if suffered for too long without something positive being seen to be done to drive the attackers off, could grind morale dangerously fine. As well as probing the quality of an enemy army in battle array, these basic chariot tactics could be used for two other purposes. They could pin down the enemy while the

The 'great king' dismounts from his chariot, bow and quiver at the ready and flanked by his vigilant pair of shield-bearers. Detail from the north palace of Assurbanipal at the Assyrian capital of Nineveh

main army deployed for its own attack; and they could avert total disaster by 'freezing' an enemy pursuit, giving infantry shaken by an initial setback time in which to rally and save the day.

In itself, the chariot was a mass of contradictions. The basic vehicle was a bouncing one-man cockleshell mounted on two wheels and a rear-slung axle, with the emphasis on lightness and speed. But a war chariot had to carry an archer or javelin-thrower with his gear and ammunition as well as the driver. This made the chariot bigger, heavier, and slower, a useful combination for the armed passenger, who needed a comparatively stable firing platform. On the other hand, once the driver had brought his passenger within arrow-shot of the enemy, his chariot was within arrow-shot itself. Assyrian chariots of the New Kingdom were built even bigger, to accommodate one and sometimes two shield-bearers.

Of more importance than its speed, a chariot's most useful characteristic must have been good handling qualities and elusiveness. A chariot was of most use when its crew concentrated on staying alive to be a repeated nuisance, not getting themselves gloriously but pointlessly killed. And the good chariot crews — the ones who stayed alive — must have developed an instinctive trust and teamwork, with the driver giving his archer just enough time to fire a couple of shafts before sharply changing course and taking off to throw out the aim of enemy marksmen.

Looking back, it is tempting to wonder why nobody thought of shooting the horses. If this had become the classic anti-chariot tactic the chariot would not have lasted very long as a viable proposition, but it was clearly not so simple as it sounds. In any event, horses were highly prized as useful and valuable war booty, and deliberately killing them does not seem to have been generally encouraged. From most angles the crew of a chariot would have made just as good a target as the horses, and a lucky shot or two could make the whole contraption useless by incapacitating either the driver or his passengers. Emergencies, of course, brought forth exceptions. At Arzashkun in 856 BC cornered Haldian infantry did make a desperate charge, singling out the chariot horses and cavalry of Shalmaneser III's army, but it did them little good. The Assyrians beat back the Haldians and went on to win the battle with great slaughter.

Undoubtedly the chariot had a tremendous psychological potential. It could panic good troops, just as German troops were occasionally to panic when charged unexpectedly by Polish and Russian cavalry in the Second World War. This psychological aura made it a classic symbol of military might, as even the most casual reading of the Old Testament makes abundantly clear. 'Their land is filled with horses,' laments Isaiah, 'and there is no end to their chariots'. (*Isaiah* 2:7–8). The biggest chariot force encountered by the Assyrians seems to have been at Qarqar in the Orontes valley of Syria (854 BC), when they tackled a coalition army of Syrians, Phoenicians, Hittites, and Egyptians which had 4,000 chariots. The Assyrians captured the lot.

Apart from their expertise with the war chariot, the Assyrians were also noted for the formidable horsed cavalry which they developed. They no more invented the horsed soldier than they invented the war chariot, but they were the first to make systematic use of cavalry. Anathema though it may be to the *élite* 'cavalry mentality', efficient mounted troops can be created in a surprisingly short time, as T. E. Lawrence pointed out in *Seven Pillars of Wisdom*:

Maulud, the fire-eating A.D.C., begged fifty mules off me, put across them fifty of his trained infantrymen, and told them they were cavalry. He was a martinet, and a born mounted officer, and by his spartan exercises the much-beaten mule-riders grew painfully into excellent soldiers, instantly obedient and capable of formal attack! They were prodigies in the Arab ranks. We telegraphed immediately for another fifty mules, to double the dose of mounted infantry, since the value of so tough a unit for reconnaissance was obvious.

The Assyrians seem to have made similar experiments and started to apply the results by the end of the reign of Tiglathpileser I. At first they treated the horse very much as a more economical substitute for the chariot: mobile seats on which groups of armoured soldiers could be switched rapidly about a battlefield. Each mounted, armoured archer was given a mounted attendant or shield-bearing groom to help direct the horse and hold it when the archer dismounted to shoot. These were not true cavalry but mounted infantry, and they followed the triple grading of the foot soldiers: heavy, medium and light.

It took centuries of trial-and-error for the full potentialities of horsed troops to be appreciated. The most obvious advantages would have been the first to be absorbed, foremost among these being the fact that a horse and rider can go places where a chariot cannot, and a good deal faster than a chariot. This gave horsed troops the vital role of reconnaissance, as the eyes of the army, which was to remain a primary cavalry task until the advent of aircraft. Another obvious role was the pursuit of a beaten enemy, keeping fugitives on the run and preventing them from rallying.

But it seems clear that the way in which the Assyrians used their horsed troops in battle was dictated by their basic tactic of relying on the central mass of foot archers and spearmen *and looking after them*. This meant launching chariot and cavalry attacks to deter the enemy from any swift advance, which might – regardless of losses – get in among the Assyrian foot archers and cut them down. The Assyrians used the mobility of the horse to keep the enemy at a range where massed arrow fire could be most effective. By the time of Tiglathpileser III, Sennacherib, and Assurbanipal – the eighth and seventh centuries BC – Assyrian horsed soldiers no longer depended on mounted attendants and had ousted the chariot as the most numerous mobile arm in the Assyrian battle array. Though they remained a 'service department' for the foot archers, the cavalry of Assyria had achieved the first true marriage between the *mobility* provided by the horse and the *long-range fire-power* provided by the bow. Before it was finally recovered in the twentieth century in the form of the tank, this potent combination was destined to be ignored or overlooked by succeeding military supremacies.

The reverse applied to the horsed spearman or lancer, another

Assyrian lancers charge into action, riding down the beaten foe

Assyrian innovation, who was still riding into action in the Second World War. Assyrian lancers came into their own during the pursuit of broken armies, harrying the fugitives at point-blank range where archers were not merely ineffective but vulnerable to desperate counter-attacks.

The Assyrians not only excelled in the pitched battle in open country: they were masters of siege warfare as well, and without this skill their conquests would have been ephemeral if not impossible. Having beaten an enemy in the field and chased him into his strongest walled city or fortress, the Assyrians smoothly shifted gear into 'siege tempo' and finished the job within the enemy walls. This was the pattern of every one of the thirty-four key campaigns fought by the Assyrians between 1270–648 BC, and their siege tactits boiled down to the pursuit of four basic objectives.

First came *isolation*, cutting off the beleaguered army from all hope of relief, and shutting off the water supply if this ran into the besieged city or fortress by stream or aqueduct. The next phase was *preparation* of the approach to the area of wall selected for the main breach (or breaches). This was achieved by levelling ground, and building whatever bridges, ramps or causeways were necessary to get the siege-engines up to the walls without overturning *en route*. The third phase was *penetration* of the masonry by the concentrated use of picks and rams at the point of the breach. If the soil permitted, this might well be assisted by *mining* under the wall to bring it down. And the assault on the wall was accompanied by the *suppression*, by the maximum possible concentration of arrow-fire from the ground and the siege-engines, of effective countermeasures by the garrison.

The Assyrians' method in attaining these objectives was balanced by their other dominant talent: flexibility. They did not invariably sit

down for a full-dress siege. There were repeated instances of Assyrian armies storming a city or fortress in a single day, proof that they knew when to try their luck with an *escalade* — the massed use of scaling-ladders to swamp the defenders. In its campaign to suppress rebel Babylonia in 710 BC, Sargon II's army stormed the improved defences of Babylon in a single day and later stormed Samuna and Bab-Duri as well. But where circumstances permitted or demanded, the Assyrians were quite happy to starve out a city rather than squander valuable troops and equipment in excessively wasteful assaults. Assurbanipal laid siege to Babylon in 648 BC and it took three years to starve the city into submission, during which time the bulk of the Assyrian army was left free with ample time to reduce every other major city in Babylonia.

The siege-engines shown on Assyrian memorials were impressive structures, sheathed in wickerwork to protect the crews and mounted on four or six wheels. They are shown with two variants of head: a flat-headed conical ram for cracking masonry, and a pair of spear-headed picks for gouging out chunks of wall by leverage after being driven into cracks. The ram was so slung within the framework of the engine that it could be directed upwards as well as horizontally, and so hurled at a wide area of wall.

The biggest danger to the crews engaged in battering a wall was plunging fire from the defenders up on the battlements, particularly in the form of incendiary missiles. To counter this threat, the most elaborate Assyrian siege-engines featured a tower with a fighting-top from which archers could shoot down on the defenders. This tower sometimes included a water tank for the quenching of incendiaries before they could set the whole structure ablaze. But of course the effort needed to move these giant structures was immense, even when the approach to the wall had been levelled and smoothed in the preparation phase. By the time of Tiglathpileser III, the Assyrians were contenting themselves with lighter and smaller siege-engines, which were run up

ABOVE: A siege. This is one of the lighter, six-wheeled Assyrian siege engines, here accompanied by heavy archers in strength to keep down counter-fire from the walls. The men on the right seem to be preparing to fire a mine driven under the walls

high ramps; the ramps themselves being built under the cover provided by shield-bearers.

Siege-engines, with all the labour and manpower needed for their use, were used to the end of the Assyrian supremacy, but they used miners as well. These are shown crouching at the foot of the wall, spade in hand and protected by the inevitable shield-bearers. The miners' task was to drive a short tunnel under the foundations, pack it with wood and fire it, the resulting subsidence bringing down or at least severely weakening a section of wall.

Out of the many campaigns which studded the Assyrian epic and which make fascinating study, the Kutha campaign of 706 BC is particularly interesting because it brought the Assyrians up against troops very like their own. It was fought to crush one of the frequent attempts by the Babylonians to throw off Assyrian rule, and was triggered by the death of Sargon II of Assyria in 706 BC. Merodach-baladan, the vassal-king of Babylonia, had revolted against Sargon only to be defeated and driven into exile. On Sargon's death Merodach-baladan returned to Babylon and brought in the Arameans and Elamites as allies in a new war against Assyria. The Elamite army seems to have been particularly important because it consisted of 80,000 archers. The Babylonians and Arameans contributed infantry spearmen and cavalry, and awaited the inevitable Assyrian counterblow on the plain outside the city of Kutha.

The scene was set for what the allies must have hoped would be a most evenly-balanced struggle. Sennacherib, the new Assyrian king, must have marched into Babylonia with an almost identical army. But the accounts of the ensuing battle at Kutha record victory for the Assyrians almost as a matter of course. It cannot have been a very costly victory, for Sennacherib was able to march straight on to capture Babylon and then to mop up all the major cities of Babylonia. The Assyrians went home leaving Babylonia thoroughly cowed for the time being, having captured 208,000 prisoners and 7,200 horses.

BELOW: The lords of defeated Lachish pay tribute to Sennacherib

Given the allied strength in archers, the only reasonable explanation for this easy Assyrian victory must be that Sennacherib used his mounted archers to do as he pleased with the allied infantry centre, repeatedly engaging at ideal bowshot range and shooting the allies to pieces. In all other respects the campaign was a typical Assyrian *tour de force*, with the battle only serving as a prelude to an all-out pursuit and subjugation, not as an end in itself. Nineteenth-century military theorists were to hail this method of waging war as 'Napoleonic', It certainly ranks the Assyrians among the most celebrated military innovators in history.

As the New Empire spread ever wider in the eighth and seventh centuries BC, culminating in the reduction of Palestine and Egypt, so the Assyrians had to face the ever-increasing problem of nationalist revolts on the fringes of the empire. They tried to counter this with mass deportations of the defeated populations, colonizing the evacuated territory with exchanges of settlers from Mesopotamia. This was the fate which eventually befell the kingdom of Israel in northern Palestine, as the Old Testament makes clear in *2 Kings*:

In the ninth year of Hoshea [772 BC] the king of Assyria [Sargon II] captured Samaria, and he carried the Israelites away to Assyria, and placed them in Halah, and on the Habor, the river of Gozan, and in the cities of the Medes . . . And the king of Assyria brought people from Babylon, Cutha, Avva, Hamath, and Sepharva'im, and placed them in the cities of Samaria instead of the people of Israel; and they took possession of Samaria, and dwelt in its cities. (2 Kings 17:6, 24).

The fall of the Assyrian empire was amazingly rapid, and was due as much to the Assyrians' earlier respect for the national identities of subject powers as to out-and-out military defeat; the centralized power of the empire failed before the energy of the provinces. As with the Babylonian revolt of 706 BC, the last act was precipitated by the death of a strong Assyrian king – the greatest of them all, Assurbanipal, whose massed archives of cuneiform records at Nineveh and Nimrud preserved not only the Assyrian but the Akkadian and early Sumerian stories for posterity.

When Assurbanipal died in about 626 BC, none of his successors proved able to step into his shoes. The provinces revolted again, this time on a massive scale. The whole of subject Mesopotamia joined forces against Assyrian rule. The new upsurge was headed by Nabopolassar, a Chaldean prince who declared himself king of Babylon in 626 BC and sealed a powerful alliance with Cyaxares, King of Media. Together Nabopolassar and Cyaxares flung the massed armies of Babylonia and Media, with powerful Arabian and Persian aid, against the Assyrian heartland.

Shinsharishkun, the son of Assurbanipal, never came near to halting the flood. Beaten at Kablini and Arrapha, he fell back on his capital, Nineveh, in the centre of the Assyrian heartland on the upper Tigris. The *coup de grâce* came in 612 BC when Nineveh was stormed and destroyed by the confederate host after a three-year siege.

There is no assuaging your hurt,
your wound is grievous.
All who hear the news of you
clap their hands over you.
For upon whom has not come
your unceasing evil?
(Nahum 3:1–4, 14–15, 19)

Though understandable as a paean of revenge, this does the Assyrians less than justice. The first military nation to put warfare on a scientific footing, their talents extended far beyond mere soldiering into the arts of civilian administration (well out of the scope of this book). In their heyday, thanks to the good intelligence readily obtainable from the civilian governors and officials of the empire, Assyrian kings always knew where to find the weak link when faced with revolt. At times they certainly earned their reputation for ferocity in war, practising the deliberate terror tactics known in the twentieth century as 'frightfulness'; flaying, burning alive, impaling, and other atrocities were a

A grisly trophy takes shape: heaping up the severed heads of the enemy dead after the Chaldean campaign of Sennacherib. Cruelty and 'frightfulness' were calculated elements in the Assyrian military repertoire

calculated part of the Assyrian repertoire. But this dark reputation was more than balanced by remarkable qualities of leadership and fitness for imperial rule. Without their flair for methodical improvement in all fields, civilian as well as military, the Assyrians would have been nothing.

In the wake of Assyria's collapse, Nabopolassar of Babylon founded the Chaldean dynasty which lasted less than a century, but which rose for a while to emulate the glory of the Assyrian empire under Assurbanipal. Nabopolassar (626–605 BC) seems to have rebuilt the Babylonian army on the Assyrian model; he certainly began the reconquest of the western Assyrian empire, defeating Necho of Egypt at Carchemish in 605 BC and reducing Syria. His son Nebuchadnezzar 'The Great' (605–561 BC) crushed the last flickers of resistance by the kingdom of Judah in Palestine, razing Jerusalem in 587 BC and deporting its population to Babylonia in true Assyrian style. But within 25 years of Nebuchadnezzar's death the 'Neo-Babylonian Empire' which had risen from the wreck of Assyria had fallen intact to a greater power in the east: the united empire of the Medes and Persians created by Cyrus 'The Great'.

CHAPTER TWO

Warlords of the Nile

Thanks largely to the old testament — supported in the cinema by the efforts of Cecil B. de Mille and others — the Egypt of the pharaohs has gained the reputation of having been a great military power, an awesome repository of military might. But this is a false reputation. The ancient Egyptians were not a military people, in the sense that the Assyrians, Macedonians, or Romans were military peoples. Out of the 2,330 or so years of Egyptian history down to the Persian conquest of the late sixth century BC, less than 250 years were spent in successful wars of conquest or defence. Indeed, one of the main reasons for Egypt's long survival as an independent power, so far from military invincibility, was the country's unique geographical position, on the south-western periphery of the ancient world.

Rivalling that of Mesopotamia as the world's oldest, Egypt's civilization enjoyed geographical advantages denied to Mesopotamia. The people of the Nile lived within natural frontiers — the Red Sea to the east, the Mediterranean to the north, the desert to the west. And Egypt's land link with the rest of the civilized world, the Isthmus of Suez, only eighty-five miles wide, could be defended against anything but an all-out invasion in overwhelming strength.

Though full of gaps and inconsistencies which continue to attract the criticism of historians, the conventional chronology of Egyptian history remains that of Manetho, an Egyptian priest of the third century BC who reckoned his country's history in thirty ruling dynasties. These are grouped into three main phases. The *Old Kingdom* (c. 3100–1990 BC) included Dynasties I–XI; the *Middle Kingdom* (c. 1990–1680 BC) consisted of Dynasties XII–XIV and ended with the conquest of northern or 'Lower' Egypt by the invading Hyksos, who made up the XV and XVI Dynasties. Dynasty XVII (southern or 'Upper' Egypt) began wars against the Hyksos around 1600 BC and Egypt was finally liberated by Dynasty XVIII, the first of the *New Kingdom* (Dynasties XVIII–XXX, ending in the Persian conquest of 343 BC).

The period of the Old Kingdom saw recurrent attempts by a succession of rulers to unite the two kingdoms of Egypt. Lower Egypt stretched upstream from the Nile Delta as far as El-Amarna/Cusae; Upper Egypt reached south to the First Cataract at Aswan. Success in

OPPOSITE: Battle scene on the ivory handle of a flint knife from Djebel-el-Arak, late third millenium. Amazingly primitive soldiers (armed only with clubs and virtually naked) are depicted in a sophisticated art form

37

this policy of unification was marked by the union of the two crowns: the White Mitre of Upper Egypt and the Red Crown of Lower Egypt. One of the earliest 'documents' in early Egyptian history is a slate bas-relief dating from around 3000 BC; it shows King Narmer of Upper Egypt, crowned with the White Mitre, defeating the men of the lower Nile. It was during Egypt's first four dynasties (c.3000–2500 BC) that the Pyramids and the Sphinx were built by Narmer's successors. But over the following millennium the two kingdoms repeatedly parted company, later to be reunited by some other powerful king.

Compared with such marvels of scientific engineering as the Pyramids, Old Kingdom troops and weaponry seem astonishingly primitive. Soldiers wore nothing but a stiffened linen kilt, with no helmet or armour. The wooden shields they carried were modest in size and covered little more than the trunk. The weapons were round- or pear-headed maces, short thrusting-spears, and simple axes made by lashing a semi-circular copper plate to a handle. Photographs of Zulu warriors 4,000 years later look far more formidable. Certainly not one Egyptian memorial of the third millennium shows anything as menacing as the Sumerian phalanx on the Stele of the Vultures.

The reason for this paradox seems to be that no Egyptian army of the third millennium had to fight anything more formidable than another, similarly-equipped Egyptian army, in the wars between Upper and Lower Egypt. In the absence of foreign invasions, or of any vital stimulus to adopt new weaponry and tactics, the art of war made virtually no progress at all. That a great nation's military resources could remain so unchanged *for a thousand years* – the period separating, say, the Viking invasions and the Vietnam war – is a concept almost impossible to grasp. Yet it is true for all that.

The most advanced item of war gear depicted on King Narmer's victory tablet of 3000 BC is a suggestion of moulded greaves to protect the king's legs – and that could well be nothing more than the artist's representation of human musculature. The king is armed with nothing but a mace. And evidence from around 2000 BC shows only one significant change. This evidence is from the splendid display of model soldiers found at Asyut in the tomb of Prince Emsah, a feudal warlord of

ABOVE LEFT: The earliest known portrait of an Egyptian king as warlord – Narmer, wearing the White Mitre of Upper Egypt (slate bas-relief)

ABOVE: Narmer after his victory, now wearing the Red Crown of Lower Egypt, with courtiers and standard-bearers

RIGHT: A warlord's monument – the miniature 'private army' unearthed in Prince Emsah's grave at Asyut. This shows spearmen on the march, accompanied by Nubian archers. Their most obvious feature is total reliance on the shield for protection

Dynasty XII during a period when the royal supremacy was in eclipse and 'private armies' predominated. Though not 'model soldiers' in the modern sense – they are 'grave-goods', and not children's toys or the products of a highly-skilled hobby – Emsah's soldiers are probably the oldest military miniatures in the world. They show the same austerity in dress and equipment as Narmer's tablet 1,000 years before: semi-naked, kilted soldiers carrying medium-sized shields, armed with short thrusting-spears and protected by no armour or helmets.

When not fighting Lower Egypt, the army of Upper Egypt campaigned against the negro warrior tribesmen of Nubia in the northern Sudan. The Nubians were to ancient Egypt what the Pathans and Afridis of India's North-West Frontier were to the the British Raj: a military nuisance to be periodically crushed or, where possible, channelled by alliance. The Nubians were archers who used a lightweight stave bow. Primitive foot archers could not stop a well-drilled army of spearmen from marching through their territories and burning their settlements – but when recruited as mercenaries, drilled, and deployed as companies of foot archers operating on the flanks of the spearmen, they were a potent force against an army relying on spearmen alone. Nubian archers could hold their ground, safely out of missile range, and allow their spearmen to advance against the enemy line under a hail of covering fire. And if the charge of the spearmen should be repelled, the archers could save their discomfited comrades from being routed by a decisive enemy riposte.

When it came to recruiting Nubian archers, Upper Egypt, bordering on Nubia, had a decisive advantage over Lower Egypt. This may help to explain why nearly all the victory monuments of the Old Kingdom wars of union and reunion show the triumphant king wearing the White Mitre of Upper Egypt. Half of Prince Emsah's model 'army' was made up of Nubian archers, who were to provide Egypt with an easy source of infantry fire-power right down to the Persian conquest. This makes the Nubians the earliest-known participants in a long line of specially-recruited foreign troops, reaching down the ages to units like the Gurkhas in the British Army or North African *goums* in the French.

ARMIES OF THE MIDDLE KINGDOM

By the time of the Middle Kingdom in the early second millennium, the knowledge that enemy archers were a force to be reckoned with had brought about several refinements. The mass of shield-carrying spearmen in the centre remained the real battle-winner, but the spearmen now carried huge, wide shields which covered them from head to foot. This gave Egyptian armies the phalanx of heavy infantry, some 500 years after the Sumerians had developed the formation in Mesopotamia. The spearmen remained without any other form of armour. More than likely all their energies were required to handle the enormous shields; an Egyptian phalanx struggling to control its shields in a sudden squall of wind must have been quite a sight. One of the most favoured shield shapes resembled that of a Gothic church window: a vertical rectangle with a pointed top, round which the spearman could peer. These shields were flat, braced wooden structures, covered with stretched hide with the hair still on and able to stop any arrow from a stave bow.

Supplementing the heavy infantry of the phalanx, there were now several types of *light infantry*, all carrying the traditional, smaller shield. The task of these light infantrymen would have been to charge enemy archers under cover of their shields and drive the archers back out of range. Unprotected foot archers subjected to such a charge were highly vulnerable; each man would have known full well that he would only be able to get off two or three arrows before the charging spearmen were on him. Apart from light infantrymen equipped with thrusting-spears, others were equipped with a dual-purpose spear. This could be used as a short-range javelin without ever leaving the thrower's hand, a large knob on the end of the spear-shaft enabling him to retain and recover the weapon. Then there was a light infantryman who carried a poleaxe instead of a spear. This weapon, a quarter-staff shod with a narrow cutting edge about seven inches long, must have been a most unpleasant prospect when unleashed in a sudden, flailing charge.

By the end of the Middle Kingdom, it seems that archers were an essential element of any Egyptian army. The native Egyptians had adopted the bow themselves and there were now companies of native Egyptian archers, though the recruitment of Nubian archers continued. Their 'side arms' now included the dagger as well as the light axe with its half-moon blade. Though the Egyptians had moved on from copper to bronze, they seem to have been very slow in mastering the art of casting solid bronze axeheads and blades in the Sumerian manner. They relied instead on thin, hammered plates of metal, realizing that the

RIGHT: A relief from Amarna shows a spearman carrying the light axe normally slung from the belt, with a slinger on his right

narrower a blade is fashioned from soft metal the less chance there is of its buckling. But they still used pure copper for arrowheads and spearheads. Copper was hard enough to make a sharp point for penetration but soft enough to buckle on hitting bone, thus being agony to extract. And enough arrows or involuntarily-yielded spears jammed fast in enemy shields would add mightily to inconvenience and fatigue in the enemy ranks.

Though details of army organization are scanty for the Old Kingdom, the simplicity of the troops and their weapons would seem to have been matched by an equally simple military establishment: a small standing force, bulked out in time of war by contingents of provincial militia. This militia was given some kind of peacetime training and was supplied on demand by the *nomarchs*, governors of the *nomes* or provinces; but the king's treasury fed the men during their period of service. Unit breakdown seems to have been on a decimal basis, the usual description of the strength of an Egyptian army being 'many ten thousands'. Allowing for the almost inevitable exaggeration required for eulogizing a king's power, this does make some kind of sense. Taken literally and using twentieth century unit nomenclature for the sake of clarity, it would suggest basic squads of 10 men, platoons of 50, companies of 100, battalions of 500, brigades of 1,000, and a couple of divisions of 5,000 making up a corps of 10,000. Two or more of these corps would have made up the army.

The appointment of senior officers was the king's prerogative, with the royal family and nobility providing a useful pool of candidates. An army consisting of spearmen with support from archer companies would not have had a very demanding tactical repertoire, and the drill for converting a marching column into battle formation would have been straightforward enough. With no fast mobile forces with which to strike at enemy communications, the main tactical objective would have been a deliberate collision with the enemy field army. And the side with the steadiest troops, and the most training in smooth deployment for a line attack before the other side was ready, would probably win. Tactical genius was therefore hardly required of generals in the Old Kingdom. Nor can supply, normally a headache for any general, have posed a serious problem. During the Old Kingdom, Egyptian armies marched and fought either within the country's frontiers or within easy reach of them, with the more than adequate resources of the civilian administration at their disposal.

As the Old Kingdom decayed, feudalism in Egypt flourished to such an extent that nomarchs and rich provincial warlords maintained their own private armies. The fact that Prince Emsah was prepared for eternity with a symbolic army among his grave-goods speaks for itself. Although these private armies did little for the country's internal security – the chronicler Manetho claims that at one point Egypt had seventy kings in as many days, which seems excessive by any standard – they did add to the country's state of military readiness under a king effective enough to command the loyalty of the provincial rulers. As Prince Emsah's miniatures show, the private armies were armed and drilled as well as the best force that the king could raise.

With the parallel development of light and heavy infantry under the Middle Kingdom, tactics changed with the composition of the army. The standing nucleus maintained by the king had to include light infantry as well as phalanx spearmen, for both needed extensive training to reach full co-ordination. And as generals now had to concert the movements of the central phalanx, light infantry wings, and archer companies, the resultant deepening of the command structure posed new problems of communication. This seems to have been tackled by using runners to relay orders.

Crack regiments began to emerge. One of the most important (dignified in the New Kingdom with the title 'Braves of the King') was an elite light infantry shock force, 300 in number and earmarked for decisive attacks at the crucial moment – plus, one suspects, all-or-nothing counterattacks if things got desperate. It is likely that a soldier who repeatedly distinguished himself while serving in the shock force qualified for admission to the elite of elites: the King's Bodyguard. The Old Kingdom distinction between 'retainers' (the standing army) and 'recruits' (the yield of the provincial call-up) continued through the Middle Kingdom; and this was where the feudal autonomy of the nobility showed its positive side, for a private army like that of Prince Emsah would obviously be an invaluable contribution to the national muster in a time of crisis.

One prominent feature of Egyptian armies from earliest times was the use of standards, which were crowned with animal designs corresponding to the crests or badges of the different *nomes* or feudal lords. Standards did much more than add to military pomp during formal parades and processions. They had a very positive role to play in battle, serving as familiar marks on which shaken troops could rally.

With such armed forces at their disposal the rulers of the Middle Kingdom – most notably Ammenemes I (1991–1962 BC) and Sesostris III (1878–1843 BC) – had little trouble in extending Egypt's sphere of influence south as far as the Second Cataract and east into the Sinai Peninsula and southern Palestine. But these successes were gained at the expense of nothing more formidable than frontier tribesmen – Nubians in the south and desert nomads in Sinai – who lacked the Egyptian organization and discipline. In military terms, however, organization and discipline were the Egyptian army's sole trumps under the Middle Kingdom. Apart from those virtues it was a paper tiger. It lacked mobility; it lacked fire-power; and its soldiers lacked the protection to survive against an enemy armed with all three advantages. And all this was proved when the invading Hyksos swept into Lower Egypt around 1678 BC. It seems to have been one of the most one-sided confrontations in history, with all the impact of Cortez and his handful of mounted *conquistadores* shattering the apparent might of the Aztec Empire.

THE HYKSOS ONSLAUGHT

For all the tremendous results of the Hyksos' descent on Egypt, comparatively little is known about them. Their name, commonly used in its Greek version, stemmed from the Egyptian *hiq-khase*, 'lord of a foreign hill-country' – in this case Syria and Palestine. What turned the

LEFT: Captives of the pharaoh: bound prisoners of war (Canaanite or Syrian) decorate the feet of a royal mummy-case

RIGHT: The Egyptian empire at its height under Ramesses II, showing its tenuous hold over Palestine and southern Syria

BELOW: The pharaoh, bow in hand, mounts his chariot on the eve of battle (from the Great Temple at Karnak)

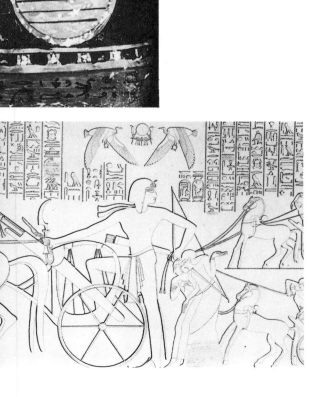

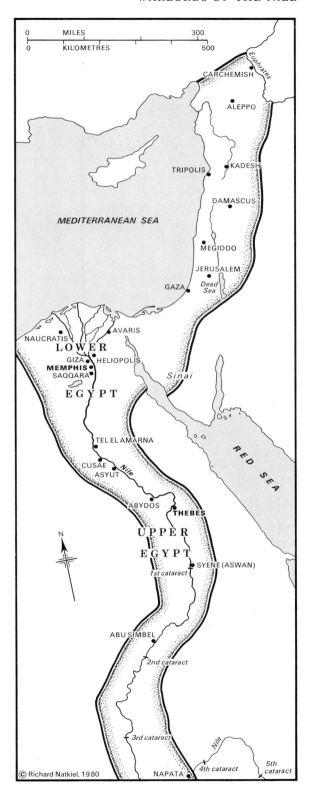

© Richard Natkiel, 1980

Hyksos against Egypt seems to have been Hittite pressure out of Asia Minor, the Hyksos having learned the essentials of chariot warfare from their aggressive northern neighbours before moving south. To a large extent the conquest of Lower Egypt by the Hyksos was the inevitable victory of their mobility, fire-power, and armoured protection over the flimsy Egyptian infantry. But this does not tell the whole story. It is like wondering how different Waterloo would have been if Napoleon had had the *Grande Armée* of ten years before, or if Wellington had had the regiments with which he had won the Peninsular War. As far as a sudden foreign invasion was concerned, it does seem that Egypt was comparatively easy meat in 1678 BC.

The last powerful king, Ammenemes III, had died in 1786 BC and Upper and Lower Egypt had parted company once again. When the Hyksos arrived, almost a century had passed since a seasoned Egyptian army, drawing on the resources of the whole kingdom, had taken the field. As a result Lower Egypt took the brunt of the Hyksos' onslaught, with green troops and no general with the unique talent required for improvising brand-new tactics on the spot. Had the Hyksos come up against sufficiently large armies of steady troops who held formation and refused to be panicked by chariots, the invaders might just have been given two or three stand-up fights severe enough to persuade them that Egypt was too tough a nut to crack.

Instead it is quite easy to reconstruct the pattern of the Hyksos conquest. Whatever troops Lower Egypt was able to muster were appalled at the clouds of Hyksos chariotry rushing against them. The Egyptian archers found themselves hopelessly outranged by the invaders' composite bows; both heavy and light infantry found that their shields offered no protection from the Hyksos arrows. Maybe the best of the retainers stood their ground, and died where they stood; more likely the recruits panicked and broke, only to be overtaken and destroyed in flight. There would have been no need to close with whatever knots of Egyptian resistance formed round the standards as the phalanx crumbled; the Hyksos archers could shoot them to pieces where they stood.

All this is a reconstructed scenario, because no detailed record of the Hyksos conquest survived. But we do know that Lower Egypt fell virtually at a single stroke, whatever force raised in its defence being wiped out without putting up a prolonged resistance. The Hyksos overran the Nile Delta with little or no trouble and settled down to enjoy life as the new lords of creation in the promised land. Like Kublai Khan's Mongols in conquered China 3,000 years later, the last thing the Hyksos wanted to do was to exterminate the native population and erase its culture. Here was a docile, well-ordered people, with an efficient bureaucracy used to getting the most out of a rich land for the benefit of its rulers. The Hyksos made the sensible decision to let it all work for them, taking over at the top as Dynasties XV and XVI. Practically their only innovation was to build a new walled capital at Avaris in the north-eastern Delta.

With their conquest of Lower Egypt complete, the Hyksos made their fatal mistake. They left Upper Egypt to its own devices. There can be little doubt that the conquerors of the Delta could have taken Upper

Egypt as well; but as far as war was concerned the Hyksos never showed the killer instinct which typified the Assyrians. Very much 'warriors for the working day' – which in their case was limited to finding a new land to live in – the Hyksos seem to have been unable or unwilling to look ahead and wonder what would happen if Upper Egypt were to adopt the very weapons and tactics which had brought Lower Egypt to grief. In addition, the Hyksos inevitably went soft during their unmilitary hundred years as the ruling caste of Lower Egypt. They lost their cutting edge as a migrant warrior race. And retribution came at the beginning of the sixteenth century BC, when Upper Egypt launched the first attacks of a crusade which swept the Hyksos clean out of Egypt in little more than thirty years.

Upper Egypt's reaction to the Hyksos challenge was that of an intelligent civilization already some 1,500 years old. In modifying their armies to take on and beat the Hyksos, the Egyptians do not seem to have made blind copies, but to have concentrated on the essentials and incorporated these into their own system. Certainly the Egyptian troops of the early New Kingdom had all the advantages which those of the Middle Kingdom had lacked. They had protection, in the form of body armour; they had more hitting-power, in the form of a new and dominant role for archers, equipped with the composite bow; they were better equipped for hand-to-hand combat thanks to a wider variety of side arms; and they now had mobility in the form of the horsed chariot.

When Egyptian troops were first given armour in which to fight the Hyksos, it was one of the earliest-known case-studies in one of the most basic laws of warfare: that the value of armoured protection depends on the inferiority of enemy weapons. Any armour is better than none at all, but as soon as the enemy adopts a weapon able to pierce your armour, you must confound him by rapidly adopting armour which he cannot pierce: 'scissors cut paper, stone blunts scissors'. The speed with which the Egyptians took to armour suggests that they started by making copies from Hyksos styles, for the art of the armourer is not learned overnight. Certainly the large-scale production of metal armour demanded a specialist industry which would have taken years to build up. For this reason leather, so much easier to cut and work, was probably used extensively. The most elaborate of these early New Kingdom experiments with armour is shown worn by chariot archers: scale-armour fastened to a leather tunic, with short sleeves extending halfway to the elbow. All other styles left the shoulders and arms unprotected, a natural result of their basic simplicity.

Leather armour sounds faintly comic, but only in the age of the high-velocity bullet. It was very different in the Bronze Age. For leather has impressive protective qualities, as every motor-cyclist knows, and can take an incredible amount of battering and stabbing. Stiffened leather armour would have been reasonably proof against sword-cuts and spear-thrusts, though soldiers wearing it would get used to coming out of action blotched with vicious welts and bruises. It would not stop a blow from a heavy axe or the tremendous punch of an arrow fired from a composite bow, if either struck squarely, but would certainly help deflect a glancing blow. The new body armour was accompanied by added protection for the head, but it is hard to tell of precisely what type because the traditional draped headdress, falling to the shoulders, was not abandoned. This may have concealed a simple bronze pot helmet or skullcap. Given the other instances of methodical thinking which the Egyptians were applying to weaponry at the same time, it is hard to accept that they relied simply on padded or quilted fabric head-dresses. At least, one suspects, leather replaced patterned cloth as the outer covering, with the traditional designs being painted on the leather.

Apart from the importance of the composite bow and protection for the troops, the most important lesson which Upper Egypt learned from the Hyksos was the value of the horse in war — not merely for pulling chariots, but for scouting and the fast relaying of orders. The Egyptians never developed a heavy cavalry of their own, but once they had learned to use *mounted scouts* properly there could be no danger of their main army being taken completely by surprise. Egyptian scouts were never intended to enter the battle; their role must have been simply to stay out of trouble and get back safely with the news. They are shown riding bareback, naked but for close-fitting 'briefs'. The scout carried a bow with a quiver slung across his back. This would give him the chance of silencing enemy scouts whom he might encounter, but very little else in the way of combat value.

Thus provided with long-range intelligence, the new Egyptian army adopted mobility in the form of the horsed chariot. Egyptian chariots were unique of their kind, the ultimate lightweights, resembling nothing so much as the skeleton 'cars' used in modern trotting races, with none of the solid construction or heavy wheels seen in the war chariots of other nations. The Egyptian chariot wheel was elegant to the point of flimsiness: spoked, with a narrow rim of jointed wooden arcs shod with a stretched 'tyre' of leather. This suggests that the Egyptians had thought through the problems of chariot warfare to a point beyond that reached by the Hyksos. In the lands where chariots were used in ancient warfare there is so much hostile terrain of all descriptions that it is hard to understand how chariots could have operated at all without bogging down in soft sand, or losing their wheels on rocks. The Egyptians seem to have met this problem head-on by deliberately making their chariots as light as they could, so that the charioteer alone could lift the car clean off the ground and carry it clear if need be.

The Egyptian chariot crew was limited to driver and armoured archer, whose quiver was mounted on the side of the car. Sensibly, the Egyptians do not seem to have embarked spearmen in chariots. Their way with chariots was almost the reverse of the Assyrians', whose chariots carried spearmen or archers, with further deadweight added by a shield-bearer for the warrior and later for the archer as well. Thus Egyptian chariotry pursued speed, agility, and fire-power, to get into action and out of trouble as swiftly as possible.

Such were the improvements developed in Upper Egypt to drive the Hyksos out of the Delta. The first attacks on the Hyksos seem to have been made around 1600 BC under Dynasty XVII, the most successful of whose warrior-kings was Kamose. The reconquest of Lower Egypt was not accomplished overnight, for the Egyptians were learning as they went. They most probably stuck to a methodical advance, never exposing their new troops unnecessarily and gaining vital combat experience with each encounter. By about 1570 the Hyksos had been driven back to their fortress-capital at Avaris, which fell in or about that year to Amosis, first king of Dynasty XVIII. The loss of Avaris robbed the Hyksos of their last foot-hold in Lower Egypt and effectively completed their expulsion. But the efforts needed to oust the Hyksos proved far-reaching for Egypt. The country had been transformed into a state tuned for waging wars of conquest, and the years which followed were known as those of the New Kingdom: the years of empire.

The expulsion of the Hyksos was followed by a century of reconstruction at home and consolidation of the frontiers at the expense of the Nubians in the south and Libyans in the north-west, at the beginning of which the beaten Hyksos were pursued into Palestine. This period was followed, from 1479, by the imperial conquests of Tuthmosis III. Born around 1504 BC, Tuthmosis grew up in the shadow of his formidable mother, the Regent-Queen Hatshepsut. During her 30-year reign Tuthmosis devoted himself to service in the army and raised it to a high peak of efficiency. But he also thought as a strategist and future monarch, deciding that Egypt would not enjoy full military and economic security until the whole of Palestine and Syria were under Egyptian control.

THE CAMPAIGNS IN PALESTINE

When the opportunity came he wasted no time in putting his imperial plan into effect. In his first year as sole ruler, 1479 BC, Tuthmosis marched into Palestine with an army of three divisions. Facing him was a slightly smaller army (about 10–15,000) assembled by a coalition of Canaanite and Syrian rulers. The decisive clash took place at Megiddo, east of Mount Carmel – a natural meeting of the ways where so many battles have been fought that the place gave the word 'Armageddon' to posterity. The battle of 1479 BC seems to have been won by the initial charge of the chariots, before which the coalition army broke and ran for the city of Megiddo. After a brief siege Megiddo surrendered, yielding 924 chariots, 2,238 horses, and 200 suits of armour as spoils for the victors.

This was only the beginning, for Tuthmosis launched annual campaigns into northern Palestine and Syria for year after year until he was satisfied that Egyptian supremacy was unchallenged. He reached Kadesh on the Orontes in 1474 BC, and three years later crossed the Euphrates to pillage the kingdom of Mitanni in a deliberate campaign of 'frightfulness'. Apart from Syria Tuthmosis also campaigned in the south, annexing Nubia and extending Egyptian control up the Nile as far as Napata and the Fourth Cataract.

The conquests of Tuthmosis were energetically maintained by his successors Amenophis II and Amenophis III, but Amenophis IV (1379–1362) proved completely unconcerned with the imperial programme. He was a religious reformer whose overriding mission was to make worship of the sun's disc, or *aten*, the new religion of Egypt. To that end he changed his name to 'Akhenaten' and let every other interest go to the wall. The army was neglected together with the new provinces in Palestine and Syria, which broke away in revolt – aided and abetted by the growing power of the Hittite Empire in the north. The only glories of Akhenaten's jarring and divisive reign were the splendid temples and palaces he built. His son Tutankhamun died childless in 1351 BC, and order was not restored until the reign of Horemheb, former 'General of the Armies' (c. 1347–1319). Horemheb's accession as pharaoh (from *per'o*, literally 'great house', a title adopted by Tuthmosis III), reflects the heightened status of the New Kingdom's army. Horemheb's successor Ramesses I was another former general, but when he died in about 1319 Egypt was spared from the rule of a third general by the smooth accession of Ramesses' son, Sethos I (c. 1319–1304), who restored not only dynastic rule but the imperial programme of Tuthmosis III.

Like Tuthmosis, Sethos I inherited a country and an army which had been put in excellent order. He managed to recover Palestine and pushed through Syria as far as Kadesh, only to find that there was no chance of restoring the northern frontier of Tuthmosis III without an all-out war against the Hittite Empire. The showdown finally took place in the fifth year of Ramesses II, 'The Great' (1304–1237), who marched against the Hittites in 1298 BC. The armies clashed at Kadesh on the Orontes. To meet the four divisions under Ramesses, the Hittite King Muwatallis seems to have had an almost identical infantry strength and a slight advantage in chariots, perhaps about 3,500 to the Egyptians' 3,000. It was the Hittites who took the initiative and attacked, throwing the Egyptians into some disarray. According to the boastful inscriptions of Ramesses which commemorated the battle, the Egyptian army was so big that the rearmost division never got into action at all. The Hittite attack panicked the leading Egyptian divisions and the day was only saved by the personal valour and inspiration of the pharaoh. Put straightforwardly, Ramesses' army seems to have been let down by its scouts and forced to withdraw to the north, away from its line of communication. It deployed hurriedly to meet the Hittite attack but the Egyptian right wing was driven in by a mass charge of Hittite chariotry, and disaster was only averted by desperate counterattacks. Ramesses and his bodyguard were in the forefront of the action, but the dominant feature of the battle was the collision between the Egyptian and Hittite chariotry.

Chariots were never intended to fight enemy chariots; they were a device for wearing down the nerves of enemy infantry, and the massed dog-fight at Kadesh was almost certainly an emergency measure. The frail Egyptian chariots were ill-suited to a head-on collision with the more solid Hittite vehicles, but against that must be set the superior fire-power of the Egyptian chariot archers. Ramesses, however, still had his rearmost division to throw into the fight and it was probably this that caused the Hittites to break off the action. The monuments of Ramesses claimed Kadesh as a great victory, but honours were clearly even. Both sides certainly appear to have accepted that the two empires were so well matched that there was no point in prolonging the struggle. The eventual outcome was a formal Egyptian-Hittite peace

An Egyptian view of the
rout of the Hittite chariots
at the battle of Kadesh.
Note the number of
casualties from Egyptian
arrows

treaty which settled the Eleutheros valley (Lebanon) as the frontier
between the empires.

Ramesses II's accommodation with the Hittites after the battle of
Kadesh marked the furthest limit of Egypt's imperial expansion. The
Egyptian provinces of Palestine and Syria were not retained for long.
Egypt was finding it increasingly difficult to maintain large armies and
administer her outlying provinces. It would seem that manpower was
the biggest problem, and this helps explain why either Ramesses or his
father, Sethos I, as recorded in the Old Testament, imported large
numbers of Jewish workers from Palestine. This, in time, only saddled
Egypt with the additional trouble of a dangerously dissatisfied immi-
grant population vital to the economy. It seems that the Jews and their
families had decamped from Egypt *en masse* and headed for Palestine by
the reign of Ramesses' son Merneptah (1237–1225 BC), but the
immediate aftermath of the Exodus is obscure. The famous disaster to
the pursuing Egyptian army described in *Exodus* is not mentioned in any
known Egyptian source; similarly, readers of the Old Testament will
search in vain for any mention of the victory over 'Israel' recorded on the
'Stele of Merneptah'. In any event, Merneptah did not restore the Jews to
serfdom, and any plans he might have had for further campaigns in
Palestine must have been short-lived. For in 1232 BC Egypt was
menaced by a far greater crisis: a massive invasion from the west.

Across the Mediterranean the phenomenon known as the 'migration
of the Sea Peoples' was fast taking shape by the end of Ramesses II's
reign. Southern Greece and the Aegean Islands were teeming with
vigorous warrior tribes willing to cross the sea and find new lands to
conquer and inhabit. Tough, well-armed, and willing to form alliances

with any power likely to help them, the Sea Peoples overran the declining Hittite Empire in Asia Minor and were the final instruments of its destruction. They were a most dangerous military phenomenon, and nothing like them was to be seen until the mass Teutonic migrations which flooded the Western Roman Empire in the late fourth and fifth centuries AD. In 1232 BC a confederation of Sea Peoples – named as Sherden, Sheckelesh, Lycian, Teresh, and Eckwesh tribesmen – crossed to north Africa and allied themselves with the Libyans on Egypt's western frontier. Then, over 20,000 strong, they swarmed into Egypt itself. Merneptah met them in a battle which he seems to have won mainly with the composite bow, a weapon given great prominence in Egyptian memorials of this period. The invaders suffered great loss: over 8,500 killed and as many captured. For the moment, Merneptah's victory was a 'battle without a morrow', and neither the Libyans nor the Sea Peoples gave Egypt any more trouble before the turn of the century. But early in the reign of Ramesses III (about 1190–1156 BC) the menace returned in even greater strength.

THE LAST BATTLES OF ANCIENT EGYPT

Ramesses III was the last of Egypt's great warrior pharaohs. His reign marked the last occasion in Egyptian history when the hour produced the man. One of the great captains of history, he was a master not only of defensive land warfare but also of combined operations. A realist and a diplomat, he had no hesitation in recruiting mercenaries from the ranks of his country's enemies. Above all, he was the first-known ruler to have grasped the importance of sea power, giving Egypt a fighting navy and smashing her enemies at sea. The actual date of Ramesses III's accession is uncertain, but seems to have been just before 1190. No sooner had he become pharaoh than he was faced with an enemy alliance almost identical to that defeated by Merneptah: Libyans and Sea Peoples. Ramesses saw at once that the Sea Peoples were the prime movers; the Libyans alone could give Egypt little trouble. This time the enemy alliance advanced on the Nile Delta by land and sea, their ships carrying reinforcements and, presumably, supplies. If this seaborne cover could be destroyed, the enemy land forces would be isolated.

Though the Egyptians had never had to fight a sea war before, they were no mean sailors. Old Kingdom tombs have yielded models of the oared sailing ships with which the early Egyptians cruised the Nile; Queen Hatshepsut had sent a fleet of vessels in a famous trading voyage to the land of 'Punt' (possibly Somaliland) in around 1500 BC. By 1190 BC Egyptian sailors knew the eastern Mediterranean well and were thoroughly at home on the coastal waters from Libya to Syria. As the warships Ramesses needed had to be built fast, they were almost certainly conversions from merchant coaster types. His basic aim was to destroy the ships of the Sea People, so the new Egyptian warships were fitted with rams. They had to have enough oars on each side to give them manoeuvrability for ramming attacks. And they had to carry enough fire-power, in the form of marine archers, to destroy the masses of warriors in the enemy ships.

Detail from Medinet Habu
of the great sea victory of
Ramesses III over the fleet
of the Sea Peoples

Ramesses met the first onslaught on land, probably before the new
fleet was ready. As it turned out, the Sea Peoples had not modified their
tactics since Merneptah's victory over them and this time the carnage
wrought by the Egyptian archers was even greater: over 12,000 killed
and 1,000 taken prisoner. These captives were probably the Sherden
mercenaries who had taken service with the Egyptians by the time of the
second attack later in 1190. Ramesses seems to have used the Sherden
troops as a shock force, presumably to disconcert their former comrades
and husband the regular Egyptian troops as much as possible. The
Sherdens fought as doughtily for their new masters as could have been
hoped and Egyptian records were generous in giving the Sherdens the
lion's share of the credit for the second victory.

The third of the great battles of 1190 BC was fought at sea, and is
shown on the walls of Ramesses III's temple at Medinet Habu – the
earliest-known illustration of a sea battle. Points stressed on the Egyptian side are the rams, tipped with snarling animals' heads, jutting from
the ships' bows; and the archers mowing down the enemy crews. The
Egyptians are shown manoeuvring under oars, with sails brailed up to
the yards. Each Egyptian warship has a firing-platform at bow and stern,
plus a small 'fighting-top' up the mast from which individual marksmen could shoot down. Lacking rams, the Sea Peoples would have tried
to close and board the Egyptians, whose tactics – almost exactly like
good chariot drivers – would have been to frustrate this by manoeuvre
and retain the best possible range and field of fire for their archers. The

battle seems to have been a thoroughgoing *mêlée*, with individual Egyptian captains going in to ram, backing straight out and turning to let the marine archers pour their arrows on to the decks of the stricken victims.

The location of Ramesses' sea battle is unknown, but if it had been fought off the mouth of the Nile, silt deposits over the centuries would account for the fact that no wrecks have been found. Despite this uncertainty, Ramesses III's triumph at sea was clearly decisive. The Sea Peoples never troubled Egypt again, though some of their tribes, most notably the Philistines, settled in southern Palestine to become a major thorn in the side for the Jews.

Five years after the great sea battle, Ramesses completed his splendid work against the Sea Peoples by turning on Libya. His objective was not conquest but the destruction of the Libyan army, and once again this was accomplished by the Egyptian archers. Their supremacy now stood so high that the Egyptians went into action with the archers massed in front of the heavy infantry. This would have been a suicidal tactic against an enemy able to charge home, accepting losses, and close with the archers. In fact the Libyans seem to have tried this, only to lose their entire chariot force — ninety-three chariots fell to the victors. Libyan losses were in the usual proportions: over 2,000 killed and about the same number captured.

After Ramesses III Egypt entered a period of uninterrupted decline, with an unbroken succession of unmilitary and feeble rulers increasingly dominated by the priesthood of Amun-re. This decline (Dynasties XX–XXI) continued without a break for over 200 years, during which time Egypt abandoned all imperial ambitions east of Sinai and the splendid Israelite kingdom of David and Solomon flourished in the former Egyptian province of Palestine. Solomon's queen was an Egyptian princess, making him not only the political equal but the brother-in-law of the pharaoh. But when Solomon died in 922 BC and his kingdom split into the rival states of Israel and Judah, Egypt was presented with new opportunities in Palestine.

These opportunities were greedily seized by Sheshonq I (c.935–914 BC), founder of Dynasty XXII. In about 918–917 BC Sheshonq raised an army and invaded Judah, plundering all the major cities and ending with the sack of Jerusalem, looting Solomon's Temple of its golden treasures. This glorified (and admittedly highly lucrative) raid was Egypt's last offensive foray into Palestine as a conqueror — an inglorious tailpiece to the great expeditions of Tuthmosis III, Sethos I, and Ramesses II. By the reign of Sheshonq's grandson, Osorkon II (c.860–832), Egypt was apprehensively sending what aid she could to the Palestinian and Syrian states in their fight against the Assyrians at Qarqar in 854 BC, only to share in the allied defeat. In the late eighth century BC the Ethiopians conquered Egypt and set up a new ruling dynasty, XXV; but its rulers could do no more to check the Assyrian menace than encourage the kings of Judah to fight on, while sending little or no effective aid. When Sennacherib besieged King Hezekiah in Jerusalem in 701 BC, the Assyrian king sneered at Pharaoh Shabaka as a useless ally, a 'broken reed of a staff'.

ABOVE: In the early twelfth century BC Egyptian power still extended east of Sinai. This detail from the palace of Ramesses III shows a captured Canaanite prince

Egypt was finally conquered by the Assyrian kings Esarhaddon (689–670 BC) and Assurbanipal (669–627 BC). With their typical method, the Assyrians did not repeat the error of the Hyksos: they pushed up the Nile to sack Thebes and reduce the whole of Egypt to the status of a vassal kingdom. Their puppet-king was Necho I, former governor of Sais, who founded Dynasty XXVI. Necho's son Psammetichus I (663–609) saw very well that Assyria was facing a mounting sea of troubles and that her claim to be overlord of Egypt was little more than nominal. In his last years Psammetichus took no part in the destruction of Assyria, but his son Necho II (609–594 BC) clearly realized that the Neo-Babylonian Empire of Nabopolassar was an even bigger long-term threat to Egypt than Assyria had been. In 609 BC Necho led an Egyptian army into Syria, ostensibly in support of the dwindling Assyrian cause, and when checked by King Josiah of Judah defeated Josiah at Megiddo. After four years of trying to prop up the western remnant of the Assyrian Empire as a buffer against Nabopolassar, Necho was eventually driven out of Syria after being defeated at Carchemish by Nebuchadnezzar, the Babylonian Crown Prince. Even so, Necho managed to defeat Nebuchadnezzar's attempt to break into Egypt in 601 BC, which suggests that Necho was no mean general and had led a fighting retreat out of Syria with his army substantially intact. The same cannot be said of Necho's grandson Apries (588–568 BC) who encouraged the last revolt of the kingdom of Judah only to withdraw immediately from Palestine on his first encounter with Nebuchadnezzar's army. Nebuchadnezzar, however, contented himself with the final conquest of Jerusalem (587 BC) and the extirpation of the kingdom of Judah; he made no attempt to invade Egypt. This was finally accomplished by Cambyses, son of Cyrus of Persia, in 525 BC; and Egypt became subject first to Persian, then Macedonian, and finally to Roman rule.

The military supremacy of ancient Egypt was like a dinosaur: very impressive and successful in its heyday, and developing some novel features, yet somehow failing to evolve far enough to survive. One of the most obvious of these failures was the ever-increasing reliance on the foot archer without giving the infantry formations adequate protection in the form of mobile archers. As we have seen, an important feature of the Assyrian war machine was an obsession with protecting the key troops; and the Egyptian failure to make the transition from the horsed chariot to horsed cavalry, as the Assyrians did, was fatal.

Egypt's true genius was limited to the peaceful arts, invariably practised on a breathtaking scale; her military successes were ephemeral. This characteristic makes ancient Egypt one of the most fascinating, and sympathetic, of the world's lost civilizations. But in the end Egypt's failure to develop military defences strong enough to foil her attackers proved the country's undoing. The peaceful arts were not enough, and two thousand years of splendid independence were succeeded by another two thousand years of servitude. And this, along with all the artistic masterpieces, must surely be counted one of Egypt's greatest legacies to posterity: a supreme object-lesson in the results of military inadequacy.

CHAPTER THREE

Syria and Palestine

SYRIA AND PALESTINE played a strange role in the wars of the ancient world. Because of their geographical position as the 'Fertile Crescent's' western arc, they made up a vital link in world land and sea communications – between Africa and Asia, between the Mediterranean and the Euphrates. This also made them a conduit for every current of military pressure that flowed.

Sooner or later, Syria and Palestine became an essential objective for every power making a bid for international supremacy. At the same time the region frequently acted as a receptacle for new military ideas introduced by successive waves of migrant peoples – military ideas which sometimes proved excessively inconvenient for neighbouring powers. The Hyksos invasion from Palestine changed the entire course of Egyptian history. Syria and Palestine played their parts in the collapse of the Hittite and Assyrian empires. And, in the Israelites, the region produced one of the most extraordinary military peoples of all time.

THE FIRST CITY-STATES

As an early focus of urban civilization, Syria-Palestine was close on the heels of lower Mesopotamia. At the time of writing, research is continuing on the enormous haul of records and other artifacts unearthed at Ebla, 35 miles south of Aleppo, in 1975. Written in Sumerian characters, Eblaite records tell of a swarm of city-states in Syria-Palestine, many formerly thought to have emerged much later than the third millennium – Beirut, Damascus, Gaza, even Sodom and Gomorrah.

Ebla itself dominated a powerful confederacy of city-states around 2400 BC, strongly reminiscent of the Sumerian confederacies of Lagash, Uruk, and Ur conquered by Sargon the Great. Ebla was probably strong enough to treat on equal terms with Sargon the Great. Sargon claimed a victory over the forces of Ebla during his westward advance to the Mediterranean, but seems to have exacted no more than nominal tribute. Ebla certainly challenged the Akkadian Empire around 2300 BC and Naramsin mounted a special expedition which stormed and burned the city. The significance of the feat may be judged from the fact that one of Naramsin's victory inscriptions hails him as 'the conqueror of Ebla, never before subdued in history'.

OPPOSITE: Gorgeous decoration adorns a Phoenician gold knife of the eighteenth century BC. Though the enduring talent of the Phoenicians was trade rather than war, their immense wealth made them invaluable allies for the powers battling for mastery in Syria and Palestine

What sort of troops did the Akkadians beat in Syria during their short-lived imperial tenure? So far the digs at Ebla have suggested that the Syrians were far more of a trading than a military people, for no visual evidence as good as the 'Stele of the Vultures' has been turned up. But the voluminous tablet-archives at Ebla have yielded one startling written account which is an unmistakable military despatch. This is a report by a third millennium general, Enna-Dagan by name, of his triumphant march to the city of Mari on the Euphrates around 2480 BC. It yields little military detail, being hardly more than a catalogue of gory slaughters on the march to Mari with the refrain 'Piles of corpses I gathered'. But it does show that when occasion demanded the leading Syrian city-states could send an irresistible army at least 250 miles.

This puts Ebla and its satellites in the same category as the leading Sumerian city-states: capable of spasmodic military action when roused, yet incapable of developing a defence system strong enough to beat off greedy rivals. Like Lagash and Ur, Ebla enjoyed a brief renaissance after the Akkadian Empire fell to pieces – but the old order in both Syria and Mesopotamia went under to overpowering waves of Amorite nomads around 2000–1900 BC.

The ethnic reinforcement of Syria-Palestine referred to above had begun in earnest when refugees from Naramsin's conquests in Syria headed south into Palestine. The Amorites added another layer, and this had barely made the transition from nomadic to urban when a third layer was added, starting from about 17–1500 BC. This third layer was the result of the overspill of the migration of the Hurrians south-west from the Caucasus. The Hurrians had learned the use of horse and chariot from the steppe peoples to the north; by 1500 BC they had permeated the whole of the 'Fertile Crescent', and the southward drift they triggered off in Syria-Palestine resulted in the Hyksos invasion of Egypt (pp. 42–7). Pressure on Syria from the north intensified by the expansion from the Hittite Empire from Asia Minor.

Egypt was the first civilization to take shape outside the 'Fertile Crescent'; the Hittite Empire was the second. Like the Egyptians, the Hittites developed their own culture, language, and hieroglyphic script, but there the similarities ended. For the Hittites were a fighting people of great energy and imagination. The power of the empire they carved out reached east into Upper Mesopotamia and south into Syria, thus giving Syria-Palestine the last injection of foreign influence it received before the Israelites embarked on their remarkable career as a martial race.

THE HITTITE EMPIRE

After its emergence around 1600 BC the Hittite kingdom had a shaky first century until the throne was made hereditary by King Telepinus after 1500. Hittite kings were made and unmade by a powerful aristocracy, and although the king combined in his person the roles of high priest, lawgiver, and supreme warlord he seems to have been replaced with distressing frequency. For this very reason no Hittite king of the sixteenth century BC remained at peace for long, war being a natural antidote to mischief and conspiracy at home. But even without this

ABOVE: Hittite gold figure from the fourteenth century BC, probably of a warrior – note the sword at his belt

domestic stimulus the Hittites had far too many hostile neighbours ever to be troubled by too long an outbreak of peace.

Khattusas, the Hittite capital (modern Boghazkoy), lay in the arc of the Halys river in central Asia Minor, and the first Hittite campaigns on record were west and south of the Halys, expanding towards the Mediterranean. From about 1580 BC King Khattusilis II began the process of south-easterly expansion into Syria, conquering Alalakh. And his successor, Mursilis I (c. 1550–1530 BC) brought off one of the most resounding military feats in ancient warfare.

After overrunning northern Syria and taking Aleppo (Haleb), which had replaced ruined Ebla as the key city between the upper Euphrates and the Mediterranean, Mursilis took the Hittite army on a breathtaking march down the Euphrates, captured Babylon, looted it bare and levelled it to the ground. He then marched home with the spoils. If Mursilis had hoped that destroying and plundering the most prestigious city in the world would cement his authority at home, it was a ludicrous miscalculation: he was assassinated soon after his return. But the biggest question is how he managed to do it at all.

It was 500 miles from the Hittites' Syrian base at Aleppo to Babylon. Mursilis' plan must have depended on covering those 500 miles as quickly as possible and attacking before the Babylonians had time to raise a defending army. For this he must have had help, active or passive, from Babylon's northern neighbours; no army can be force-marched 500 miles through hostile territory and emerge in perfect fighting trim, ready for instant action, at the end of the road.

Mursilis seems to have had a choice of two plans for the all-important approach. The first and most likely would have been to set up a chain of advance depots as far down the Euphrates as possible, in the territory of allied cities or friendly neutrals who had agreed to give the Hittite army passage through their lands. Mari seems a likely 'advance base' depot: it was half way to Babylon from Aleppo and well within range of an army approaching from the Aleppo region, as the Eblaites had proven 950 years before. Such an assisted approach by easy stages would have left the Hittite army in prime condition for a 250-mile march on Babylon. It would also make Mursilis the 'Duke of Marlborough' of the second millennium BC, a not inappropriate title, given the audactiy of the venture. Faced with similar distances to cover, Marlborough used just such a chain of advanced depots to march his army across Germany in his Blenheim campaign, 3,235 years later.

The only alternative which seems at all feasible would have been a direct approach by water, with the Hittites commandeering every boat and raft on the upper Euphrates and swarming downstream in an awesome armada. Once again, Mursilis would have needed a good deal of advance preparation, not only to collect enough troop transports but to recruit enough pilots who were familiar with the vagaries of the Euphrates. But such a voyage would have been so extraordinary that it would surely have been remembered, even in the laconic Hittite chronicle which records little more than that the expedition took place.

One fact is clear: this was not an attempt at conquest and occupation but the biggest and earliest commando raid on record. Nor was it – like

57

Mobility and firepower

OPPOSITE: Two of the greatest warlords in their chariots: Ramesses II of Egypt (*top*) and Assurbanipal of Assyria (*below*). The lightweight Egyptian chariots were built for the speediest possible movement of archers, whose arrows were carried in quivers fixed to the side of the car. With their emphasis on protection for all grades of troops, the Assyrians built bigger and heavier chariots carrying at least two shield-bearers in addition to driver and archer.

LEFT: Pharaoh Ramesses II, whose chariot battle with the Hittites at Kadesh, though the most dramatic chariot engagement recorded in ancient history, ended in a strategic draw

so many commando raids – a glorious failure. The objective, Babylon's pillage and destruction, was completely achieved and the assault force successfully withdrawn, surprise having been virtually complete. Few campaigns in military history have been crowned with greater success, or have received so little recognition.

The Babylon campaign was a splendid achievement, but its immediate aftermath made it look like a brilliant flash in the pan. After the assassination of Mursilis, the Hittites were ruled by a number of brief-lived kings, five of them in thirty years. Instability at home was compounded by defeat abroad: the powerful Hurrian Kingdom of Mitanni threw the Hittites out of Syria and pushed them back into Asia Minor. In the fifteenth century things went from bad to worse. The Hittite Kingdom came close to extinction, its old enemies in Asia Minor forcing the Hittites back into their original heartland east of the Halys. At one time, wild Kashka tribesmen from the north sacked Khattusas itself. But from these humiliations and perils the Hittite kingdom was first saved, then raised to imperial power by King Suppiluliumas I, who took the throne around 1380 BC.

Suppiluliumas gave the people strong government and confidence for the present by rebuilding Khattusas and fortifying it. As far as security for the future was concerned there could only be one formula: a reconstructed army capable of beating not only marauding tribesmen but the troops of Mitanni as well. And the Hittite army built up by Suppiluliumas eventually proved eminently capable of performing both tasks.

Unlike the troops of the Egyptian New Kingdom, Hittite infantry did not depend on large formations of foot archers. The accent was on axemen, spearmen, and swordsmen, helmeted but with no body armour to slow them down – ideal troops for forcing a close-quarter action after a charge, relying on their iron axes and swords to beat down the opposition.

The trump card of the new Hittite army was its chariot force, which correctly blended the elements of mobility and fire-power. Hittite chariot warriors were archers and their main purpose was to decimate enemy infantry with their fire, thus taking excessive pressure off the Hittite infantry formations. But that was not the only function of the chariot forces. Compared to the lightweight speedsters favoured by the Egyptians, Hittite chariots were solid trucks carrying three men, where an Egyptian chariot could never carry more than two. The third man was a spearman, enabling a Hittite chariot formation to engage in close-quarter fighting as well as hit-and-run attacks, if need be.

These new troops enabled Suppiluliumas to smash the ring of tribesmen around the Hittite heartland and begin the reconquest of Syria, but the Hittites' first clash with the army of Mitanni under King Tuishrata resulted in defeat. Suppiluliumas reacted to this setback by modifying his tactics and calling in allies, including Artadama, a prince of Mitanni who was challenging Tuishrata for the kingship. The price which Artadama had to pay for Hittite sponsorship and aid in his bid for the throne of Mitanni was agreement that northern Syria should pass from Mitanni to Hittite control. Thus aided by shrewd diplomacy and

Egyptian chariotry met its match in the epic battle with the Hittites at Kadesh (1298 BC). Perhaps it is significant that the Egyptians made the loudest claims of victory in what was clearly a strategic draw – this relief showing three-man Hittite chariots is a detail from Ramesses II's temple at Abydos

foreign contingents, Suppiluliumas struck at Mitanni again and captured its capital, Washukkani. Artadama duly became King Artadama II of Mitanni and the cities of northern Syria had no choice but to accept Hittite rule again.

The last gift of Suppiluliumas to his people was the stability bestowed by a long reign; he finally died of plague in 1346 BC. Unfortunately his heir, Arnuwandas II, succumbed shortly afterwards from the same cause. The resulting disruption in the smooth transition of power in the Hittite ruling house encouraged the subject peoples of Asia Minor to break out again. Fortunately the eventual successor to the Hittite throne, Mursilis II, proved equal to the crisis, fighting innumerable campaigns against the Kashka to the north and the warriors of Arzawa to the south-west; he also had to put down a revolt by the city of Carcemish in Syria. When he died in 1316, Mursilis left his successor Muwatallis an empire with secure frontiers and a seasoned army in excellent fighting trim.

Meanwhile, the New Kingdom Pharaoh Sethos I was pushing ahead with the Egyptian reconquest of Palestine, a programme enthusiastically maintained by Ramesses II when he succeeded to the Egyptian throne in 1304. Watching the Egyptian tide rising inexorably northward towards Hittite Syria, Muwatallis refused to fritter away his army in piecemeal efforts to help the Palestinians. He kept the army concentrated, waiting for the Egyptians to come within reach; and the inevitable moment of truth occurred at Kadesh on the Orontes in 1298 BC.

Apart from the fascinating tactical aspects of Kadesh (see pp. 48–9), the battle is particularly interesting from the strategic viewpoint. (Assessing who 'won' at Kadesh is like conducting the debate over who won the Battle of Jutland after an interval of 3,214 years.) Here was unquestionably the biggest single head-on clash between two military empires the world had ever seen, and there was no decisive outcome. Ramesses made the loudest claims for victory, although his bid to drive the Hittites out of Syria had obviously failed. On the other hand, neither Muwatallis nor his successor Khattusilis II made any subsequent attempt to push the Egyptians further south.

The fact was that Kadesh was a climacteric for both empires, and their rulers knew it. There was no point in wrestling a second or third fall. Neither Egypt nor the Hittite Empire could benefit from a protracted struggle on their mutual Syrian frontier, with each side having to keep its army operating at maximum distance from home. Common sense prevailed (in a way that it has rarely done in the wars of the last few centuries) and the *impasse* was officially recognized in the treaty of 1283 between Ramesses and Khattusilis.

This treaty did much more than merely settle a mutually acceptable frontier between the Hittites and Egyptians in Syria. In the fifteen years since Kadesh, rapidly-changing events in Upper Mesopotamia had made some kind of formal arrangement with Egypt essential for the Hittite Empire. The first great burst of Assyrian expansion had begun. By the 1280s, Adadnirari I had assaulted feeble Mitanni, once Assyria's overlord, and conquered it. A frightening new power now menaced the Hittite Empire across the Upper Euphrates. But the Hittite-Egyptian treaty of 1283, removing the biggest bone of contention between the two powers, created a new power bloc in the west which deterred the Assyrians from a drive to the Mediterranean. The Kassite dynasty of Babylon, not Hittite Syria, was their next victim.

So it was that the aftermath of Kadesh kept Syria-Palestine under joint Hittite and Egyptian rule until the death of Ramesses II in 1237. From then on events leaped forward again, impelled by the migrations of the Sea Peoples who swept east across Asia Minor and had overrun the Hittite heartland by about 1230. Because of the need to keep troops in Syria to watch the Assyrians, the Hittites found it impossible to raise a strong enough army to fight off the Sea Peoples in the west. But even if they had been free of the incubus of empire, the Hittites would have stood little chance in a stand-up fight. The warriors of the Sea Peoples revelled in hand-to-hand fighting and the major weakness of the Hittite army was in infantry fire-power, with its ability to kill at a distance. As we have seen (see pp. 50–2) the Egyptian armies of Merneptah and Ramesses III, relying on their foot archers, were the only imperial troops which managed to keep the Sea Peoples in check.

With the Hittite homeland gone, the provincial forces in Syria found themselves in much the same position as the French colonial forces in North Africa after the fall of France in 1940. They stayed where they were because there was nowhere else to go, and kept Hittite culture alive in Syria. Meanwhile the Egyptian withdrawal from Palestine, in order to fight off the Sea Peoples, created a vacuum to be filled by the Israelites, transformed from serfs into a ferocious warrior people inspired by a god of wrath.

THE ISRAELITES

The accounts of the Jewish Exodus from Egypt and conquest of Canaan, as given in the Old Testament, make chilling reading. Here is warfare waged at a new level only too familiar in our own era. In their blind obedience to the orders of their god to take 'the land which I give to you', the Israelites practised total war with a ferocity which not even the Assyrians surpassed – cleaning out lands they conquered with systematic massacre. Their holy books argue that whenever the Israelites tried to defy the 'word of the Lord' and spare conquered populations – in other words, to imitate every other military people of the ancient world, and content themselves with being the new rulers – they were punished with military defeat, humiliating tribulation, or both.

The great books of the Pentateuch – *Genesis, Exodus, Leviticus, Numbers,* and *Deuteronomy* – describe the patriarchal origins of the Jews or 'children of Israel' (the patriarch Jacob), and how they came to servitude in Egypt. Then, in the late thirteenth century BC, with Moses acting as God's interpreter, the Israelites set out from Egypt to regain their long-lost homeland, Canaan. During their forty-year Odyssey in the Sinai and Negev deserts, Moses gave the Israelites a draconian code of civil law and religious observance, welding the disparate Israelite tribes into a close-knit league. *Numbers* and *Deuteronomy* describe the process in detail, providing a comprehensive answer to one of the most crucial riddles in history: how a pastoral nomad people can be transformed into a warrior race.

Numbers explains that this transformation began with a census taken in Sinai which yielded a grand total of 603,550 men, women, and children – excluding the tribal elite known as the Levites, 22,000 strong, who tended the shrine of God itself: the Ark of the Covenant and its tabernacle. The population was grouped into twelve tribes named for the twelve sons of Israel, each tribe with its standard and allotted place in camp. This amounted to a four-square deployment shielding the Levites and the Ark: the tribes of Judah, Issachar, and Zebulun to the east of the Ark, Reuben, Simeon, and Gad to the south, Ephraim, Manasseh, and Benjamin to the west, and Dan, Asher, and Napthali to the north. The order of march read counter-clockwise: Judah/ Issachar/Zebulun – Reuben/Simeon/Gad – Ephraim/Manasseh/Benjamin – Dan/Asher/Napthali. Each tribe was called upon to supply a contingent of fighting men when required. These contingents were made up on a decimal basis, officered by 'commanders of thousands' and 'commanders of hundreds'.

Though subject time and again to incidental delays and diversions, the Israelites knew precisely where their destination lay – and they did not march blindly to gain it. They relied on detailed intelligence reports brought in by reconnaissance parties and spies. The first close reconnaissance of Canaan, carried out by a detail of twelve spies, one from each tribe, was not promising. 'The people who dwell in the land are strong, and the cities are fortified, and very large . . . we are not able to go up against the people; for they are stronger than we.' (*Numbers* 14:28–31). A lucky victory over one southern Canaanite ruler, Arad, failed to tempt the Israelites into heading straight into Canaan. Instead they crossed the

Negev desert, skirted the northern tip of the Gulf of Akaba, and headed north through the Amorite kingdoms of Edom and Moab, east of the Dead Sea. This line of march involved the Israelites in their first war of conquest, against the Midianites of southern Edom, and this gave a fair indication of what the invaders had in store for their enemies.

The Israelite muster was 12,000 strong: 'of every tribe a thousand, throughout all the tribes of Israel'. It successively annihilated the armies of five Midianite kings, all of whom were taken and killed. There were no hostages and no prisoners. The Midianite women and children were rounded up as part of the spoils, but not for long. On the orders of Moses and Eleazar the priest, all boys and male babies were murdered, together with all women who had lost their virginity. Virgins were handed back to the fighting men to 'keep alive for yourselves'.

The slaughter of the Midianites was repeated with each city that fell to the Israelites east of the Jordan – Aroer, Heshbon, Rabbath-Ammon, Edrei: 'men, women, and children, we left none remaining; only the cattle we took as spoil for ourselves, and the booty of the cities which we captured'. (*Deut.* 2:34–35). And the same fate was laid down in advance for the kingdoms west of Jordan: 'when the Lord your God gives them over to you, and you defeat them, then you must utterly destroy them; you shall make no covenant with them, and show no mercy to them'. (*Deut.* 7:2). This was not the way in which the Akkadians, Babylonians, Egyptians, or Hittites had administered their empires, adapting to and tolerating – after the ferocity of battle – to the culture and religions of their new subjects. Even the Assyrians, who later became a byword for alien cruelty in Israelite lore, never applied themselves to the deliberate extinction of conquered populations.

The subjugation of east-bank Jordan gave the Israelites combat experience which they badly needed before crossing the Jordan and tackling the city-states and kingdoms of Canaan. Joshua, Moses' successor, proved a most able war leader; the *Book of Joshua*'s account of the Israelite invasion and conquest of Canaan is an intriguing blend of resounding miracles and highly sophisticated military tactics.

Before he led the Israelites across the Jordan, Joshua had already reconnoitred his first objective: the walled city of Jericho, which the Israelite host besieged as soon as they were across the river. Whether the famous collapse of Jericho's walls was the result of a timely earthquake or of intensive mining operations remains a matter for endless debate, but the ease of Jericho's capture and the riches of the spoils tempted the Israelites into a rash gamble. An inadequate force of 3,000 men failed ignominiously to take the nearby city of Ai. Joshua announced that this was God's punishment for one man's theft from the loot of Jericho, and had the man stoned to death along with his entire family and all his livestock. Having thus atoned for the crime and restored morale, Joshua then turned on Ai with the full muster of Israel, 30,000 strong.

The attack on Ai was a tactical gem. Joshua posted a strike force of 5,000 men in ambush to the west of Ai. He then advanced on the city with the main body and, by feigning retreat, lured the army of Ai out into open country. As Ai emptied in pursuit of the retreating Israelites, the strike force swept in from its ambush, seized the city and set it

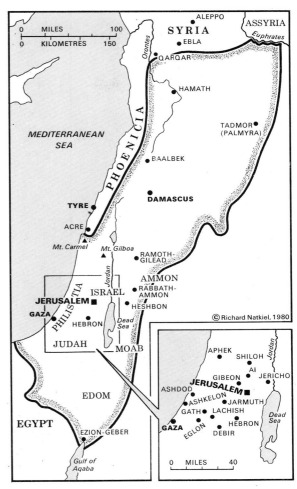

ABOVE: Statuette of a
Canaanite war god, from
Megiddo. Though under
divine orders to
exterminate the 'idolaters'
of Canaan and their
neighbours, the victorious
Israelites soon found
themselves making
alliances with them
instead

ABOVE RIGHT: The
kingdom of David and
Solomon at its greatest
extent

ablaze. Meanwhile Joshua turned the main body to the attack; the strike
force advanced from the burning city and completed the total envelopment of the army of Ai. The usual massacre followed, with the victims –
battle casualties and civilians combined – totalling 12,000.

The Canaanite rulers reacted to the invasion by forming a defensive
alliance – 'the Hittites, the Amorites, the Canaanites, the Perizzites, the
Hivites, and the Jebusites'. This was weakened at birth by the defection
of a confederacy headed by the city of Gibeon, which lay within a mere
three days' march of Ai and was clearly next on the Israelites' list.
Appalled at the destruction which the Israelites had dealt out at Heshbon, Jericho, and Ai, the Gibeonites escaped by a clever trick. They
hastily made up a fake embassy to look as if it had come from a long way
off, and sent it in to the Israelite host with the offer of an alliance. Joshua
and the tribal leaders were fooled into swearing an alliance with the
Gibeonites, only to discover within days that the Gibeonites were close
neighbours. There was a popular clamour to exterminate the Gibeonites, but the Israelite leaders did not dare break their oath. They
compromised by sparing the Gibeonites but setting them to work as
serfs – 'hewers of wood and drawers of water for the congregation'.

The reaction of the Canaanite league – the kings of Jerusalem, Hebron, Jarmuth, Lachish, and Eglon – was to march against Gibeon in punishment for its defection. The Israelite host had set off to the north-west to reduce Gilgal, but the Gibeonites managed to get a message through in the nick of time. Joshua came racing back with the Israelite army in a gruelling forced march through the night, fell on the Canaanite host at Gibeon and destroyed it in a running battle with immense slaughter. The victory at Gibeon was followed by a gory victory march by the triumphant Israelites through Makkedah, Libnah, Lachish, Eglon, and Debir – a march of destruction all the way.

The news of the seemingly unstoppable juggernaut down in Canaan prompted another defensive alliance, this time assembled by the principalities and the Hittites of Syria. This coalition army included an element which the Israelites had not encountered before: chariots. Joshua and his captains, however, tackled the new menace practically and introduced an anti-chariot tactic summed up in *Joshua* 11:6 as 'hamstring the horses and burn the chariots' – presumably with fire-arrows. It sounds suicidal until one remembers the versatility of steady infantry. At Hastings in AD 1066, for instance, Harold's axemen stood their ground in the face of Norman cavalry charges until they could kill the knights' horses at point-blank range. Joshua seems to have met the charge of the northern chariots with a barrage of fire-arrows, which must have had a most disconcerting effect on the chariot crews. A screen of light infantrymen armed with poleaxes could then have dodged the chariots which did get through, hewing at the horses' legs as they swept past.

The battle with the northern league and its chariots took place at Merom, north of the Sea of Galilee; it ended in total victory for the Israelites and, like the battle of Gibeon, was the prelude to a second relentless victory march which cleaned out the lands on both sides of the Jordan as far as Mount Lebanon.

The *Book of Joshua* claims that a total of thirty-one Palestinian city-states fell to the Israelites between the crossing of the Jordan and the annihilation of the northern league at Merom. The account has its 'grey areas', the most obvious being the question of how long this period of invasion and conquest lasted. We are told that it took 'a long time', a phrase which hardly makes for precision. But it is nevertheless helpful, for it indicates that this was not a runaway conquest with the victims falling overnight like a row of skittles. There was certainly a pattern in the conquest – a battle, followed by systematic exploitation. In the main the conquest seems to have been a long, slow grind in which the Israelites probably had to modify their tactics more than once. Only one outright Israelite defeat – the failure of the first attack on Ai – is described in any detail; there may have been many more. But enough is said in *Joshua* to indicate that Israelite tactics were flexible enough to overcome every enemy state or league who tried to make a fight of it, and that Joshua himself was an outstanding general.

The important point is that during the conquest the Israelite tribes stayed concentrated, able to field armies of up to 30,000 which were far too strong for the opposition. The turning-point came when the conquered territories were shared out between the twelve tribes and settlement began, which seems to have happened early in the twelfth century BC. Settlement not only dispersed the Israelite host of the conquest: it marked the end of the massacres. 'When Israel grew strong, they put the Canaanites to forced labour, but did not utterly drive them out' (*Judges* 1:28). This was a process which was bound to have begun sooner or later, but it also stripped the Israelites of their most potent psychological weapon: terror. It also saddled them with resentful subject populations, always ready to break out and exact revenge on the hated aliens. (Much the same thing happened in Saxon England when the Great Army of the Danes, after terrorizing the entire land for over fifteen years, broke up and began to put down permanent roots — it reduced the invaders to human proportions.)

Sharing out the conquests was Joshua's last achievement and there is a hint that he did it reluctantly, knowing the conquest was incomplete but yielding to pressure. Certainly he made it clear, when delineating the tribal boundaries, that the divine plan as revealed to Moses was far from its completion. Syria remained to be conquered and there were still pockets of unconquered territory to the south-west — Gaza, Gath, Ashkelon, Ashdod.

Joshua's death deprived the Israelites of their supreme warlord and national leader, and as they struggled through the twelfth century trying to hold on to their conquests they remained in desperate need of both qualities. They were assailed by enemies understandably out for revenge, foremost among them the Midianites and Moabites in the south, and the Syrians in the north. Israelite survival during the twelfth century BC amounted to a hand-to-hand reliance on individual military leaders; occasional injections of national inspiration and leadership were provided by the random charismatics whom the Israelites called 'judges'. Thus Ehud the assassin put an end, with his dagger, to the ascendancy of the Moabite king Eglon; Gideon waged highly successful guerrilla warfare against the invading Midianites. The prophetess Deborah, who 'judged Israel' from the shade of her famous palm tree, urged the northern tribes of Zebulun and Napthali to combine against a powerful Syrian army commanded by Sisera, who had a formidable force of 900 chariots. Led by Barak, the Israelite muster of 10,000 remembered the anti-chariot tactics which had won the day at Merom and smashed Sisera's army on the Kishon river, east of Mount Carmel. Sisera himself, forced to abandon his chariot and flee on foot — a significant ignominy for a commander of chariots — met a particularly gruesome fate at the hands of Jael the wife of Heber, whose prowess with hammer and nail immediately made her a national heroine (*Judges* 4:15–21).

As if there were not enough foreign enemies to worry about, Gideon's son Abimelech tried to seize power and rule as a king, and there were other outbreaks of civil war between tribes dissatisfied with the territorial allocations. A semblance of unity was only restored to the Israelites by that time-honoured prescription for internal discord: an overwhelming menace from outside. And this was provided by the most tenacious enemies the Israelites had to face before the Assyrians came west: the armies of the Philistine league.

As we have seen (see p. 52) the Philistines were Sea Peoples who settled in south-west Palestine after the wars of Ramesses III in defence of Egypt. There is a striking similarity between the story of Philistia and that of the Duchy of Normandy. Both were founded by sea warriors; both retained an aggressive military caste; and both, after consolidating their original foothold, caused the peoples of the hinterland increasing trouble.

The Philistines first appear as a military threat to the Israelites in the period of the judges, neighbours of the apprehensive tribe of Judah. The most famous Israelite champion against the Philistines is named as Samson, a maverick hero with the status of a judge in Israel. With Samson's story the comparison of the Philistines with the Normans becomes particularly apt because his adventures (*Judges* 13–16) are not unlike those of Hereward the Wake and Robin Hood. (Also like Hereward the Wake and Robin Hood, he was brought down in the end by female treachery.) By the middle of the eleventh century BC, border raiding and reprisals had escalated into a full-blown power struggle between the Philistines and the Israelites, who finally sank their differences and raised a national army to break the Philistines in battle.

The result was catastrophic. At Aphek, on the northern border of Philistia, the first engagement resulted in 4,000 dead for the Israelites. Their army, however, stayed in the field while the Ark of the Covenant was hastily brought up from its shrine at Shiloh, in confident hope of receiving divine reinforcement for a second attack. This proved a fatal error. The Israelites' blind faith in the powers of the Ark was no longer matched by the combat ferocity which had brought victory to the armies of Moses and Joshua. It was the Philistines who took the initiative and attacked. The morale of the Israelites collapsed at the first shock and their ranks melted in a general rout. The Philistines, following up hard and fast, made an immense slaughter – 30,000 Israelites were cut down as they fled or cowered in their tents. The Philistines' masterstroke was in capturing the Ark itself. When they carried the Ark off in triumph they had not only annihilated Israel's only field army: they had carved out the heart and soul of the Israelite people.

The Old Testament does not give the name of the Philistines' supreme warlord, but the terms he dictated to the beaten Israelites were as effective as they were simple. The Israelites were prostrate, numbed with horror at the loss of the Ark, but there was no need for the Philistines to occupy the entire country. Disentangling the highly confused sequence of events in the *First Book of Samuel*, it seems that the Philistines contented themselves with imposing a total ban not only on the making and carrying of weapons by the Israelites, but on any kind of smithing. The effect of this was that 'every one of the Israelites went down to the Philistines to sharpen his ploughshare, his mattock, his axe, or his sickle'. (*I Samuel* 15:20). To add insult to injury the Philistines levied a scale of charges for these repairs.

Driving metal-working underground and banning weapons was a most effective way of preventing a conquered people from launching an armed rebellion against the invaders, who could in turn patrol the country from a handful of garrisons. In addition, the Philistines had the sense to return the Ark of the Covenant, thus depriving the Israelites of the most obvious motive for revolt and a holy war. They could have their totem back – it had done them little good at Aphek.

Disarmed and humiliated, the Israelites reacted by looking for a permanent fighting leader. They brushed aside the homilies of Samuel, their current judge, who advised them to stick to the Law, repent their sins, and await divine guidance. They wanted a king, and they ordered Samuel to produce one. 'We will have a king over us, that we also may be like all the other nations, and that our king may govern us and go out before us and fight our battles.' (*1 Samuel* 8:20). Samuel's nominee was Saul, of the tribe of Benjamin, who was duly anointed as the first King of Israel around 1020 BC. In trying to mastermind a national guerrilla movement against the Philistines, Saul had a formidable task. For a start there was the lack of weapons, a fundamental deficiency which took time to remedy. Then there was the human material. The Israelites were a fickle people, easily discouraged by setbacks. They demanded instant victory, and when Saul could not provide it they looked for other leaders who could. But above all Saul lacked the human qualities which a guerrilla leader must have – the magic touch which inspires men to follow a leader through thick and thin, instantly responsive to his orders. Saul was also unlucky as a commander, and although this was not always his fault nothing destroys morale faster than a string of failures.

As the first Book of Samuel makes clear, Israelite resistance to the Philistine occupation was therefore bedevilled by internal discord. Saul's mind gradually gave way under a constant barrage of frustration and suspicion. The three-cornered saga of Saul, David and Jonathan needs no repeating here but one of its most famous episodes, the single combat between David and the Philistine champion Goliath, contains many aspects of no little relevance.

For a start, the combat itself symbolized the underlying plight of the Israelite guerrillas, still starved of adequate weaponry with which to confront an excellently equipped foe. At the same time, it showed that the confrontation was by no means a hopeless one. Here, in miniature, is all the fundamental viciousness which characterized warfare until the emergence of efficient firearms in the last two centuries. This viciousness was conferred by the *permanent efficiency* of cutting and thrusting weapons. In the modern era a captured enemy rifle often has an unfamiliar action, and once that has been mastered the rifle becomes useless as soon as its ammunition supply runs out. But an abandoned sword or spear, once snatched up, could be instantly turned against its former owner.

On the purely descriptive level, the David-and-Goliath story gives us an excellent description of a Philistine warrior at the turn of the eleventh century BC (setting aside the superhuman weights and measures used to convey Goliath's stature). He wore, we are told, a bronze helmet and a 'coat of mail'. As this was made of bronze it must have been scale armour and not mail; mail consisted of interlinked rings for which bronze was an inferior metal. His legs were protected with bronze greaves, and in addition to a long sword at his side he carried a huge spear with a weighty iron point. As a crowning touch, 'his shield-bearer went before him'. (*1 Samuel* 17:5−7). Here is a figure which could have stepped straight out of Homer's *Iliad*; Goliath could certainly have joined the ranks of either side in the Siege of Troy without exciting comment. Bearing in mind the original homeland of the Sea Peoples who settled in Philistia − Greece and the Aegean − the presence of such an apparition in Palestine becomes less surprising.

Thus David's victory over Goliath typified the gradual rearmament of the Israelites by means of successful ambushes and hit-and-run raids, both of which provided the victors with more weapons and armour. This was a war of attrition, with time on the side of the Israelites. It saw many of the Mediterranean features of the Philistine war machine rub off on to the Israelites. Apart from using the same armour and weapons, the Israelite warriors naturally came to ape their Philistine counterparts. This happened quite early on in the struggle. To give one example, Saul had employed David as his armour-bearer *before* the duel with Goliath.

Apart from his personal failure to control his own deficiencies of character and to give his people genuine unity, Saul's last and greatest mistake was the one which many a guerrilla leader has made. The process of transforming guerrillas into regular troops fit for pitched battle takes time, and Saul challenged the Philistines long before his forces were ready. The Philistines, for their part, acted with all the resolution they had displayed at Aphek, marching out to crush the resurgent Israelite menace before it grew too strong; they attacked Saul before his muster was complete. Saul himself was cut off with his sons and bodyguard on Mount Gilboa and perished in a heroic last stand:

The battle pressed hard upon Saul, and the archers found him; and he was badly wounded by the archers. Then Saul said to his armour-bearer, 'Draw your sword, and thrust me through with it, lest these uncircumcised come and thrust me through, and make sport of me'. But his armour-bearer would not; for he feared greatly. Therefore Saul took his own sword, and fell upon it. And when his armour-bearer saw that Saul was dead, he also fell upon his sword, and died with him. Thus Saul died, and his three sons, and his armour-bearer, and all his men, on the same day together. And when the men of Israel who were on the other side of the valley and those beyond the Jordan saw that the men of Israel had fled and that Saul and his sons were dead, they forsook their cities and fled; and the Philistines came and dwelt in them. (1 Samuel 31:3−7).

Though it appeared catastrophic at the time, Mount Gilboa only accelerated the Israelite recovery. It did not destroy the Israelite army, and the deaths of Saul and his adult sons only swept the field clear for David, by far the most respected guerrilla leader after Saul's son Jonathan (killed with his father on Mount Gilboa) to take the crown. The tribes rallied to David *en masse* in a joint crusade against the Philistines who were forced back into the coastal strip between Gaza and Ashkelon. After border campaigns east of the Jordan to put down those warlords who cherished notions of independence, David began his splendid reign as the first king of a united and independent 'Israel' (c. 1000−961 BC).

Despite the power and the glory still associated with the reigns of

Mount Gilboa, where
King Saul was cut off and
killed, together with his
sons and bodyguard, by
the triumphant Philistines

David and his splendid heir Solomon (961–922), the kingdom they
ruled was a contradiction in terms. David and Solomon were trying to
build an enduring state out of fundamentally unsuitable materials. The
kingdom had been born in battle, the only cement capable of bringing
the tribes together. But the opulent monarchy built up by David and
Solomon gambled on the Israelites' sense of a common heritage proving
stronger than their fierce tribal loyalties. The new monarchy was a direct
challenge to the tradition of the founding fathers who had followed
Moses out of Egypt, and seemed a decadent innovation by comparison.
The passage of time and the removal of all foreign perils only made the
situation worse. A centralized state with a rich capital city; an ever-
growing bureaucracy; an undreamed-of host of taxes; forced labour;
alliances with idol-worshipping foreigners – it all seemed hopelessly at
odds with the gaunt simplicity of the Law of Moses.

In the short term, however, the monarchy meant splendour and
supremacy for a people sick of war; and Solomon's reign widened the
kingdom to its greatest extent. The Syrians recognized him as overlord
from the Euphrates to the Red Sea. Although Solomon's reign was a
reign of peace, the king underpinned his diplomatic triumphs by
building up the Israelite army to unheard-of strengths, transforming it
in the process. 'He had fourteen thousand chariots and twelve thousand
horsemen, whom he stationed in the chariot cities and with the king in
Jerusalem.' (2 *Chronicles* 1:14). The chariots and horses were imported

from Egypt but were not manned by mercenary troops. 'Of the people of Israel Solomon made no slaves for his work; they were soldiers, and his officers, the commanders of the chariots, and his horsemen' (2 *Chronicles* 8:9). Quite apart from the exorbitant cost of Solomon's building projects, such as the new Temple and the fortification of Jerusalem, the price of these military improvements plus the forced labour for building new garrison towns throughout the kingdom were particularly resented.

Thus when Solomon died in 922 BC his son Rehoboam was faced with immediate opposition. The northern tribes particularly resented the way in which Judah, the tribe of David, had assumed the monopoly of power as the ruling house. Now they demanded less taxes and more autonomy, and when Rehoboam refused, it was 'To your tents, O Israel! Look now to your own house, David.' The northern tribes seceded from the union created by David, and formed the Kingdom of Israel. Rehoboam and his successors ruled over the southern Kingdom of Judah. As Solomon's army had been garrisoned throughout 'all the land of his dominion', both of the new kingdoms reaped the benefits of his military reforms. Each had an army in which the accent was placed on mobility, and of which the strength was reckoned in chariots and horsemen rather than in foot soldiers. The infantry contingents, however, were still provided by the old tribal levies.

The turbulent story of the two kingdoms is told, in lavish and often contradictory detail, in the four Old Testament books of *Kings* and *Chronicles*. Judah and Israel frequently fought each other; each kingdom also had its full share of internal trouble, the latter encouraged in no little measure by a succession of charismatic 'prophets'. The struggles between the prophet Elijah and the evil King Ahab and Queen Jezebel are among the best-known Bible stories, but they naturally overshadow Ahab's talents as a general.

Solomon's pattern of foreign alliance broke up with his kingdom, leaving Israel exposed to the ambitions of Syrian rulers – the kings of Damascus in particular. Ahab of Israel (869–850) and Ben-hadad of Damascus fought repeated wars in the first of which Ahab did quite well, breaking two Syrian thrusts across the Jordan in the hill country of Samaria. The two adversaries then shelved their quarrel to meet the westward advance of the Assyrians under Shalmaneser III. A coalition army formed by the powers of Syria-Palestine, to which Ahab and Ben-hadad both led contingents, gave the Assyrians a tremendous fight at Qarqar in the Orontes valley (854). Qarqar was an Assyrian victory, but so painfully won that Shalmaneser abandoned the idea of further operations in Syria.

Qarqar was followed by a three-year truce between Damascus and Israel, which Ahab finally broke. He planned an advance across the Jordan to retake Ramoth-Gilead from the Damascenes, and made an alliance with Jehoshaphat, king of Judah, to make sure of this limited objective.

The account of the battle in *I Kings* represents Ahab as going into the action in fear of a prophecy that he would die in battle, and disguising himself in vain. The tactics agreed between Ahab and Jehoshaphat, however, seem to have been much more subtle and came within an inch of success. Ben-hadad, drawing up his forces for yet another battle with his old enemy, had decided to make a quick end by ordering his chariot commanders to concentrate on the King of Israel — but it did not work out like that:

The king of Israel said to Jehoshaphat, 'I will disguise myself and go into battle, but you wear your robes.' And the king of Israel disguised himself and went into battle. Now the king of Syria had commanded the thirty-two captains of his chariots, 'Fight with neither small nor great, but only with the king of Israel'. And when the captains of the chariots saw Jehoshaphat, they said, 'It is surely the king of Israel'. So they turned to fight against him, and Jehoshaphat cried out. And when the captains of the chariots saw that it was not the king of Israel, they turned back from pursuing him.

Ahab meanwhile was in the thick of the action, leading his own chariots and presumably seeking to exploit the disruption of the Syrian chariot attack. His disguise had held and the Syrians were still not clear which was the key element of the Israelite plan — but Ahab's chances were ruined by that eternal hazard of battle, the random shot.

A certain archer drew his bow at a venture, and struck the king of Israel between the scale armour and the breastplate; therefore he said to the driver of his chariot, 'Turn about, and carry me out of the battle, for I am wounded'.

Black though his character has been painted, nobody can deny Ahab credit for great courage and tenacity. He deserted neither his men nor the enemy:

And the battle grew hot that day, and the king was propped up in his chariot facing the Syrians, until at evening he died; and the blood of the wound flowed into the bottom of the chariot. And about sunset a cry went through the army, 'Every man to his city, and every man to his country!'

Though the battle of Ramoth-Gilead ended in an Israelite withdrawal it did not spell a Syrian victory. Ben-hadad's army was in no condition to pursue, even though the death of Ahab offered a golden opportunity for striking a decisive blow at the Kingdom of Israel while it was leaderless.

Tiglathpileser III of Assyria, whose armies crushed the northern kingdom of Israel in 736–32 BC

THE CONQUEST OF ISRAEL AND JUDAH
Qarqar had proved that only combined action could check the Assyrians, but the jealous rivalries which had broken Solomon's kingdom survived to ruin both Israel and Judah.

Israel was the first to go, rent by dissension between those who wanted to survive by paying tribute to Assyria and those who wanted to fight. The latter faction, headed by King Pekah (736–732 BC), prevailed in Israel but Ahaz of Judah refused to join a coalition to fight the Assyrians. Pekah promptly attacked Judah and Ahaz appealed to the Assyrians for protection. This division in Syria-Palestine was a godsend for Tiglathpileser III, who responded with an invasion which crushed

both Damascus and Israel. Tiglathpileser turned Samaria over to Israelite rule as a puppet state under Hoshea (732–723), who made the great mistake of relying on Egyptian urgings to revolt and promises of assistance. Hoshea duly rebelled in 725 but found himself on his own; Shalmaneser V overran Samaria and captured Hoshea. Samaria itself fell after an epic but futile three-year siege concluded by Sargon II, who succeeded Shalmaneser in 722.

The Kingdom of Judah survived its northern neighbour and rival by 135 years, most of them as an Assyrian vassal state. Hezekiah (715–687) imitated Pekah of Israel's ill-fated attempt to form an anti-Assyrian league, but again the Egyptian contingent let down its Palestinian allies. All Judah was overrun by Sennacherib's forces, and Hezekiah was besieged in Jerusalem. In *2 Kings* and *2 Chronicles* Sennacherib's failure to take Jerusalem is represented as a total defeat for the Assyrians, while at the same time it is admitted that Hezekiah made formal submission to the Assyrian king and paid an enormous tribute. It would seem that the Assyrian forces found the walls of Solomon too strong for them and that sickness broke out in the siege lines, Sennacherib thereupon saving face by naming Hezekiah as Assyria's vassal king in Judah.

Hezekiah's heirs, Manasseh and Ammon, never had a chance to rebel against Assyria, even if they had been so inclined. Their reigns coincided with those of the last great Assyrian kings, Esarhaddon and Assurbanipal, who used Judah as the base for the Assyrian conquest of Egypt. But the reign of Josiah (632–609) coincided with the crumbling of the Assyrian Empire after Assurbanipal's death in 627. Here was an ideal

The full weight of the Assyrian war machine is thrown into the siege of a city: siege engines, scaling-ladders, and prisoners impaled on stakes to crack the defenders' morale. Nevertheless, although Sennacherib's army overran the whole of Judah, the city of Jerusalem held out under King Hezekiah

chance for Josiah to accelerate the process by launching a revolt in the west, but he refused to do any such thing. He was obsessed with internal reforms and restoring the Law of Moses as it had been observed by David and Solomon, and he seems to have pledged nominal allegiance to Assyria in order to assure Judah of a spell of peace as a neutral.

So far from joining the insurgents, he tried to prevent Necho II of Egypt from marching to attack Assyria in 609 BC, interpreting Necho's ambitions as a greater danger. The armies met at Megiddo. Necho asked for free passage through Judah – 'What have we to do with each other, king of Judah? I am not coming against you this day, but against the house with which I am at war'. (2 *Chronicles* 35:21). Josiah, however, rejected Necho's overtures and attacked, only to be mortally wounded by an Egyptian arrow.

This was the real end of the Kingdom of Judah, though twenty-two ignominious years lay ahead. Judah became subject first to Necho and then to Necho's destroyer, Nebuchadnezzar of Babylon. Ill-advised attempts at revolt – depending as usual on Egyptian aid, and as usual disappointed – led to the capture of Jerusalem by the Babylonians, first in 597 and again ten years later when Solomon's Temple was destroyed. The Babylonian and Chaldean rulers who completed the ruin of the Israelite kingdoms sought to end the problem of revolts by mass deportations of the population to the east, a process reversed by the Persian emperor Cyrus.

Once the eastern empires had mastered the administrative skills enabling them to rule from Mesopotamia to the Mediterranean, there was never any chance that an independent Israelite nation could remain for long at peace in Palestine. The extraordinary military history of the Israelites contained nearly all the essential ingredients for survival: the willingness to learn, to adopt new tactics and weapons. But one they never learned, and that was the need to supplement military readiness with flexible diplomacy and alliances made to suit the crisis of the hour. Their undoubted military virtues as a fighting people were not enough, by themselves, to enable the ancient Jewish Kingdom to survive. But the ancient Jewish traditions were quite another matter. They enabled the Jewish people to survive over 2,600 years, until their homeland became a nation again.

CHAPTER FOUR

The Persian Colossus

A MAP OF THE PERSIAN EMPIRE in 500 BC, when it stood at its zenith under the rule of Darius I, shows a breathtaking phenomenon. The effect is heightened if the earlier 'world empires' of Akkadia, Assyria, and Babylonia are superimposed in all their comparative modesty. To put it plainly, they look like pygmies. None of them do more than connect the Mediterranean with the Persian Gulf or the Red Sea. But the Persian Empire stretched from the Mediterranean to India, and from Turkestan to the Indian Ocean. It was the biggest, richest, and (especially in the modern, humanitarian sense of the word) most civilized power on the face of the planet.

One might well imagine that such a colossus must have taken centuries to grow, but this was not so. In 500 BC the Persian Empire had been in existence for less than fifty years. It was a most paradoxical monster. Military conquest had carved it out, like all its other predecessors on the world stage, yet the empire's own military effectiveness was actually less than that of many of the warrior races — the Assyrians being the prime example — which it had subjugated. What is more, the subject warrior races, once engulfed, remained digested without constantly breaking out in revolt. The Persian emperors (or 'great kings', to use their correct title) did not spend their time hurrying from one end of the empire to the other, forever smashing provincial rebels. They sat in their palaces and directed the operations of an army of civil servants.

Precisely how this was achieved is not clear. It was certainly not a question of virtual self-government for the provinces, which remained firmly connected to the central government and its bureaucracy. Yet somehow it *was* done. Entire subject nations such as the Medes, Babylonians, and Assyrians, all resilient civilizations with centuries of military trouble-making behind them, remained reconciled to the imperial Persian system. Had this not been the case the Persian Empire would never have outlived its founder, Cyrus 'The Great', with whose achievement this chapter is largely concerned.

CORE OF THE EMPIRE: MEDIA AND PERSIA

The map of the Persian Empire shows a central 'waist' or land bridge, slanting south-east from the Caspian Sea to the mouth of the Persian

LEFT: An archer-spearman of the elite Persian guard corps – the Immortals – portrayed on glazed tiles on the palace walls at Susa. Though superbly equipped and drilled, the Immortals could have done with a little less ostentation and a little more practicality. For instance, the ornate silver pomegranates decorating the spear-butts made it impossible for the Immortals to jam their spears in the ground and form a protective hedge from behind which they could shoot. RIGHT: From the Oxus treasure – gold model of a Persian king or satrap in his chariot. BELOW RIGHT: Scythian warriors on an electrum vase found in the tomb of a Scythian chief

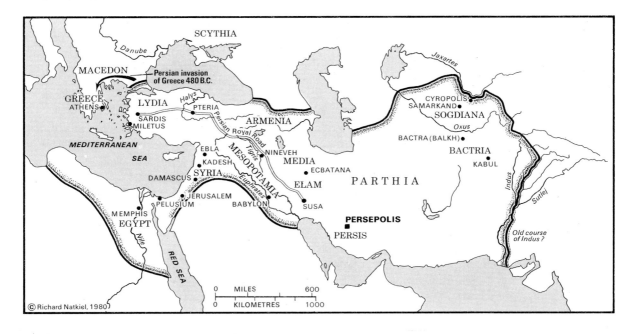

Gulf. This land bridge represents the homelands of the Medes and Persians on the Iranian plateau. It favours expansion to the west and south-west (Asia Minor/Syria/Palestine, ending up in Egypt); to the east and north-east (India/Bactria/Sogdiana, ending up in Turkestan); and finally a converging descent on Babylonia and Assyria. That, roughly, was how Cyrus built the Persian Empire in under thirty years. It was an achievement which owed much to the wars of the previous century, out of which had emerged a uniquely favourable alignment of powers. At the beginning of Cyrus' career the site had been cleared, as it were, and all essential materials lay stacked and waiting.

Cyrus' first debt of gratitude should have been to the Assyrians, who had destroyed the oldest and most dangerous power east of the Tigris. This was the Kingdom of Elam, which had been a blood foe of Mesopotamia (hillmen versus plains-dwellers) since the days of Sargon the Great. Elam had been destroyed and its capital, Susa, razed by Assurbanipal of Assyria in 646–640 BC. At this time Assyria still controlled Media, the highland province east of Upper Mesopotamia; but after Assurbanipal's death Cyaxares of Media fell on Assyria with the help of the Babylonians. This alliance of Media and Babylonia dealt Assyria its death-blow in 612 BC, with Babylonia subsequently engulfing Assyria west of the Tigris, and leaving Cyaxares to found an empire of his own. By the time of his son Astyages (585–550 BC) the Median Empire extended to the Black Sea and the Caspian. To the south-east it exercised sovereignty over the Persian principality of Anzan, which had grown up in the vacuum left by the destruction of Elam. Astyages of Media married his daughter to Cambyses of Anzan, and Cyrus was their son.

Destiny and drama cling round the story of Cyrus, even if it does seem to have been borrowed from that of the young Moses. Astyages is said to have been terrified by a dream that his grandson would supplant him, and to have ordered Harpagus, the royal general, to kill the baby. The kindly Harpagus, however, exchanged the infant Cyrus for the dead baby of a herdsman and left Cyrus in the herdsman's care. When the fosterling grew up, of course, his princely bearing won him the favour of Astyages, who avenged himself on Harpagus by killing Harpagus' son. Vowing revenge of his own, Harpagus placed himself and the army of Media at the disposal of Cyrus, who overthrew his wicked grandfather but mercifully spared him his life.

For all the melodrama, here at least is an explanation of the rebellion of Cyrus against Astyages in 553, which ended three years later with Cyrus master of the Median Empire. It was less of a direct Persian takeover than a new partnership, a restatement of the power balance between the Median and Persian aristocracies, who now went forward together under a joint 'King of the Medes and Persians'. A programme of further conquests was not only the most obvious expedient for cementing this partnership; it naturally continued the expansion begun by the Medes under Cyaxares and Astyages. All this bears remembering because as the empire continued to grow its armies became less and less 'Persian'. The armies of the 'great kings' after 500, in the heyday of the Persian Empire, were no more 'Persian' than the Imperial and Commonwealth forces of 1939–45 were 'British'. Having made this important point, it has to be admitted that there is no simpler alternative description, and so the word 'Persian' will be used in this book in the sense of 'Persian and imperial forces'.

The cutting edge of the Median-Persian army of Cyrus in 550 was its strength in horsed cavalry. The Medes had built up this arm from experience gained first from Assyria and extended in prolonged fighting against the Scythians, horse-riding warriors from central Asia. Chariotry, and infantry formations of unarmoured spearmen, completed the Median array. It was an army with great hitting-power and mobility, experienced both in fighting nomad tribesmen from the east and the more sophisticated, 'regular' armies of the western powers. During the rapid expansion of the new empire, more and more units were recruited from its former enemies, who as provincials were required to supply troops for compulsory service with the 'great king's' army. As all provincial contingents retained their customary weapons – swords, axes, or adzes; thrusting-spears or wooden javelins with hardened points; short bows or long – the overall *manpower* of the Persian army rose dramatically but its overall *fighting efficiency* did not keep pace. This the Greeks eventually demonstrated with world-shattering effect. But in the original Median-Persian army whose victories created the empire of Cyrus, the ratio of fighting efficiency to manpower was high and there was no stopping it.

The first move of Cyrus as ruler of the Medes and Persians was to establish friendly relations with King Nabonidus of Babylon. This secured the southern flank for a resumption of expansion in Asia Minor. Under Cyaxares and Astyages the Medes had advanced as far as the Halys river, once the innermost defence line for the capital of the Hittites. West of the Halys lay the kingdom of Lydia, a rich state fed by Aegean trade. An uneasy peace had reigned along the Halys since Alyattus of Lydia and Cyaxares of Media had agreed to an immediate and indefinite truce on 28 May 585 BC. This date is known for certain because it was the first known occasion on which a total eclipse of the sun was accurately predicted. The man responsible was Thales of Miletus, one of the earliest 'worthies' of Greek philosophy and science. Whether it was the awe inspired by the accuracy of Thales' forecast or by the eclipse itself, both sides were so impressed that they refused to go on fighting, agreeing to accept the Halys as the Lydian-Median 'front-line'.

The truce was broken in 547 when King Croesus of Lydia took the field against the growing menace in the east represented by the accession of Cyrus. The Greek historian Herodotus, writing within a century of the Lydian war, states that Croesus had consulted the famous Oracle of Delphi before deciding on war. The Oracle had foretold that 'Croesus would destroy a great empire if he crossed the River Halys'. With all the touching faith of a modern politician making a fateful decision on the strength of an opinion poll, Croesus interpreted the Oracle in his own favour, never suspecting that the 'great empire' might turn out to be his own.

Herodotus believed that written history should point a moral while entertaining its readers; he was, above all, not a soldier. But when allowances have been made for all this the following campaign emerges from his narrative. Croesus invaded Median territory and an indecisive battle followed, after which Croesus withdrew in disappointment. Cyrus did not follow up at once, but gave the Lydian army time to get home and to disband. He then launched a whirlwind invasion of Lydia and swept right through to Sardis, the capital. An attempt by Croesus to stop the invaders with mounted troops was foiled when Cyrus ordered forward camels, whose unfamiliar stink panicked the Lydian horses. With the last of his field army scattered, Croesus prepared to sit out a siege behind the massive walls of Sardis which presented, on the face of it, far too tough a proposition for an army consisting mostly of horsed archers. Cyrus and his men were indeed baffled by the defences. Then came the day when a Lydian soldier was observed climbing back in after accidentally dropping his helmet and scrambling down to retrieve it. A stealthy assault party, following the soldier's route, got over the wall, broke into the city and took it, with Croesus himself being captured.

The overall pattern of the Lydian campaign was determined by Cyrus' weakness in regular infantry and siege equipment. He was attacking a kingdom studded with fortified cities and his strategy was to force a quick decision by a high-speed strike at the enemy's vitals, *blitzkrieg*-fashion. Once Croesus had lost all his forces in the open, the cities could be tackled at leisure. The reference to camels describes one of many occasions when these animals have been deliberately used to upset enemy cavalry. Cyrus could have recruited camel-riders either from Arabia by courtesy of the Babylonians, or from the nomads of Asia to the east of Media and Persia. But the siege of Sardis is perhaps the most significant part of the story, showing the impotence of horsed archers before stout walls and gates until the weak link in the defences was found and exploited.

For all his dependence on fast and fluid improvization during the campaign, Cyrus carried out the occupation of mainland Lydia with method and sensitivity. The conquered cities were not razed and plundered: they were brought into the imperial system which Cyrus was developing. This was particularly true of the scatter of Greek colonial cities round the western coast of Asia Minor, formerly tributary to the Lydian kingdom, which were now persuaded to accept not only Persian rule but Persian patronage. This was the direct result of Cyrus' deep respect for Greek civilization. There was one exception: Miletus, the city of Thales, which retained the independence it had enjoyed ever since Thales' *tour de force* in the year of the eclipse.

After securing Asia Minor as the western bastion of his empire, Cyrus turned about to repeat the process in the east. Here there was no natural stop-line, no delineating coast – only thousands of square miles of emptiness on the threshold of the central Asian steppe, rising to the mountains of Afghanistan and the Hindu Kush and finally reaching the Punjab and the civilization of the Indus. Only an army of horse soldiers could have roped in this vast area in six years (545–539 BC); only a ruler with unique confidence and vision would have attempted it at all. The eastern campaign of Cyrus gave Persia and Media a shield from nomad invasions from Asia. It gave the Empire vast new recruiting-grounds for light cavalry and mountain troops. But in return the eastern tribesmen were offered the benefits of imperial security under the 'great king' – irrigation schemes and agriculture, permanent roads for trade. As for the garrison cities which Cyrus planted in the eastern provinces – Kabul, Herat, Balkh, Samarkand – they became in later centuries rich staging-posts on the overland trade-route between Europe and China. But the whole process had barely begun when, in 539 BC, Cyrus suddenly descended on Mesopotamia and took Babylon with almost ludicrous ease.

BABYLON AND EGYPT

In 539 BC no city in the world had a more embattled history than Babylon. The city had fallen to the Sumerians, the Akkadians, Elamites, Hittites, and Assyrians, more often than not after a murderous siege and sack. The Chaldean rulers Nabopolassar (626–605) and Nebuchadnezzar 'The Great' (605–561) had rebuilt the city and given it the strongest fortifications in the world. Studded with bastions every twenty yards, the outer walls stretched three miles by two, enclosing the summer palace of Nebuchadnezzar and running for over a mile along the eastern bank of the Euphrates. The river itself was straddled by the even more formidable defences of the inner city, two miles by one in extent, surrounded by a moat fed by the Euphrates. In 539 BC the Persian army lacked any equipment with which to crack these defences, but Cyrus never intended to mount a traditional siege. There was no need. Under-cover diplomacy had done its work well and he was relying on that notorious military expedient, the 'fifth column' or enemy within.

Nabonidus, the Babylonian king, was a jarring and unpopular monarch reminiscent of Akhenaten in Egypt: a religious eccentric who alienated the priesthood and practitioners of the established creed. But

Akhenaten had succeeded to his throne. Nabonidus was a usurper and it was particularly stupid of him to let his religious quirks blind him to the necessity of keeping the establishment happy. Cyrus had kept himself well informed of all this and had assured the incensed Babylonian priesthood of Bel-Marduk that he would champion their cause. He was rewarded by the news that the city would not resist him; but Belshazzar, the Babylonian crown prince, remained loyal to his father. When the Persian army approached it found the gates shut and the walls manned.

Cyrus' problem was, therefore, how to get into Babylon without doing any serious damage to a city prepared to accept him as king. At Sardis an easy way in had been found at a weak spot in the defences where the wall was low enough, but the fortifications of Babylon were far too well planned to permit this. Instead of concentrating on the walls, Cyrus and his general Gobryas turned their attention to Babylon's water defences. The Euphrates was channelled through the city in two streams, and by diverting one of these the Persians were able to expose enough river bed for troops to get in by the watergates. Once the Persians were inside the walls, resistance collapsed at once and Cyrus was hailed by the priests of Bel-Marduk as the new ruler of Babylon and its provinces – Assyria, Syria, Phoenicia, and Palestine.

The last ten years of Cyrus' reign were spent in pushing forward his policy of reconciling a host of subject peoples to the Persian 'new order'. His success in this may be judged from the fact that he was remembered with affection and gratitude by the captive Jews as well as the Babylonians. The latter hailed him as the great defender of Mesopotamian tradition – 'Cyrus, king of all, the great king, the powerful king, the king of Babylonia, king of Sumer and Akkad, king of the four regions of the world'. But to the Jews, out of their humiliation by the Assyrians and Babylonians, Cyrus was the instrument of the Lord who restored the looted treasures of Jerusalem and sent the exiles home to rebuild their holy city. As we have seen, the Israelite kingdoms had, before their final dissolution, repeatedly revolted against Assyrian and Babylonian rule – but they never gave the Persians any trouble. To the Jews, Cyrus and his successors were more than indulgent patrons: they were lords to serve in loyalty and gratitude.

The reason for the success of Cyrus can be traced back to the way in which Cyrus used war as an empire-building instrument. Other conquerors, the Assyrians being the prime example, had made full play with the brutality of war, stitching their empires together after gory bouts of ferocious surgery. By contrast, Cyrus was a master with the scalpel. His wars were quick, deft, and thorough, leaving behind no lingering source of infection and creating hardly any scars.

The reverse was the case with Cambyses, who succeeded Cyrus in 529. A vicious and unstable character, Cambyses began his mercifully brief reign by having his brother Bardiya murdered, to remove any threat to his own supremacy. He then resumed the project which had occupied him during the last years of his father's life: preparing for the invasion and conquest of Egypt. He seems, however, to have had the sense not to attack Egypt prematurely and was rewarded in 526 BC with the death of Pharaoh Amasis. This was the moment to strike, before the new pharaoh could establish his authority or, more to the point, do anything to strengthen Egypt's defences. A lover of peace and, like Cyrus, a great respecter of Greek culture, the late pharaoh had reigned for forty-two years; but he had done little or nothing to overhaul the Egyptian military machine.

Psammetichus III had barely mounted his throne in 526 when the Persian army came flooding out of Palestine. There was only one battle, fought at Pelusium east of the Delta, in which the sole Egyptian field army was shattered. It was a resounding demonstration of the supremacy of the mounted archer over the foot archer, for the Persians lacked the heavy armoured infantry which was the only other arm capable of breaking an army relying on foot archers. The victory at Pelusium was followed by a trouble-free occupation of the Delta and Nile Valley upstream as far as the First Cataract. Frontier garrisons were left to guard the southern extremity of the occupied zone, together with a population of Jews who had volunteered to settle in the area under Persian protection.

Cambyses' behaviour towards his new subjects could not have been more different from that of Cyrus. He violated the tomb of Amasis and outraged the priesthood of Apis at Memphis by having the sacred bull, incarnation of the god Ptah, slaughtered. Had he continued with these stupidities Egypt would probably have staged a nationalist revolt against Persian rule, but in 522 BC his career was abruptly cut short. Cambyses died in Syria by his own hand, according to Herodotus as the result of accidentally wounding himself with his own sword — an explanation with a cynically modern ring. It may well have been an assassination. What is certain is that when Cambyses died he was on the way east to cope with a dangerous rebellion which his own ruthlessness had unleashed.

The revolt of 522 was not a mass bid for liberty by the kingdoms which Cyrus had conquered. It was led by a Median mystic named Gaumata, who claimed to be Cambyses' brother Bardiya and won enough support from the provincial governors (*satraps*) to make good his claim to the throne. Gaumata ran up a lot of short-term support with his promises to drop all taxation for three years and abolish military service, but the mainspring of his revolt was as much religious as political. He stood for the purity of Zoroastrianism in a crusade against the old gods of the kingdoms and provinces, whose toleration was one of the strongest props of the empire. The revolt was finally put down by Darius, the younger brother of Cyrus, vassal-king of the Medes. Gaumata had set a compelling example, however, and in his first year as king, Darius had to cope with several other would-be messiahs, one of whom turned up in Babylonia claiming to be a reincarnation of Nebuchadnezzar The Great.

Having restored the authority of the Persian ruling house, Darius proceeded to complete the work of Cyrus by giving the empire a permanent administrative framework. The swarming details of this administration and what it achieved — coinage, taxation, roads, canals, the imperial post — are too numerous to list here. But the way in which the civil and military life of the empire was directed is of the greatest

Gold plaque from the treasure of Oxus shows a Scythian warrior and his formidable armament: ribbed leather armour, battleaxe, spear, and enclosed bowcase slung from the waist

importance for an understanding of the empire's strengths and weaknesses in time of war.

First came the separation of the civil and military authorities. None of the twenty satraps of the empire held a military command, and no military commander exercised civil authority. This deterred the rise of self-sufficient military governors with an eye on the imperial throne. It was taken a stage further by appointing fewer military commanders than satraps, which prevented the development of dangerous partnerships. A military commander might have under him the troops of four or five satrapies. All satraps and military commanders received their appointments and subsequent orders direct from the king and reported to him individually. And an independent survey of the civil and military administrations was kept by special crown inspectors, who travelled through the empire and reported direct to the king on what they saw.

The satraps saw to the raising of revenue and were answerable for the loyal administration and maintenance of the king's peace; the military commanders saw to the raising of troops for military service and were answerable for the readiness and efficiency of the army. In both spheres, the aristocracy of Persia enjoyed unique privileges. As the cradle of the dynasty, Persia provided the empire's ruling *élite* and was exempt from taxes. From this *élite* the king appointed the satraps and the military commanders. The regional contingents provided their own NCOs and officers up to the equivalent rank of company commander; above that all officers in the army were from the Persian landowning aristocracy. A good example of this separatism at work may be found in the building of the new imperial palace at Susa, a mighty imperial project demanding labour contributions from all over the empire — Greeks and Lydians from Asia Minor, Syrians, Babylonians, and Medes. All these were listed on the inscription marking the completion of the palace, in which the Persians are conspicuous by their absence. They did not contribute: they supervised, and the splendours of the new palace formed the most abundant proof of Persian supremacy.

Every empire in history has functioned to the ultimate benefit of the motherland. But in the case of the Persian Empire the pro-motherland bias was put on an official footing very early on, by Darius, and had particularly unfortunate results on the fighting capacity of the army. The supremacy of the Persian-Median 'hard core' was preserved, which was only to be expected after the sobering experience of the Gaumata revolt. But this supremacy was preserved by *deliberately limiting* the efficiency of the provincial contingents. Instead of expanding the original Persian-Median army by raising provincial corps equipped and trained to fight in the same manner, Darius and his successors contented themselves with adding more and more low-grade infantry and light cavalry units impressive only in their aggregate size.

This explains why the Assyrian contingents in the imperial Persian army were neither horsed nor heavy infantry archers — the arms in which the Assyrians had always excelled. Instead the Assyrians supplied heavy infantry — phalanx spearmen with large shields. Nor was any use made of the traditional excellence of Egyptian archers; Libyan and Ethiopian light spearmen were recruited instead. These are only two instances of a

Gold seal of Darius I shows the great king hunting lions in his chariot, protected by the winged-disc symbol of Ahuramazda

general policy of 'levelling down', of keeping up paper strengths by relying on troops which could be recruited with maximum ease and at minimal expense. Only strong doses of all-out war could have stopped this particular rot from creeping in – but after the accession of Darius the empire remained at peace for over thirty years, and no army is immune to the subtle ravages of peacetime routine and complacency.

The Persian Empire blocked out by Cyrus was a grouping of the most efficient military nations in the world, and by no means an enforced one. It gave the Persians a unique pool of military talent from which to draw, but they failed to do so. The imperial Persian army which took the field against Greece in the early fifth century BC was a bloated travesty of what it could have been; fat had become confused with muscle. The quality of the Persian and Median 'original cast' remained largely intact, but it was diminished by the masses of inadequate 'stage extras' which had been added to the strength since the death of Cyrus.

ORGANIZATION OF THE ARMIES

The imperial Persian army as described by Herodotus – over one and three-quarter million soldiers tramping into Greece – is a stark impossibility. It is impossible on two counts: the dislocation of the life of the empire which such a ferocious siphoning-off of manpower would have caused, and the overwhelming problem of supplying such a host in the field. Even if it had been invading the richest farming lands in the world instead of barren Greece, such a monstrous army, if forced to 'live off the country', would have had little or no time for fighting.

It is important to make this point at the outset because exaggeration is far too strong a word for the figures given by Herodotus, who has often been sneered at as a pro-Greek propagandist trying to make the Greek victory even more impressive than it undoubtedly was. But Herodotus

Persian archer and medium spearman. In contrast to the system evolved by the Assyrians, the Persian war machine failed to co-ordinate the roles of the missile troops (slingers and archers) and the shock troops (heavy infantry phalanx). Relying on one élite corps was not enough: the imposing but brittle mass of the imperial Persian host remained vulnerable to determined infantry or cavalry attacks

was not – like Thucydides, Xenophon, or Julius Caesar – a soldier writing about war. He was a civilian who failed to distinguish between overall 'paper strengths' and the actual sizes of the army contingents in the field.

The basis of the imperial Persian army was the national contingent, or corps, made up of decimal units – squads of 10, companies of 100, battalions of 1,000, and brigades of 10,000. Herodotus states that there were twenty-nine of these corps (apart from the household guards and 'Immortals', of which more below) and that each of them had a strength of 60,000. Here is the real source of his exaggerated assessment of the army's total strength. It makes no distinction between raw recruits, half-trained soldiers and fully trained and battle-worthy troops. Recruiting and training was a continuous process in which garrison duties within the empire played an important part. It was impossible to strip every garrison town and recruiting depot of every soldier on the strength: a permanent establishment was needed, both to assist in the training of recruits and to carry out its duties as the local guarantor of peace and security. Out of its overall 'paper' complement of 60,000, therefore, a corps garrison town could hardly have supplied the army with an instant draft of more than 6,000 fully-trained men, if that. By the time reinforcements were needed at the front, the next batch of recruits would have finished its training and be ready to go. With troops such as heavy spearmen, whose combat efficiency depended on extensive training, the first draft could easily be as low as 2,000.

In the whole army there was only one unit to which this did not apply: the Persian guards corps and household regiments, usually lumped together and described as 'The Ten Thousand Immortals'. The Immortals are one of the oldest-named crack regiments in military history – indeed, the only one in the ancient world whose name was still being used 2,500 years later in the nuclear age. Recruited exclusively from Persia, the Immortals formed the most carefully selected and lavishly equipped corps in the whole army. Whatever their losses in action, their numbers were always kept at precisely 10,000 – a fetish which, if observed in time of war, meant that the Immortals were the only corps to go on campaign with adequate reserves. They were, of course, the *ne plus ultra* in the Persian war machine, the assumption being that when they moved forward to attack the battle was as good as won.

The splendid pictures of Immortals on the glazed walls of the imperial palace at Susa all feature the flowing, calf-length Persian tunic. This was probably worn only on ceremonial parades, being replaced on campaign by the more practical breeches favoured by Median troops. A corselet of scale armour was worn under the tunic. For all their sartorial splendour, the troops themselves were the result of a somewhat clumsy attempt to give archer fire-power to armoured shock infantry. They were archer spearmen, intended to form a bristling shield-wall which could roll forward to the accompaniment of massed archery. In practice all archers carried spears, but the spearmen who formed the shield-wall could not carry bows as well. The archers carried their ornate quivers slung on their backs, with the composite bow over the left shoulder and a seven-foot thrusting spear in the right hand. The latter was probably grounded when the archer was shooting; it could not be stuck in the ground because the butt ended in an elegant silver pomegranate.

The troops who formed the shield-wall, the front ranks of the Immortals' battle formation, were armed only with spear and shield. Two very different shield patterns are shown, indicating a further step away from uniformity in the corps. One of these shields is an elegant oval, three feet long, with curved cut-outs on each side, the latter making it possible for the men to lock their shields together when advancing under a hail of missiles. The other shield is a five-foot convex rectangle, direct descendant of the *gerrhon* favoured by the Assyrian heavy infantry in its heyday (see p. 27). These tall shields enabled the front ranks to form 'windbreaks' behind which the archers could shoot in comparative safety.

Within the Immortals was the élite of élites: the two household regiments which formed the royal bodyguard, one of 1,000 infantry, the other of 1,000 cavalry. The troopers of the household cavalry were shield-carrying archer-spearmen, another burdensome forced marriage of incompatible weapons. The household troops sparkled with gold — gilded scale armour, and gold pomegranates on their spear-butts.

The richness of the Immortals' equipment fails to conceal two obvious weaknesses. They wore no head protection at all — just an ornamental fillet to keep their carefully-braided hair out of their eyes and serve as a sweat-band. And they carried no side-arms. This left the archers completely dependent on the shield-wall. If the shield-wall broke the archers would be defenceless unless they managed to sling their bows, close ranks and form a hedge of spears in time. Even this desperate expedient would not suffice to keep determined infantry armed with stabbing-swords from thrusting in between the spear-shafts.

The point was, of course, that the Immortals anticipated Queen Victoria — they were not interested in the possibility of defeat: it did not exist. They were assault troops *par excellence*, their speciality being the unstoppable advance. Only when they *were* stopped did the flaws in their armament become glaringly apparent. In Greece the Immortals came up against infantrymen who were better armoured; who had the advantage of longer spears in a collision between shield-walls; who could break formation and, in a stabbing charge, tear open the Immortals' shield-wall like hounds going through a hedge, as happened at Plataea (see p. 128).

The heavy 'line infantry' of the Persian army consisted of six corps recruited from Persia and the provinces of the old Median Empire: Persians, Medes, Hyrkanians from the southern Caspian, Kashites from Armenia and eastern Asia Minor, Assyrians, and 'Exiles'. The latter were recruited from the many conquered peoples transported to Mesopotamia by the Assyrians and Babylonians. These people, a high proportion of whom had lost their natural identity with their homelands were very useful to the empire and the example of the Jews who went to help settle southern Egypt has already been quoted (see p. 85).

The heavy infantry of the Persians, Medes, Hyrkanians, Kashites, and Exiles had the same basic armament as the Immortals, being archer-spearmen whose front rank formed a shield wall; but they lacked the glitter and glamour. Their scale armour was of iron, their spears lacked the gold and silver ornaments. The clothing looks unbearably hot and cumbersome, but the garments were light-weight and served to keep the sun off the scale armour. The Assyrians wore no scale armour; they favoured the quilted tunic. Nor were there any archers at all in the Assyrian corps. But its soldiers wore conical bronze helmets with ear-protectors, carried tall *gerrhon* shields and had side-arms — clubs and daggers.

The most versatile light infantry came from the eastern satrapies. There was a combined corps of Bactrians and Scythians (also known as

'Informal' study of a Scythian archer blowing a trumpet. These horsed archers could have made the Persian army invincible – but failure to expand the horsed archer elements of the army during the long reign of Darius I allowed the army to go dangerously to seed

'Sakae') archers who carried bow and arrows in a dual-purpose bowcase and quiver slung at the hip. The Scythians also carried the *sagaris*, a nasty-looking chopping weapon like a long-handled carpenter's adze; the Bactrians had thrusting-spears as their alternative weapon. Other corps from the east, similarly armed, were Sogdian, Arian, Parthian/-Chorasmian, and Gandarian/Dadicae. All carried short stave bows except the Arians, who had the composite bow; but none wore armour or carried shields.

The bulk of the light infantry units – ten corps in all, one-third of the entire army – consisted of the easiest of all troops to raise: unarmoured spearmen and javelin-throwers. They were recruited from all over the empire and they featured a variety of regional dress and weaponry. The javelins flung by the Libyans, and by the Mysians (hillmen from western Asia Minor) were simple wooden shafts with fire-hardened points. The Paphlagonians, from the southern coast of the Black Sea, carried a thrusting-spear as well as javelins. With all these troops the dagger was the only side-arm, when one was carried at all. Some units, though not all, carried small round shields, while the

Thracians from the Bosphorous fought with the *pelta*, a small crescent-shaped shield with a cutting edge.

The army was almost as well equipped with light infantry archers: seven corps in all, recruited, like the light spearmen, from all over the empire. Most were armed with nothing but long-stave bows, like the corps made up of Indians from the Punjab and 'East Ethiopians' from Makran province in what is now south Pakistan. The real Ethiopians, from the other end of the empire, were straight out of the Stone Age, using obsidian for arrowheads and gazelle horn for spearheads. They formed a corps with Arab bowmen from the wild lands south of the 'Fertile Crescent'. The Sarangians of southern Afghanistan, however, formed a corps of their own and were almost light infantry imitations of the Immortal archers, being armed with both compound bow, back-pack quiver, and thrusting-spear. None of these light archers wore any armour or carried side-arms. They were skirmishers, fit for nothing more ambitious than harassing fire, who would stand no chance at all if charged down by enemy infantry.

For all its infinite variety and magnificent appearance, the infantry

Assyrian horsed archers in action with camel-mounted Arabs. Instead of recruiting the most effective troops from their martial subject peoples, the Persians deliberately restricted them, recruiting no Assyrian cavalry but only heavy infantry

of the Persian Empire introduced nothing new in either weaponry or tactics. Sadly lacking in either cohesion or tactical efficiency, it represented an attempt to get the best out of traditional warfare by concentrating on numbers. Its biggest failing was that it had far too many units which could not defend themselves in hand-to-hand fighting against well-protected opponents — and this was precisely what the Persians got when they invaded Greece in the fifth century BC.

The Medes and Persians had created the first mobile army of what might be called the 'post-chariot era', in which horsed cavalry replaced the chariot as the dominant arm of mobile warfare. By 500 BC the chariot had been relegated to ceremonial duties, the status transport for monarchs and generals; and it seemed that the true efficiency of horsed cavalry — particularly horsed archers — had been accepted at last.

As we have seen, however, the Persians were simultaneously building up a huge, unwieldy, and dangerously vulnerable infantry force. What they did not do was to increase the numbers or the efficiency of the horsed archer divisions in order to guarantee protection to the infantry. In short, after all they seemed to have learned under Cyrus, the Persians fell into the unaccountable error of regarding their cavalry as an extension of the infantry — as foot soldiers on horseback rather than as a separate arm with its own tactical role. The Persians were the first military nation to make this mistake: they were to be by no means the last. The mistake continued to be made down the centuries, right into the modern era. (The most recent example occurred between the world wars, when tank design was crippled by the misguided obsession with producing 'infantry' tanks in large numbers.)

Thus Persian imperial cavalry came to reflect faithfully the main types of infantry soldier being recruited at the same time. The Persian, Mede, and Cashite cavalry corps were archer-spearmen, though they must have found it impossible to manage a shield as well. True horsed archers were provided by the Bactrian, Caspian, and Paricanian corps, who rode unencumbered by spears. There was a seventh cavalry corps recruited of Indian archers with their long stave bows. The Persians certainly failed to make the best use of the Scythians, by far the most effective horse-riding nomads who had been incorporated into the empire. Scythian horsed archers were recruited but only formed part of the Bactrian corps.

In addition to these seven corps of horsed cavalry there were two oddities. The first, recruited from the Arabs, was a camel corps. Illustrations have been unearthed of a two-man team — a driver directing the camel and a pillion archer — though it was quite possible for a single archer to operate from camel-back. And the second, operating in support of the Persian cavalry corps, was an 8,000-strong detachment of Sagartians. These were nomad *gauchos* from eastern Iran whose main 'weapon' was a lariat of plaited leather. The Sagartians used their lariats to snag a victim and haul him in, to be despatched with a dagger-thrust. Precisely how they managed to do this without the help of a saddlebow is not known. Clearly they can only have been of any use against a broken and fleeing enemy, and the way the Persians used their cavalry did not create many opportunities for these 'cowboy' tactics.

93

It is natural to think of the Persian Empire as a monstrous land animal, but its possessions and ambition in the eastern Mediterranean made it a sea power as well. Control of the Phoenicians' sea-trading empire, together with the Phoenician colony of Cyprus, meant that the Persians had to build and maintain a navy; and this was a task naturally entrusted to the maritime provinces in the west. There was never any question of the Persians failing to understand the importance of sea power, or of being hopelessly outclassed at sea because of their inability to produce adequate warships. As well as having the biggest army, they also built the biggest navy in the world. Without this navy they could never have contemplated the conquest of Greece and the Aegean in the fifth century BC.

Naval warfare had changed very little since the days of Ramesses III and the Sea Peoples of 700-odd years before. The only way to sink an enemy ship was to ram it; the only way to disable an enemy ship was to smash its oars off; the only way to take an enemy ship was to close it and board. A warship therefore needed strength, manoeuvrability, and enough room to carry a detachment of marine soldiers. The heavier a ship was built the more devastating it would be in a ramming attack but, at the same time, the harder it became to move. By 500 BC the *trireme* war galley, propelled by three banks of oars, had replaced the two-banked *bireme* as the most effective fighting ship. The Persian navy had 600 triremes, plus transports suitable for carrying horses.

Providing the ships, oarsmen, and marines was the task of the maritime provinces. The Phoenician contribution was the highest: 300 ships, with marines equipped with Greek-pattern helmets, stiffened-linen cuirasses, and small round shields. They were armed with javelins and a short sword. Next came the Egyptians with 200 ships; their marines wore similar tunics and fought with heavy axes, supplemented with long spears and swords. The Lycians of Asia Minor, whose coast supplied 100 ships, provided the most effective marines in the form of armoured archers. They fought with long stave bows and javelins and wore scale body-armour with greaves on their legs.

But these three types only provide another instance of the Persians' failure to think out military problems and apply them to reality. The weaponry of the marine forces, apart from the bows of the Lycians, was of little use for shooting at enemy crews: it was essentially *defensive* and positively encouraged offensive enemy action. Because of the vulnerability of its banks of oars, a fighting galley was emphatically not a floating fortress for luring enemy ships to their doom. It was an offensive weapon, and its marines needed offensive weapons as well. As Ramesses III's navy had proved against the Sea Peoples, the trump card in long-distance sparring between galleys was massed archery for decimating enemy crews, and the Persian navy was woefully deficient in archers.

Despite this serious tactical shortcoming, however, the Persians had undoubtedly grasped the strategic importance of sea power and their fleet was perfectly capable of fulfilling one of the most important functions of any navy: serving as a catapult for the troops. They could take a powerful expeditionary force anywhere they liked and could ensure the army's communications by sea.

One highly important innovation, which served both the military and civilian life of the Persian Empire, should be mentioned here. This was the great trunk road built by Darius between Sardis in western Asia Minor and the capital at Susa. The road was furnished with a highly efficient imperial post, with messages carried by official gallopers, enabling information to be flashed from one end of the empire to the other in a matter of days. As a military aid the road was invaluable for the rapid and easy marching of troops; when the great expeditions were being prepared against the Greeks, the road served as a funnel for all the troops coming west from the eastern satrapies. At its western end it was within easy reach of all embarkation-ports for amphibious operations and enabled massive troop concentrations to be built up for an invasion of mainland Greece.

The road also helped in the flow of supplies furnished from the satrapies, as well as troop reinforcements. In all it was a most efficient adjunct of the Persian military machine during the years of the empire's greatness. When it was planned and built it was impossible to imagine what a deadly weapon the road would prove when used by a determined and fast-moving invader.

BALANCE-SHEET: THE PERSIAN WAR MACHINE IN 490 BC
Perhaps the biggest individual weakness in the Persian army has been left until last. This was the retention by the Persians of obsolete foot

Phoenician war galley: a bireme. For all the faults in their land forces, the Persians understood the benefits of seapower and maintained a formidable navy at the expense of their maritime subjects — Ionians, Phoenicians, and Egyptians

soldiers a century after the Greeks in the west had developed a totally new type of infantryman – the hoplite, better protected, better armed and more versatile than any other foot soldier in the world. The Persian attitude to the hoplite brings us back to the description of the Persian Empire as a 'paradoxical monster' on p. 77. The empire was second to none when it came to centralized government and discipline – yet its army was a hotch-potch mass parade of wildly different fighting men and weaponry. The Greek city-states, by contrast, were exultantly disorganized. Ferocious rivals one with the other, they were at each other's throats as often as not. Yet it was the Greeks – not the well organized Persians – who produced soldiers of a standard type, who combined against the common enemy in the nick of time and fought with the disciplined energy of a meat-grinder.

So far from being caught unawares by the sudden emergence of the hoplites as a military force, the Persians knew all about them. Hoplites, in the form of Lydian heavy infantry armed in virtually identical fashion to the Greeks, were actually serving in the Persian army – a living lesson in the new order. Yet the lesson went unheeded; Lydian troops being given no more prominence than any other provincial contingent in the army. Even after the Persian defeats in Greece, the hoplite formula was never studied, copied, or adopted by the Persian army. The Persians hired hoplites as mercenaries instead.

Nothing else offers such convincing proof that the Persians, like the Egyptians, lacked the killer instinct as a martial race. They did not have the itch to experiment and perfect the efficiency of their army, as the Assyrians had done. Instead they took enormous pains to go to war in gorgeous costumes and ostentatious luxury, stressing the endless resources of their empire in manpower and wealth. It was a perfect example of a great institution, in the absence of an immediate threat, coming to believe in its own publicity.

PART TWO

From Cyrus
to Alexander the Great

CHAPTER FIVE

Greece: The Power and the Glory

IN THE EPIC POEMS OF HOMER, who dictated his version of ancient legends some time between 750 and 700 BC, the Greeks looked back to a heroic Bronze Age when kings and princes fought mighty wars in which the gods themselves took part. One of the most famous military legends of this heroic age emerged in writing as Homer's *Iliad*, the epic ten-year war between Greece and Ilion, or Troy. But other Greek legends – in particular the legend of Theseus of Athens and the Minotaur – looked back even further to the earliest-known Mediterranean civilization: Minoan Crete.

This vibrant and colourful Bronze Age civilization was a far-ranging sea power at about the time of Hammurabi's Babylon. From their capital at Knossos the Minoans traded with New Kingdom Egypt and planted thriving colonies on the islands of Cythera, Thera, Ceos, Rhodes, Miletus in Asia Minor, and many sites of the Greek mainland. The Athenian Theseus legend implies that these Minoan outposts were part of a sea empire whose dependencies paid tribute to Crete. The grave-finds at Mycenae showed an unmistakable Cretan influence and included weapons – knives and swords – as well as objects of art. But from around 1500 BC, when a shattering volcanic eruption devastated the Minoan settlements on Thera with unknown but probably far-reaching effects on the Minoan homeland, the political supremacy of Crete waned rapidly. It was soon overtaken and eclipsed by that of Mycenae on the mainland, with the former Mycenean dependants of Crete invading and conquering the island, overthrowing the Minoans by the end of the fifteenth century BC.

Mycenae replaced Minoan Crete as the arbiter of the western Aegean, extending its supremacy as far as the Dardanelles. These straits owe their name to the 'Dardan land' across the water in north-west Asia Minor: the lost empire of Troy. When the city of Troy was finally excavated (1872–1874) it turned out to be the usual layer-cake of vanished supremacies, with Homer's Troy being tentatively identified as 'Troy VIIa' in the dry language of the archaeologist. But where Troy remains nebulous, Mycenae was very real. Hittite and Egyptian records mention Mycenae as a power to be reckoned with and treated, if not on equal terms, at least with respect.

OPPOSITE: A glorious tradition of the Greek heroic age – a seventh-century vase from Mykonos shows Greek warriors manning the Wooden Horse of Troy (mounted on wheels)

As the Myceneans eventually went under to the Sea Peoples (Mycenae itself had been destroyed by 1100 BC) the Trojan War can be placed between the fifteenth and thirteenth centuries BC. And according to the legends transmuted by Homer there was no doubt that the Greeks combined to attack Troy under the supreme command of the King of Mycenae: Agamemnon, son of Atreus.

'His following', says the Iliad, *'was by far the finest and most numerous. He was a proud man as he took his stand among his people, armed in gleaming bronze, the greatest captain of them all, in virtue of his rank and as commander of by far the largest force'.*

The *Iliad* is the supreme battle hymn of the Bronze Age. No other work comes anywhere near to capturing the lust and menace, almost the worship, of the metal. Homer himself, in his opening prayer for inspiration to do justice to his theme, appeals for a heart of bronze, not a muse of fire. Nothing tests his versatility as a poet more than the endless range of similes he uses for the role of bronze in battle. The massed glitter from the army's bronze armour and weapons is compared to the glare in the sky from a forest fire. 'The bronze rang grimly on the prince's breast'; 'victims to the bronze of man'; 'the penetrating bronze'; 'the shining bronze'; 'the relentless bronze' — the appearance, sound, and deadly effect of bronze rings through the entire poem. Even the chariot wheels of Hera, Queen of Heaven, are made of bronze. When iron is mentioned it is as a rarity, a substance fit for royal gifts; or used as a device to point attention to some great warrior, particularly worthy of note for using arrows with iron heads.

Those who may be inclined towards a dismissal of the *Iliad* as nothing more than a poet's fancy would do well to remember that it has been used as a reference-book in one of the most exciting quests in the history of archaeology. Heinrich Schliemann, a lover of *Iliad* stories from boyhood, refused to accept the assurances of the scholars that the *Iliad* was a web of myths. In his hunt for the ruins of Troy he referred constantly to Homer's epic, pacing out the distances quoted by Homer, and finally choosing a hill site much closer to the sea than the one regarded by Turkish locals as the traditional site of Troy. (He did this because, in the *Iliad*, the Greeks return to their camp by the ships two or three times a day.) And he did find Troy. So far from being a romance with little or no historical relevance the *Iliad* is in fact the master-key for understanding the Greeks and their military tradition.

Apart from its eternal tribute to the Bronze Age, the *Iliad* gives a very detailed picture of how eighth-century Greeks believed the warriors of the heroic past to have fought. Whether Greek or Trojan, the typical warrior encountered in the *Iliad* wears a bronze helmet with a 'grimly-nodding plume'; a bronze cuirass 'blazing like fire'; a reinforced apron protecting his groin; and greaves on his legs. The most important item of the protective armour — invariably given more prominence than the cuirass — is the huge round shield, made up of a bronze shell and overlaid layers of ox-hide. Usual weapons are a heavy javelin which can be used as a thrusting-spear, and a sword.

Reconstruction of a Mycenean dagger, based on the inlaid blade unearthed in one of the graves at Mycenae. Warriors with massive 'figure-of-eight' shields can be seen hunting lions

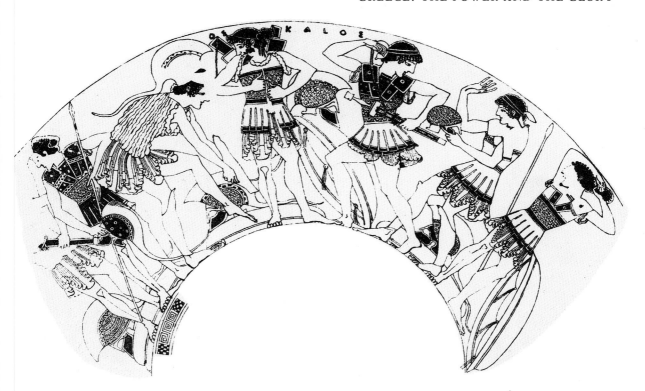

An *Iliad* scene on an early fifth-century Athenian drinking-cup depicts hoplites of the time of the Persian wars arming for battle. Apart from the striking similarity to the process as described in the *Iliad*, this scene packs in a wealth of informative detail – greaves are put on first as the corselet makes bending difficult; a thick garment is worn under the corselet. The figure carefully braiding his long hair at far right suggests that these are Spartans

Thus equipped and armed, the *Iliad* warrior rides to the battle in his chariot (driven by a fellow-warrior or trusted driver) and dismounts to fight on foot. He marks down his victim and tries for a quick kill with the javelin, by throw or by thrust. If the attack is successful the warrior recovers his javelin and looks for more prey; if the javelin has been stopped by the victim's shield or armour the warrior goes in to finish the job with his sword. Sometimes, in the turmoil of battle, there are deliberate encounters between enemies who have been looking for each other. If both parties have spread the word that such a 'grudge fight' is imminent there will be an impromptu truce, both armies looking on while the rivals engage in single combat.

Archery is an extremely specialist trade, left to marksmen who are often of the highest rank. These marksmen are frequently called upon to 'snipe' at some enemy warrior who is having matters too much his own way. While the highest respect is paid to archers for their skill – they are, of course under the special favour of the Archer-God Apollo – there is nevertheless a tendency to regard the bow as a slightly underhand weapon. It is noted that Prince Paris of Troy – the man who abducted Helen and started the whole war – is an archer, and normally fights as a sniper from the rear. Only once does Paris accept combat with shield and javelin, and that is a humiliating defeat from which he is only saved by divine intervention.

Chariots are used mostly for transport to, from, and on the battlefield. A hard-pressed warrior on foot will summon his own chariot like a tired modern executive calling for his chauffeur, or appeal to a

friend to give him a lift out of danger. The only hint of formal chariot
tactics is given when the veteran Greek commander Nestor briefs his
charioteers on the eve of battle. 'Do not think,' he said, 'that his bravery
and skill entitles a charioteer to break ranks and fight the Trojans on his
own. And don't let anybody drop behind and weaken the whole force.
When a man in his own chariot comes within reach of an enemy car, it is
time for him to try a spear-thrust. Those are the best tactics.' The
formation approach of the chariots is not intended to bowl over the
enemy ranks, but to deliver a concentrated body of warriors to the
'start-line' where they will dismount to fight in earnest. It will be noted
in passing that Homer, or whoever may have added Nestor's briefing to
Homer's original work, was generously endowed with military common
sense. 'Don't try any heroics; keep formation and hold your fire until you
can't miss — it might be a squadron briefing from the Battle of Britain.

In addition to their readiness to accept battle, the Greeks also show
that they are masters of the less glamorous art of fortification. Realizing
that if the Trojans ever manage to destroy the fleet drawn up along the
shoreline the entire expeditionary force will be doomed, the Greeks
throw up fixed defences to protect the ships. These defences consist of a
rampart pierced with gates to allow the chariots to sortie and retire,
screened by a deep ditch and a palisade of stakes.

Apart from the grim formalities involved in prearranged mortal
combat between individual champions, there is little chivalry in this
war. Agamemnon wants no prisoners. When the Trojan Adrestus
surrenders to Agamemnon's brother Menelaus and offers ransom,
Agamemnon swiftly intervenes. 'Why are you so chary of taking men's
lives?' he asks Menelaus. 'We are not going to leave a single one of them
alive, down to the babies in their mothers' wombs — not even they must
live. The whole people must be wiped out of existence, and none be left
to think of them and shed a tear.' After this chilling speech — intrigu-

ingly like the orders of God in the Old Testament that the Israelites must wipe out all the Canaanites – Menelaus looks on while Agamemnon kills Adrestus in cold blood.

No holds are barred in combat. Not even the most respected hero has any qualms about striking down an enemy from behind – then jeering at his victim as he lies dying and consigning his soul to Hades. Military glory is not a lofty abstract: it is the product of greed, to strip an enemy of his gear and gloat over the spoils. Even the dead are not safe from continued atrocity. After killing Hector under the walls of Troy, Achilles subjects the corpse to vicious mutilation. He slits the heels open, threads straps through and tows the body around Troy behind his chariot, instead of granting his dead enemy a decent burial.

Homer goes out of his way to stress the human imperfections of his heroes, their petty jealousies and bitter rivalries which constantly threaten disaster to both Greeks and Trojans. Agamemnon is one of the worst offenders. When he has to give up a girl captive he immediately saves face by taking the girl allotted to Achilles, the most respected warrior in the whole Greek army. Achilles reacts by going into a colossal sulk and refusing to fight, staying in his tent while the Trojans inflict a bruising series of defeats on the Greeks. When Achilles does come out to fight again it is not through loyalty to the common cause, but in a fit of crazed grief for the death of his friend and lover Patroclus, who had gone out to fight in his armour. In an insane rampage, motivated solely by revenge, not even the killing and mutilation of Hector satisfies Achilles. Here indeed is victory won for all the wrong reasons – but it is the winning of the victory that matters.

Thus the *Iliad* is a saga of the dogged pursuit of a collective aim – victory over the Trojans – in the teeth of racking individual weaknesses, jealousies, doubts, vanities, and suspicions. The story is a reminder that battle is basically a matter of countless individual combats in which mere skill in arms is not always enough. Homer is acutely aware of the moral factor in war. His camera 'cuts' from one side to the other, from the battle front to behind the lines, showing how a sudden misfortune or loss of resolution can change a promising advance into a panic-stricken rout. Fear and the acceptance of fear, its consequences and how it may be overcome, is frankly discussed. None of the great warriors is shown as immune to fear. Neither the Greek nor the Trojan warriors are drilled automata, fighting like clockwork and dying where they stand rather than retreat from a hopeless battle. Despite all the obsession with saving face, and all the appeals to friendship, kinship, and loyalty to one's lord, there are no futile gestures in the *Iliad*, and there is no 'glorious' dying to the last man.

Instead the accent is on resilience, on the realization that a lost battle does not mean a lost war. Both sides in the *Iliad* go through periods of depression – the Greeks fearing that they will never take Troy, the Trojans fearing that the Greeks will never give up and go home. But every time these fears are voiced in council someone stands up and points out that the enemy has his troubles, too; resolution creeps back and the men vote to try again.

Most depictions of scenes from the Trojan Wars show warriors and

Hard to relate to the athletic combat described in the *Iliad*: the massive but ungainly-looking suit of bronze armour found at Dendra, topped by a boars'-tusk helmet

weapons of up to a thousand years later, but one concrete piece of evidence has survived from the Mycenean heroic age. This is the suit of bronze armour from the mid-second millennium discovered at Dendra, armour which almost certainly belonged to a Mycenean chieftain and chariot warrior. It consists of overlapping circular strips of beaten bronze, and admittedly looks a most awkward proposition for a warrior intending to fight on foot, as described in the *Iliad*. The Dendra armour is, however, a tangible link with Homer and his nostalgia for the heroic age, which was of the highest importance because of its contribution to the Greek tradition.

Assuming that the Myceneans and their allies managed to stay sufficiently united to defeat Troy in the end, they failed to fight off the Sea Peoples. The latter swallowed Greece piecemeal and by 1100 BC Greece lay in the shadow of what, compared to the splendours of Minoan Crete and Mycenae, was a Dark Age. The invaders who eventually settled in mainland Greece, spreading overseas to the Aegean Islands and Crete, were the Dorians, iron age warriors who completely shattered the old order and reduced native Greek society to small local communities. From these communities there painfully emerged the Greek city state or *polis*, grouped around a hill on which stood the community's citadel or *acropolis*.

From the middle sixth
century: a Corinthian
helmet wreathed with
myrtle on a funerary urn

The post-Mycenean Dark Age (for want of a better term) destroyed
the material civilization of Mycenae but not its heroic tradition or
memories of the glorious past. One of these traditions was the city-
founding urge, the will to colonize far from home, which eventually
scattered Greek cities all over the Mediterranean from Spain to Egypt.
Calamity at home was the natural spur to colonization abroad, which
began in the dark age with the settling of the eastern Aegean and of
promising sites on the coast of Asia Minor. It was the relationship of
these colonial outposts of the Greek world to the Persian Empire which
provoked the Persian wars of the 490s.

There is no space here to describe the innumerable wars between the
city states of mainland Greece from the end of the dark age around 800
BC to the eve of the Persian wars, 300 years later. Suffice it to say that
Greece remained a patchwork of warring city-states, each one of them

BELOW: The dawn of
sea power in the
Mediterranean – a fleet of
Minoan galleys from the
frescoes discovered on
Thera. LEFT: The men
who overthrew the Minoan
empire – Mycenean
warriors, armoured
spearmen with boars'-tusk
helmets. RIGHT: The
citadel of Mycenae, capital
of Agamemnon in the
Homeric legends

fiercely determined to preserve its independence above all else. The individual fragments which made up the patchwork remained under the thumb of the most dominant cities. Thus Attica was the preserve of Athens, Boeotia of Thebes (with Plataea a strong contender), Lakonia of Sparta, Argolis of Argos, and so on. The states of the Thessalian plain remained more or less stable in a federal league. Epirus and Macedon, to the west and north respectively, were late-developing mountain kingdoms held of little account by the more sophisticated city-states of the south and east.

At the beginnings in the Dark Age the city-states had been ruled by kings, but as times improved powerful aristocracies replaced monarchy in all central and southern states except for Sparta. The inevitable next step was the rise of tyrannies (seventh and sixth centuries BC), with power exercised by rich and ambitious individuals. What is generally misunderstood today as 'Greek democracy' was the reaction from tyranny by the ruling class: the separation of military and civil power in corporate government, still retained by the aristocracy to all intents and purposes, but with safeguards to prevent the emergence of tyrants. Athens was still going through this latter phase during the reign of Darius of Persia. In 510, with Spartan help, Athens expelled the tyrant Hippias, who fled to Darius and appealed for Persian aid and reinstatement. When Athens refused all demands by Darius to take back Hippias as a Persian satrap, and then went on to encourage the Ionian colonies to revolt against Persian rule, Darius decided on military action against Athens.

SPARTA: THE ONLY MILITARY STATE

In general the Greek reaction from monarchy and tyranny sought to prevent the maintenance of a standing army, the most obvious tool of ambition. Sparta, however, emerged from the Dark Age and the ensuing wars with her neighbours on a different evolutionary tack. The Spartan *polis* took the view that if the state was going to be repeatedly embroiled in war it had better be more prepared for war than its enemies. Hence the compulsory military training for all male citizen youth from the age of seven, the barrack life and communal meals for all men of military age. Impoverished and permanently land-hungry, the Spartan state's military regime was supported by the labours of the *helots*, the serf labourers. All the austerity and iron discipline was self-imposed and was prized as a means to an end: the survival of the state to fight tyranny. Rather than entrust supreme power to a single pair of hands, the Spartans retained a monarchy consisting of two kings. Even they were kept in check by the five *ephors* or chief magistrates; one of the kings was only given unchallenged power in time of war, as commander of the army.

The toughness and discipline to which the Spartans subjected themselves became legendary, not only among the other Greek states but to all posterity. The reaction of outsiders was to coin countless anecdotes about the dreadful life the Spartans chose to live, ranging from the appalling food to the Spartan boy who hid a fox up his tunic and, rather than give way to pain, allowed the beast to chew him to death. Sophisticates and aesthetes, then as now, poured scorn on the barrenness of the Spartan regime, but they have never been able to deny it respect, however grudging. The Spartan tradition was not masochism or affectation: it was punctiliously observed in peace and war, and it earned Sparta a very special niche in the military hall of fame.

All Greeks who knew their Homer did not need reminding that the Trojan War had been fought by the massed warriors of Greece to avenge and uphold the honour of King Menelaus of Sparta. The descendants of Menelaus and his soldiers chose to endure self-inflicted hardships and set themselves standards of conduct which the heroes of Troy had never known. The Spartan ideal was not only physical and moral armour against the dangers of the present: it was a tribute to the past. In deliberately improving (as they saw it) on the standards of the heroic age, the Spartans set a unique example to the rest of Greece. Plutarch summed it all up in his story of the old man at the Olympic Games who could not find a place to sit. He was moved on and derided wherever he went until he came to the Spartans, all of whom rose to offer a seat. 'All Greeks know what is right', commented the old man sadly, 'but only the Spartans do it.'

Of all the Greek states, only the Thessalians and Boeotians produced horsed soldiers. The military strength of the Greeks was represented by the hoplite, the armed citizen-soldier, who fought on foot, wearing armour and using weapons of his own provenance. The armour consisted of round shield, helmet, cuirass, reinforced apron, and greaves; the weapons were a thrusting spear which could be thrown like a javelin if need arose, and a sword. This array immediately suggests that of the *Iliad* warriors, but there were important differences. In their compulsory spells of state military training, hoplites learned to manoeuvre and fight in close formation. Their tactical *tour de force* was a swift and disciplined charge, crashing into the enemy line with the minimum delay and breaking it up with spear-thrusts and swordplay. One Homeric feature remained unchanged: the use of the large round shield to push an enemy off balance at the first shock. Hoplites were, however, also trained in casting javelins.

The emergence of these tactics had led to several changes in armour and weaponry by the end of the sixth century. One such change was the disappearance of the heavy 'bell cuirass', which owed its name to the elegant flare given to the bronze back and breast sections at the waist to assist movement. The bell cuirass gave place to a lighter composite type; a leather waistcoat, laced at the front and armoured with iron scales, with armoured flaps extending forward over the shoulders and fastening at the front. Antique thigh armour, which, worn with a bell cuirass and bronze greaves, hardly helped the wearer to dash about the battlefield, also disappeared. Greaves survived for most of the fifth century before they, too, went out of fashion in the increasing trend towards lightness and mobility. Leather greaves had always been popular with less-well-off citizens; they gave adequate protection to knee and shin (for leather armour see also p. 45) and were of course far lighter than bronze.

Among the wealth of evidence yielded by military subjects chosen to decorate Greek vases and dishes, one curiosity is the distinctive grip

Hoplite leg armour: a splendid pair of greaves, contoured to the calf muscle. Greaves were also made of hardened leather

The hoplites of Greece

Despite their mutual rivalries, the city-states of Greece produced the best heavy infantry in the world at the time of the Persian invasions in the early fifth century BC. Most formidable of all was the army of Sparta, the only Greek state whose entire society was geared for war; but all states, to greater or lesser degrees, accepted the need for military training and preparedness. RIGHT: From the island of Rhodes, a bottle designed as a helmeted soldier's head. BELOW: Sixth-century hoplites, their commander mounted in a ceremonial chariot, form a decorative frieze on a bronze bowl. OPPOSITE, TOP: Spartan drill. One of the more straight-forward manoeuvres, this shows a *lochos* (company) of four *enomotiai* (platoons) adopting phalanx formation twelve men wide after advancing in column three abreast. OPPOSITE BELOW: Hoplites in the field. The long spear was their main weapon, but swords were carried for hand-to-hand fighting. The hoplite on the far right carries the distinctive shield emblem of Sparta: the Greek letter *lamda* for 'Lakedaemon', the correct name of the Spartan state

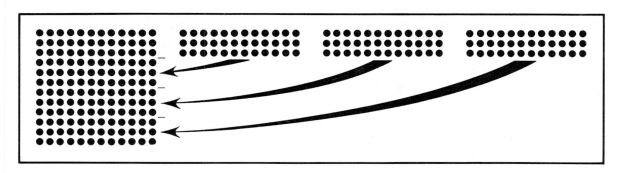

of the right hand on the javelin with the first two fingers extended. This was not an elegant affectation (like the cocked little finger of the 'genteel' tea-drinker) but a device to help the thrower improve his range and accuracy with the javelin. A thong was fastened to the javelin grip, and the thrower would grasp the weapon with this thong twisted round his first two fingers. As the hand opened to let the javelin fly, the thong would whip loose from the fingers and set the javelin spinning, giving the missile far more stability on its way to the target than an unrotated spear. This idea, plus the lightening of body armour, were typical refinements which had been adopted since Homeric times.

The Greeks never developed archery to supplement the javelin-volley, crashing collision, and swordplay of the hoplites. Small companies of archers were used, firing their stave bows apparently from the shelter of the hoplites' shields, but never in large enough numbers or with sufficiently powerful weapons to usurp the role of the hoplites. But a major change from the Homeric battle order was the recruiting of *peltast* battalions, which gave the hoplite mass a light infantry screen. Peltasts got their name from the *pelta*, the light crescent-shaped buckler which was their sole means of protection — they were completely unarmoured. Their role was to sprint in and out of enemy range making hit-and-run attacks with showers of javelins.

The Greeks certainly used horsed soldiers in the fifth century BC but the role of their 'cavalry' at this early date was ambiguous. Not every state had the resources to raise any sort of cavalry force, though armed horsemen seem to have been the normal 'eyes' for the hoplite mass. (Rich hoplites would ride to the battle on horseback, a groom taking charge of his master's horse when the time came to dismount and fight on foot.) Horsed soldiers of the fifth century are shown wearing helmet, cuirass, and sword, and carrying javelins or thrusting-spears. The antique Greek war chariot had vanished from the scene long before the end of the sixth century BC, and horsed troops never replaced it as an essential aid to tactical mobility. Instead, all the tactical eggs were put in the infantry basket and the development of the hoplite resulted. Practical and financial difficulties in raising cavalry forces, combined with the negative Greek attitude to archery, certainly explain why the horsed archer was such a total stranger to the Greek armoury.

At the time of the Persian invasions the only way in which the Greek states involved could have raised an 'instant' cavalry force would have been by alliance with the Thessalian League, the only Greek power to make extensive use of cavalry. As the Thessalians favoured appeasement of Persia, the Greek states under attack were obliged to rely on the arm in which they had the most confidence anyway: the hoplite infantry. None of the three decisive land battles of the Persian wars saw cavalry play any kind of defensive role, to the utter disadvantage of the Persians.

THE FIRST PERSIAN WAR (490 BC)

As noted in the previous chapter, the original Persian attitude to the Greek world was sensitive and pacific. The Lydians of Asia Minor had absorbed many Greek characteristics, the essentials of the hoplite panoply being an obvious example; the Ionian Greek colonies off the

Statuette of a sixth-century Spartan hoplite, wearing an unusually ornate cuirass. By the middle fifth century the Spartans had abandoned heavy body armour to give their hoplites greater freedom of movement in action

coast of Asia Minor – Miletus, Chios, Samos, Lesbos – accepted Persian suzerainty under Cyrus or, in the case of Miletus, were given privileged status. This amicable state of affairs endured under Cyrus, Cambyses, and the first half of the reign of Darius, when the Persian kings were fully occupied in building up the Persian Empire and had no desire for military adventures west of the Dardanelles. But by 510 BC, the year when the ousted Athenian tyrant Hippias and his supporters arrived at Sardis clamouring for Persian aid, the empire was secure enough for Darius to turn his full attention to the Greeks.

Artaphernes, the western satrap with his capital at Sardis, backed the suggestion of Hippias that he be reinstated in Athens as a vassal of Persia, a policy which received Darius' full approval. For their part, the Athenians, as soon as they learned where Hippias had gone and what he was up to, sent a formal embassy to Sardis to protest against Persian patronage of their arch-enemy. Artaphernes demanded instant submission from the Athenians and the Athenians rejected the demand. By the end of 510 BC a state of undeclared war existed between Athens and Persia: a tense and uneasy 'cold war'.

At first both sides hoped that the crisis would resolve itself. At this time Athens was racked with party politics and undergoing drastic political reform. The aristocratic families were jockeying for power and even the anti-Persian faction was divided by internal politics. Meanwhile Sparta was busily stirring the pot; having intervened in 510 BC to help the Athenian Alcmaeonid family expel Hippias and the Pisistratids, the Spartans sent another expedition into Athenian territory to overturn the democratic constitution set up by the Alcmaeonid Cleosthenes in 508 BC. This expedition was, however, violently resisted and the Spartan attempt at manipulation failed. As if these domestic upheavals were not enough, Athens was simultaneously expanding her zone of control into the offshore island of Euboea and trying to maintain her most distant colony on the Thracian Chersonese – the Dardanelles peninsula, on the very doorstep of the Persian Empire.

The Athenian rejection of Darius' ultimatum did not, therefore, lead to an immediate outbreak of war. The Athenians had their hands full at home and did not want to throw away their colony in the Chersonese, which would be the first casualty in an armed clash with the Persian Empire. For his part, Darius had every reason to hope that yet another political upheaval in Athens would swing back the pendulum in favour of Hippias and Persian suzerainty.

Matters were brought to a head by the revolt of the Ionian colonies in 499 BC, led by Aristagoras of Miletus. The Ionian revolt was backed by Athens and the Euboean state of Eretria. They could send their Ionian cousins little in the way of effective aid, but keeping the Ionian revolt on the boil was an ideal way of distracting Darius from their own affairs. Athens and Eretria sent a joint force of twenty-five ships, enough to encourage the Ionians to fight on but far too small a force to be of any practical use. Thus encouraged from the homeland, the Ionians pounced on Sardis and burned it, upon which Lesbos and Samos hastily quit the rebel alliance and made their peace with Darius. The Persian fleet eventually scattered the rebel fleet off Lade in 494 BC, sacked Miletus and took all the other rebel cities. The Ionian revolt was crushed, but Darius was determined to go on and punish Athens and Eretria for helping the rebels and bringing about the destruction of Sardis.

Herodotus claims that Darius employed a slave with the special job of saying, every day, 'O King, remember the Athenians!' The problem was how to get at them. A Persian army crossing the Dardanelles and advancing on Athens by land would have the enormously long march round the head of Aegean to cope with and would have to be supported by the sea. Darius tried this in 492 BC, sending his general Mardonius off on the long march with the fleet in support. This first attempt was a humiliating failure. Mardonius and his army (size and composition unknown) occupied the Chersonese which the Athenian colonists had prudently abandoned after the defeat of the Ionians. He advanced along the coast of Thrace and the Macedonians apprehensively made peace, which would have given the Persians an open road down to Mount Olympus and the northern border of Thessaly. But the Persian fleet, hugging the coast to give the army close support, was wrecked in a storm while trying to get round the rocky fang of Mount Athos. Mardonius made the sensible decision to withdraw. If he had pressed on he would have had to leave so many troops behind to safeguard his communications that he would have had nothing left to fight with by the time he reached Attica.

Two years later, having rebuilt the Persian fleet, Darius launched a second attempt. This time, instead of the overland march, he ordered an island-hopping advance through the central Aegean. It was a plan of great sophistication. The fleet of about 600 ships (war triremes and transports) would carry the army through the Cyclades group, attacking few noted pro-Athenian islands before landing on Euboea. There the army would divide, one part remaining in Euboea to settle accounts with the Eretrians while the remainder crossed to the Greek mainland to proclaim Hippias tyrant in Darius' name, receive the submission of all Greek states who saw sense, and smash any force which the Athenians might presume to put into the field.

The first part of the plan worked well enough. From its advanced base on Samos the fleet headed south-west for Naxos, which was thoroughly sacked. The next objective was the sacred island of Delos to the north, whose inhabitants were treated with ostentatious benevolence. Then the Persians made for Euboea, besieging Carystos at the island's southern tip before landing in force under the walls of Eretria, in the first week of September. The Eretrians appealed to Athens for aid; the Athenians promptly mobilized their army and sent their Olympic champion runner Pheidippides off to Sparta to enlist more help from the south. The Athenian field army was already marching north to do what it could to help the Eretrians when the news came in that the Persians had landed in the bay of Marathon.

The Persian general Datis landed at Marathon on the advice of Hippias and the Pisistratid exiles, whose original supremacy in Athens had been won in battle on the plain of Marathon after crossing from Eretria. This time, however, there was no immediate decision. The Athenians only had about 10,000 of their own hoplites and another

1,000 from Plataea and were counting on a relief force coming up from Sparta. The Persian force numbered no more than 15,000, including the bulk of the cavalry strength of about 800. Both sides, therefore, eyed each other warily, unwilling to join battle because each army was expecting reinforcements, the Athenians from Sparta and the Persians from Euboea, as soon as Eretria fell.

Eight days passed in unbroken stalemate. The Athenians had taken up a very strong position blocking the road to Athens which led inland from the Marathon plain; if the Persians should suddenly decide to take the coast road to Athens the Athenian army could attack them as soon as they strung out in a column of march. But by the end of the week the strategic balance was dipping heavily in favour of the Persians. News had come in that the Spartans would not march north until they had completed one of their elaborate religious ceremonies, which was scheduled for the next full moon – five whole days away. The ten Athenian generals elected under the latest city constitution were deeply divided about whether to attack at Marathon or fall back on Athens when the Persians made their move, The crucial debate came on the eighth day, when news arrived that Eretria had fallen: news that reached both armies at about the same time. Now all the Persians had to do was to bring the rest of the army over from conquered Euboea and they could

View across the plain of Marathon today, from the mound built by the Greeks on the site of their victory

fall on the Athenians and Plataeans in overwhelming strength.

What seems to have happened next is that Datis and Artaphernes, the two Persian generals, decided to re-embark the whole army and strike direct for Athens by sea. The Marathon force duly began to embark, sending the cavalry aboard first and moving the infantry out towards the Athenian camp to screen the withdrawal. This would explain why the Persian cavalry took no part at all in the ensuing action, even though the plain of Marathon had been specially selected because of its suitability for cavalry. And even the most hesitant Athenian general could not fail to have been tempted by the spectacle of the Persians progressively withdrawing into their beachhead, leaving their infantry isolated and open to attack.

Athenian tradition names Miltiades as the general whose urgings to attack tipped the scale at the last war council before the battle. Miltiades was certainly a master of the calculated risk: he had commanded the colony in the Thracian Chersonese and had given the order to pull out after the defeat of the Ionians. The Athenians knew that the biggest danger they would face in the attack would come from the Persian foot archers during the approach, which was therefore carried out at break-neck speed. The army broke from its camp in two dense columns which peeled outwards to form an opening 'Y' until the tails met in the centre. Then, the line duly formed, the hoplites charged.

Hoplites are conventionally depicted as carrying two javelins, and if this was the case at Marathon the shaken Persians, hastily preparing to meet the shock, could have been hit by 22,000 javelins in the first two minutes. The second flight of javelins can only just have landed when the front-rank hoplites crashed into the Persian line. During the approach of the Athenians the Persian foot archers should, by all the standards of warfare to which they were accustomed, have had the chance to wreak havoc in the attackers' ranks with their arrows. That this did not happen is attributable to two factors only: the effectiveness of the hoplites' armour and the speed with which they closed the range. The battle of Marathon is indeed one of the supreme examples of the helplessness of foot archers when attacked by armoured shock troops.

The Athenian deployment was brilliantly executed, considering that there was certainly no time for dressing and adjusting the line before the attack went in; but after all the Athenian generals had had a week in which to study the ground and work out how they would attack if the worst came to the worst. (The same, of course, applied to the Persians, but their recent decision to re-embark the army deprived them of the initiative and reduced their infantry to a screening force.) Callimachus, the Athenian *polemarch*, or supreme commander, had been determined not to let the numerically superior Persians outflank him; but extending the Athenian line to the same frontage as that of the Persians meant leaving the Athenian centre dangerously thin. This risk was worth taking, however, because the Persians deployed in the traditional manner with their heavy troops in the centre and their light forces on the flanks. Although the Persian heavy infantry in the centre not only held the Athenians but began to drive them back, the Greek flanks – Plataeans on the left and Athenians on the right – drove clean

Eternal honour to the fallen – Greek burial mound at Marathon. True to the fierce individualism of the Greek city-states, the dead of the small Plataean contingent which fought at Marathon were buried in their own ground

through the flimsy provincial troops on either side of the Persian centre. This left the triumphant Persians in the centre totally exposed. A halt, about-turn and converging attack by the Greek flanks and the Persians were trapped, with no choice but to cut their way out of the trap and bolt for the ships.

Supreme opportunity now beckoned to the tired but exultant Greeks, for if they could keep up the pressure and get in among the Persian fleet with firebrands they would be able to annihilate the entire Persian invasion force. But this splendid goal was denied them. The Persians in the ships pushed forward a strong covering force to cover the fugitives from the rout of the infantry. There was bitter fighting for the beachhead perimeter in which Callimachus died, his hand cut off as it grasped the nearest enemy ship. The battle for the ships was uncannily like the scene in the fifteenth book of the *Iliad*, in which the Trojans get in among the Greek ships and try to burn them. The result was the same too: the defenders saved themselves by the most desperate fighting. The Athenians were only able to take seven ships which had delayed too long before pushing off; the rest of the Persian fleet got away with the shaken survivors.

Persian casualties at Marathon were 6,400 killed; the total Greek loss was no higher than 192. There was an interesting tailpiece to the battle 2,460 years later, when Greek archaeologists excavated the burial mound of the Plataeans in the spring of 1970. It was found to contain eleven skeletons – all young men, between eighteen and twenty-five years old. Given the overall Greek casualty rate and the size of the small Plataean force fighting beside the Athenians, here was final proof that when it came to the sticking-point the Greek city-states could indeed sink their differences and fight with equal ferocity.

The Athenians wasted no time in celebrating their victory on the battlefield, but marched back to Athens the same day to cover the city. As they withdrew they made contact with the Spartan expeditionary force of 2,000 hoplites, which had finally arrived after its 200-mile march. Meanwhile the two wings of the Persian fleet reunited at sea and headed for Athens, arriving off the Bay of Phaleron to find the Athenian army waiting for them. Ruling out the idea of trying an opposed landing, Datis and Artaphernes agreed on a withdrawal of the entire force to Persian waters.

More than anything else, the Greek victory at Marathon proved to the world that the Persian army could be beaten. This was a fact of immense psychological importance. Apart from cracking the myth of Persian invincibility, which alone entitles Marathon to rank with the greatest battles of all time, the victory also showed the Greeks that the heroic traditions of the *Iliad* were alive and well and living in Athens. It gave the Greek world pride in a living achievement as well as in bygone glory. In the short term Marathon put an end to Persian hopes of taking Greece the easy way, piece by piece, putting in Persian client-rulers to ride the whirlpools of Greek city-state politics. It offered the Greek states an alternative to caving in to Persian demands for submission.

Naturally Marathon meant far more to the Greeks than it did to the Persians, who did not see it as a world-shattering defeat for the empire. From their point of view it was easy to work out where the campaign had gone wrong. Down to the siege of Eretria the campaign had in fact gone very well indeed, more or less precisely according to plan. Datis and Artaphernes had made a grave error in keeping the army divided for so long, but at least they had placed a powerful force within a day's march of Athens. Their fatal mistake had been to re-embark the mainland force before the rest of the army had been brought over from Euboea. As for the Greeks, they admittedly had good infantry and had used it well in a sneak attack. Next time they must be tackled with the best heavy infantry in the Persian Empire, and in overwhelming strength. The Marathon campaign should be written off as useful experience. It was a freakish setback, and nothing more, to the conquest of Greece. In the next invasion nothing would be left to chance: it would be the attack as it should be delivered.

In the ten years separating Marathon from the great Persian invasion of 480 BC, the anti-Persian lobby gained complete control in Athens. It was led by Themistocles, who had been one of the ten generals at Marathon. Themistocles was a rare blend of statesmanship and military genius, who sensed that the true security for Athens at home and abroad was sea power — a strong fleet to scatter her enemies and protect her trade. Mere strength on land would never be enough. An unexpected stroke of luck enabled his dream to be made reality in the nick of time. In 483 BC a rich vein was discovered in the Athenian state silver mine at Laurium, giving the Athenian economy a tremendous and unexpected boost. Themistocles persuaded the Athenians to spend the surplus on building a battle fleet, instead of using it to swell private fortunes and improve public amenities. It soon proved the most providential decision the Athenians ever made.

For seven years after Marathon, Persian preparations for the great invasion were disrupted again and again. Provincial revolts in Asia Minor and Egypt had to be put down before the invasion build-up could get under way. Darius died in 486 before the provinces were fully pacified, and it was not until 483 that his successor Xerxes could turn his full attention to the invasion of Greece.

Xerxes' preparations were on an immense scale. Two huge pontoon bridges were built across the Dardanelles. To save the supporting fleet from having to run the gauntlet of the Mount Athos peninsula where the fleet of 492 BC had been wrecked, the peninsula was pierced by a canal through which the ships could sail in safety. Massive dumps of supplies and munitions were built up in Thrace, which, together with Macedonia, submitted at the outset. This immediate surrender gave the Persians a clear line of march as far as the River Pineios, the northern border of Thessaly, when they set out from their main base at Sardis in the spring of 480 BC.

The choice of troops picked for the invasion was clearly the result of much hard thinking about the defeat at Marathon ten years before. Heavy infantry was the most important arm. As well as the Immortals there were four heavy infantry 'line' corps: Persians, Medes, Hyrkanians, and Kashites. In selecting the light infantry and cavalry units, Xerxes was torn between his desire to send the strongest possible cross-section of his empire's immense military resources, and the practical need – in view of the recent provincial revolts – to keep strong mobile forces at home. Even token forces from the provincial corps (examined on pp. 90–95) added up to an impressive host, the true size of which will always be open to debate. It would seem to have been in the region of 115–118,000.

THE SECOND PERSIAN WAR (480–479 BC)

Xerxes began the war by sending his envoys to every city in Greece to demand 'earth and water' in token of submission and in Athens Themistocles reacted magnificently to the ultimatum. He executed the interpreter who attended the Persian envoys, 'because he had dared to make use of the Greek language to transmit the commands of a barbarian'. By this time the great Persian build-up was all but complete, having been attended by carefully planned publicity. Herodotus claims that three Greek spies had been caught by the Persians and, on Xerxes' orders, given a painstaking guided tour of the army before being sent home to tell of the irresistible power they had seen.

This was not merely vainglorious ostentation: it was highly effective propaganda and did much to dim the hopeful beacon which the Athenians had lit at Marathon. All the northern states in the path of the Persian steamroller – Thessaly, Doris, Phocis, Boeotia – refused to give their full support to Athens but sat on the fence, allowing southern Greek forces to campaign in their territory but no more. The only help Athens received from the northern states – 400 hoplites from Thebes, 700 from Thespis, 1,000 from Phocis – were either outright opponents of their own governments or determined to fight despite the timidity of their own city fathers. Athens herself provided 8,000 hoplites, her main effort in this war being represented by her new battle fleet of 200 triremes. The Athenian fleet was reinforced to over 300 by small squadrons furnished by the southern states.

The southern Greek states of the Peloponnese naturally supported Athens, for if Athens fell they would be next on the list. But as long as a chance remained of bringing over the vacillating northern states the Peloponnesian contribution remained small. The bulk of the splendid Spartan army of 10,000 hoplites was held back, although King Leonidas came north with his hand-picked elite guard of 300 hoplites.

By the end of July, Xerxes and his host had rounded the head of the Aegean and were pushing steadily south towards the Pineios. Here Themistocles had hoped to make a stand, exploiting the confines of the Vale of Tempe; his instinctive strategy was to fight the Persians as far to the north as possible. But as soon as the allied field army of 5,200 arrived on the Pineios it was clear that it could easily be turned. The army therefore fell back on Thermopylae, where the coast road squeezed through a natural bottleneck under 200 yards wide between the mountains and the sea.

The withdrawal from the Pineios decided matters for the Thessalians, who promptly went over to the Persians. Themistocles was undismayed; this had been expected. Now he planned to take the allied fleet to sea and inflict maximum damage on the Persian armada as it rounded the northern tip of Euboea off Artemision. Unbelievably, given the magnitude of the crisis, the old bugbear of inter-city rivalry raised its head again. Themistocles had to soothe Spartan touchiness at the very idea of serving under Athenian command. He agreed to place the Athenian fleet under the command of Eurybiades of Sparta and appeased the equally outraged Athenians (whose contingent was by far the biggest in the fleet) by promising that all Greeks would soon be following the lead of Athens if they did well in the coming battle.

When the Persian fleet was first sighted off Aphetae, Eurybiades was appalled at the odds and wanted to withdraw at once; but Themistocles blackmailed Eurybiades into making a fight of it by threatening him with public denunciation. The battle off Artemision seems to have been a series of hit-and-run attacks on the leading Persian ships as they pressed through the narrows, but we know tantalizingly little about it. The action pales into insignificance beside the later triumph at Salamis, but it was vitally important. It gave the Greek crews confidence in the unfamiliar art of naval warfare. And it held up the Persian fleet long enough to prevent troops being landed in the rear of Leonidas and his Spartans, as they earned themselves military immortality in the Thermopylae gap.

The road through the Thermopylae gap was constricted by three narrow 'gates', the middle 'gate' being delineated by a half-ruined wall. Leonidas stationed his main force behind this wall and posted 1,000 local troops who knew the ground best – Phocians – on the well-known mountain road winding inland round the entire position. He then placed his Spartans in the van and awaited the Persian attack.

Xerxes and his army arrived before Thermopylae in the middle of August. A child could see that the position would be hard to force – but

Persian military relics (*left to right*) arrow-heads, spear-head, dagger, and cavalry bit

the army was running short of supplies, as the storeships were held up with the Persian fleet at Artemision. He therefore ordered a frontal assault in the third week of August, sending his heavy infantry corps against the ranked hoplites. These attacks were repulsed with ease. The Persian columns could not deploy enough to allow the archers to bring their full fire-power to bear, and in any case the flat trajectory of the composite bow was of little use against well-armoured troops skilled in the use of the shield. For two days the dominant sound at Thermopylae must have been the clang and whirr of arrows ricochetting off Greek shields — interspersed with death-cries as the Greeks launched limited but fierce counterattacks to charge down the nearest archers.

By the third day there was still no sign of the Persian fleet and the Greek hold on the Thermopylae gap was as strong as ever. It was now that Xerxes brought the Immortals into play, sending them off on their inland flank march to get in behind the Greeks and deliver the *coup de grâce*. Leonidas had foreseen this move and the Phocians should have blocked it — but instead they merely withdrew onto higher ground and let the Immortals get past. As soon as the leading Immortals came splendidly into view on the heights, Leonidas called a council of war. He ordered the mixed contingents from the Peloponnese, 2,800 in all, to retreat while they could while the Spartans, Thespians, and Boeotians held off the enemy. Less than 1,400 men were left to face the entire Persian army.

The last act at Thermopylae began with another, totally unnecessary defeat for the Persian main body. Xerxes had planned a pincer movement to catch the Greeks between the Immortals and the main body, but the latter went in to attack too early. Once again the Persians were thrown back — and this time Leonidas ordered a pursuit to the western gate. It was his last order before he was killed, and there was a ferocious struggle for his body which might have been straight out of the *Iliad*. Having recovered the remains of Leonidas the Greeks dourly pulled back onto a mound to die, with not a single Spartan surviving to tell the story.

The loss of the Thermopylae position and the immediate resumption of the Persian advance caused panic in the south. The Peloponnesian states changed their mind about marching north to help Athens fight the Persians in Boeotia, which now joined the Thracians, Macedonians, and Thessalians in submission to Xerxes. The southern states prepared to make their stand behind a wall which they frantically set about building across the Isthmus of Corinth, the land link to the Peloponnese. Athens was left on her own, apparently doomed. But once again Themistocles rose to the occasion, persuading his countrymen to migrate *en masse* to the island of Salamis, leaving Athens to the protection of Athene and a token garrison in the Acropolis.

Themistocles was virtually alone in appreciating that the odds against Athens were hopeless on land but not at sea. The fighting off Artemision had ground down the Persian fleet to about 350 ships, while the allied Greek fleet still had about 310. The allied fleet now lay inside the narrow strait between Salamis and the mainland. It could not stop the Persian army from taking Athens — but it could prevent the Persian

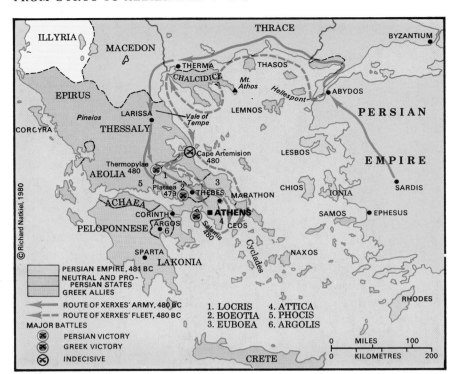

© Richard Natkiel, 1980

PERSIAN EMPIRE, 481 BC
NEUTRAL AND PRO-
PERSIAN STATES
GREEK ALLIES
ROUTE OF XERXES' ARMY, 480 BC
ROUTE OF XERXES' FLEET, 480 BC
MAJOR BATTLES
⊗ PERSIAN VICTORY
⊗ GREEK VICTORY
⊗ INDECISIVE

1. LOCRIS   4. ATTICA
2. BOEOTIA   5. PHOCIS
3. EUBOEA   6. ARGOLIS

LEFT: The Persian invasion of 480 BC. The dogged attacks of the Greek fleet at Artemision prevented the Persians from cracking the Thermopylae position by landing forces behind the Greek lines, and they were forced to make their famous inland flanking march instead

BELOW: The Thermopylae pass today. In 480 BC the coastline would have run just to the right of the road. Spurs reaching down from the hills pinched the coastal strip into the narrow 'gates' defended so magnificently by Leonidas and his men

RIGHT: Figurine of a
cloaked Spartan warrior.
'Obedient to their laws',
Leonidas and his men
fought to the last at
Thermopylae, but their
deaths were thoroughly
avenged by their
countrymen at Plataea in
the following year

fleet from supporting the Persian army. The elimination of the Greek fleet thus became the next Persian objective in the campaign.

On 21 September 480 BC the tiny but valiant garrison in the Acropolis fell at last, releasing the Persian army to move against the Isthmus of Corinth. Themistocles, however, retained the initiative in this apparently hopeless hour. He wanted to lure the bulk of the Persian fleet inside the Sound of Salamis where the Greeks could attack it on equal terms; and he did it by 'planting' false information that the Greeks were planning to escape through the western entrance to the Sound. Xerxes immediately detached the Egyptian squadrons, one-third of the whole Persian fleet, to cover the western entrance. He then set up his golden throne on the heights overlooking the Sound to watch the spectacle of the Phoenicians and Ionians going in to smoke out the trapped Greeks.

Themistocles deployed the allied fleet in such a way that it was poised for instant attack while looking temptingly vulnerable to the last moment. At dawn on the 23rd the Greek ships headed across the eastern entrance, wheeled south to face the oncoming Phoenicians and Ionians pressing into the narrows, then backed northward in a flimsy-looking arc as though unnerved by the opposition. Xerxes' captains greedily took the bait and continued into the trap. In his biography of Themistocles, Plutarch gives a most vivid account of the ensuing battle:

Themistocles appears to have chosen the time for the battle as judiciously as he had the place. He was careful not to let the triremes engage the barbarian ships head on, until the time of day when the wind usually blows fresh from the sea and sends a heavy swell rolling through the narrows. This breeze was no disadvantage to the Greek ships, which were comparatively small and lay low in the water, but it caught the Persian vessels, which were difficult to manoeuvre with their high decks and towering sterns, and swung them round broadside on to their opponents, who dashed in eagerly to the attack. The Greek captains kept a watchful eye on Themistocles, because they felt that he saw most clearly what were the right tactics to follow, and also because he had ranged opposite him Xerxes' admiral, Ariamenes, a man of great courage, who was both the most stalwart and the most high-principled of the king's brothers. He was stationed on a huge ship, from which he kept discharging arrows and javelins, as though he were on the wall of a fortress. Ameinias of Decelea and Socles of the deme of Paeania, who were both sailing in the same vessel, bore down upon his and met it bows on, and as the two ships crashed into each other and were held by their bronze beaks, Ariamenes tried to board their trireme; but the two Athenians faced him, ran him through with their spears, and pitched him into the sea . . .

The first man to capture an enemy ship was Lycomedes, the commander of an Athenian trireme, who cut off the Persian's figurehead and dedicated it to Apollo the Laurel-bearer at Phyla. The rest of the Greeks now found themselves on equal terms with their enemies, since the Persians could only bring a small part of their whole fleet into action at a time, as their ships constantly fouled one another in the narrow straights; and so, although they held out till the evening, the Greeks finally put them to utter rout. Thus they gained 'that noble and famous victory', as Simonides says, 'the most glorious exploit ever achieved at sea by Greek or barbarian, and they owed it to the courage and determination of all those who fought their ships, but not least to the surpassing skill and judgement of Themistocles'.

The Persians lost over 200 ships at Salamis, the Greeks less than forty. The battle gave the Greeks command of the sea; it left the Persian army in precisely the same situation as the invasion force of 492 BC after the wreck of the fleet, only this time far more isolated and vulnerable. Themistocles rammed home his triumph by sending an insolent message to Xerxes, advising him that the Greeks could now destroy the pontoon bridge over the Dardanelles and that the Persians had best get out while they could. Xerxes was forced to abandon his dream of conquering all Greece, and ordered a general retreat. He headed for Asia Minor with two-thirds of the army: one-third to cover his line of retreat and the other to hold down the Ionian islands. Mardonius, the Persian commander of 492, was left to take the remaining third of the army into winter quarters in Thessaly, and to carry on the campaign as best he could.

The failure of the Greeks to agree on a joint strategy during the winter and spring of 479 BC handed the initiative back to the Persians when the 'campaigning season' came round again. After the traumatic setbacks of the previous year the position of the Persians in Greece had improved considerably. The corps of Artabazus had secured the line of

A Greek bireme under sail. When a fleet was observed to be sending its masts and yards ashore, it meant that the ships were preparing for battle

communications back to the Dardanelles and was able to send consider-able reinforcements to Mardonius in Thessaly. These included the Immortals, back to full strength after the mauling they had suffered at Thermopylae, and the Median heavy infantry corps. But the most important reinforcements were in cavalry: the 1,000-strong imperial household cavalry, the Sakae corps, and a generous mixture of horsed archer and javelin units. When Mardonius opened the 479 campaign he had an excellent army of about 35,000 infantry and 12,000 cavalry. He also had the doubtful aid of about 15,000 co-belligerent Greeks, includ-ing Thessalian cavalry, whose allegiance would hardly survive another Persian defeat.

Greek rivalry and disunity was just as intense as it had been the year before. The forces of Athens, Megara, and Plataea were left unsupported while the Peloponnesian forces hesitated to move north of the Corin-thian isthmus. Mardonius took the initiative, starting with an attempt to seduce the Athenians away from the Greek alliance. There was in fact an Athenian conspiracy to overthrow the democracy, but anti-Persian feeling ran far stronger than dislike of the new regime. Diplomacy proving a failure, Mardonius invaded Attica again and occupied Athens for the second time, forcing the Athenians to make another mass migration to Salamis and the offshore islands. His objective was to prod the allied forces into venturing out from behind their defences, and it worked. As soon as the Peloponnesian forces moved into Attica, Mar-donius withdrew northwards over the mountains into the plain of Boeotia, where the terrain suited his cavalry best. The allies followed, and at the beginning of the last week in August sighted the Persians across the plain to the north-east of Plataea.

It was disconcerting to find that the Persians were based on an extremely strong fortified camp on the far bank of the River Asopus, four miles away across terrain ideally suited to their cavalry. The Greek army totalled some 40,000 hoplites and another 50,000 assorted pel-tasts and archers, but it had no regular cavalry at all. It was, moreover, not a tight-knit force like the army which had triumphed at Marathon, but a patchwork of Athenians, Spartans, Plataeans, Corinthians, Tegeans, and many other minority contingents. Even Mycenae, in 479 a ghost of its former glory, stubbornly contributed an 'army' of eighty men. Not even the most partial Greek account of the Plataea campaign and battle omits to mention the fierce quarrelling that went on between the contingents over the most honourable or advantageous deployment for each individual force.

Pausanias, the Spartan commander-in-chief, cautiously deployed the allied army on the heights of Cithaeron south of the plain. The Megarians, however, were stationed closest of all to the low ground and Mardonius opened the battle with mass cavalry attacks on this exposed detachment. The power of horsed cavalry immediately made itself felt and the Megareans suffered badly from the hail of javelins and arrows from the Persian horsemen. Aristides, the Athenian commander, sent across a picked force of 300, strong in archers, to give the Megareans fire support and a lucky shot brought down the horse of Masisius, the Persian cavalry commander. After a good deal of trouble caused by the

Hand-to-hand combat between Greek and Persian, in which the Greeks excelled due to their superior drill and armoured protection

excellence of his armour, Masisius was finally despatched by a spear-thrust into the eye-slit of his helmet, and the Persian cavalry drew off in dismay.

Pausanias then decided to move the army down into the plain, partly to improve its water supply and partly in hopes of provoking Mardonius into risking a pitched battle. This move was a bad miscalculation. For two days the Greek army lay exposed on the plain while the Persian cavalry harassed its flanks, cut off its supplies and all roads leading back over the hills to Attica and finally seized the very springs which the advancing Greeks had intended to use as their water supply. While this was going on the Persian infantry refused to budge; and Pausanias decided on a night withdrawal back to the high ground.

The withdrawal, on the night of 26–27 August, was a disorganized shambles. When day came the Athenians were still straggling over the plain, apparently hopelessly exposed. Mardonius promptly ordered in his cavalry, supported by foot archers and heavy infantry. Pausanias had made several mistakes over the last few days, but this was what he had been waiting for. The Athenians went into the classic hoplite defensive formation and stood up well to the arrow storm until Pausanias had wheeled the rest of the army into line. It was then a simple matter of waiting for the Persian infantry to work far enough forward to allow full scope for the terrible hoplite charge.

The Greeks always looked down on the Persians as barbarians and scoffed at their habit of concealing soft bodies and faint hearts behind gaudy costumes; but even the Greeks later paid full tribute to the courage with which the Immortals and heavy infantry tried in vain to fight the hoplites to a standstill. In the words of Plutarch:

Suddenly there came over the whole phalanx the look of some ferocious beast, as it wheels at bay, stiffens its bristles and turns to defend itself, so that the barbarians could no longer doubt that they were faced with men who would fight to the death. The Persians therefore set up their great wicker shields like a wall in front of them and shot arrows at their opponents. But the Spartans, keeping their shields locked edge to edge as they advanced, threw themselves upon the enemy, wrenched away their wicker shields, and then thrust with their long spears at the faces and breasts of the Persians and slaughtered them in great numbers. In spite of this the Persians fought bravely and skillfully before they fell. They seized the long spears of the Greeks with their bare hands, snapped many of them off, and then closed in to fierce hand-to-hand fighting, using their daggers and scimitars, tearing away their enemies' shields and grappling with them, and in this way they held out for a long time.

While the Spartans were tearing the Persian heavy infantry to pieces, the Athenians closed with the co-belligerent Theban hoplites and a bruising battle-within-a-battle ensued. The Thebans had already started to retreat when the Athenians heard that the Persian infantry had been destroyed and the Spartans were pressing forward to assault the Persian camp. The Athenians promptly disengaged from the Thebans and came up to help the Spartans, who were inexperienced in attacking fixed defences. As at Marathon, the survivors from the infantry killing-match put up a fierce resistance in the latter phase of the battle, but this time they failed to hold off the Greeks. The Athenians and Tegeans shared the prime honours in storming the fortifications of the Persian camp. Only a few thousand Persians managed to escape the slaughter which ensued. The Persian cavalry, which had played an unaccountably feeble role during the infantry *mêlée* compared to its excellent performance in the opening phases of the battle, covered the retreat through Thessaly into Macedonia and Thrace. Due to their own lack of cavalry the Greeks were unable to pursue and exploit, or to prevent the Persian withdrawal from Thrace into a temporary bridgehead in the Chersonese.

Plataea was one of the great 'battles without a morrow': it ended the Persian threat to Greece for ever. The bulk of the Persian army, about 30,500 in all, died at Plataea, and with the Greeks in total command of their home waters there was no course but retreat for the survivors. The Plataea campaign was rounded out by a small Spartan fleet which crossed to Samos under Leotychidas and destroyed the last Persian warships lurking in the Ionian islands in a fight at Mycale. This was not a sea battle: the Persians were so demoralized that they had beached their ships, and when the Spartans stormed ashore the Persians fired the ships rather than see them captured. Mycale was thus a symbol of the utter failure of the imposing force which Xerxes had led into Greece only eighteen months before.

Mardonius, who was killed in the Spartan assault on the Persian shield-wall at Plataea, had fought an excellent campaign and had come within an ace of cancelling the defeats of 480. It is almost certain that if he had not lost his cavalry commander, Masisius, at such an early stage of the battle, the Persian cavalry would have attacked the hoplites in the rear with the energy and skill displayed until then. In general, however, the Persian failure of 480–479 was due to the secondary role which had been assigned to the Persian cavalry; the Persian failure to retain command of the sea; and the ability with which the Greek hoplite commanders brought about the close-quarter fighting in which their men excelled. The biggest defect on the Greek side was the chronic disunity between the various regional contingents, which made itself felt in the most desperate crises. So far from being dispelled by victory over the Persians, this rivalry was only sharpened by the Greek triumph of 479. Within ten years, the victors of Marathon, Salamis, and Plataea were at each other's throats.

Sixth-century figurine of a hoplite. Plataea, death-blow of the ambitions of Xerxes, marked the climax of a glorious century for the hoplites of Greece – but the next eighty years saw them embroiled in an exhausting and futile cycle of internecine wars

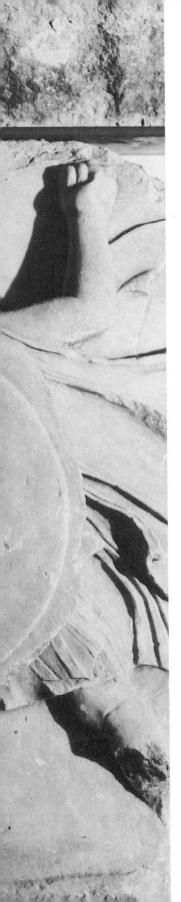

CHAPTER SIX

Greece: The Road to Ruin

T HE GREEKS HAILED THEIR VICTORY over Persia almost as a matter of course: the triumph of free civilization over despotic barbarism. They gloried in the fact that they were impossible neighbours: torn by internal rivalries that made Greece look like the ideal country to divide and rule, yet burning with ambition and aggression. The victors of 479 did not sit down to work out a glowing future of peace and harmony at home and abroad. Instead each Greek state wondered what further opportunities could be derived from the Persian defeat, and – even more important – what they should do to prevent their rivals from getting ahead.

This led directly to a virtually uninterrupted century of wars in Greece, in which the city-states, ranged behind Athens or Sparta, fought each other to the point of exhaustion. They left an enduring example of military futility to set against their earlier triumphs, and this in a century when Greek artists, writers, and thinkers were expanding the awareness of man by leaps and bounds. Great achievements in the peaceful arts were made against a background of useless war, the latter being accepted as a fact of life. Socrates, 'The Great Thinker', only left Athens twice in his life – on each occasion to fight in the ranks with the army. Neither he nor any other Greek thinker, statesman, or general anticipated Santayana in discovering that 'Fanaticism consists in redoubling your efforts when you have forgotten your aim'. In the end there was no victory either for Athens or Sparta, and it was the Macedonians – the poor relations, the semi-barbarians of the north – who scooped the pool and made themselves the overlords first of Greece and then of the world.

Sparta came out of the Persian war riding high, having directed land operations during the Plataea campaign and struck the first blow in the liberation of the Ionians with the Spartan victory at Mycale. The Spartans' last fling as allied war leaders came at the close of 479 BC when Pausanias, the victor of Plataea, commanded the Greek fleet. He broke the last Persian links between Asia Minor and Thrace by taking Byzantium and landing troops to besiege Sestos, and went on to clear the Persians out of most of Cyprus. But Pausanius was a high-handed and dictatorial supreme commander who won nothing but loathing and distrust from the Ionians. They opted for Athenian patronage, and although Pausanias was recalled to answer for his conduct, Sparta's prestige slumped. Her own dependencies in the Peloponnese – Elis, Arcadia, Messenia – broke away and formed an anti-Spartan alliance. It took Sparta until 464 to recover her supremacy in the Peloponnese and by that time Athens had taken over as the acknowledged leader of the Greek world.

The alignment between the Athenians and Ionians was strengthened in 478 when their combined forces took Sestos. In the same year they formed an alliance with the purpose of liberating all Greek colonies and territory still in Persian hands. Every city and island in the alliance was to contribute either ships or money, and send delegates to a general assembly. The island-state of Delos served as treasurer and meeting-point and the assembly took the title of the 'Delian League'. Tough and dictatorial, the League stood no nonsense from anybody and the Persians were the least of its enemies. And it inevitably became more and more a reflection of the imperial ambitions of its strongest neighbour: Athens.

The League's first military expedition was a cleaning-up operation against Eion, one of the last Persian outposts on the Thracian coast. Cimon of Athens (son of Miltiades of Marathon fame) directed the siege to its successful conclusion in the spring of 475. But the League's next three ventures had nothing to do with fighting Persians: they were instances of naked coercion. The Dolopians of Skyros were conquered and enslaved, and their island colonized anew by the Athenians. Carystos in southern Euboea – an ally of Athens in the first Persian war – surrendered and offered terms rather than suffer a similar fate. Finally, in 467, Naxos was bludgeoned back into the League after an ill-considered attempt to withdraw, suffering heavy penalties. Thucydides, the great Athenian historian of the fifth-century wars, found little wrong with this heavy-handed bullying, which he saw as the just punishment of allies wishing to enjoy all the benefits of League membership without making their proper contribution to communal defence:

The chief reasons for these revolts were failures to produce the right amount of tribute or the right numbers of ships, and sometimes a refusal to produce any ships at all . . . For this position it was the allies themselves who were to blame. Because of this reluctance of theirs to face military service, most of them, to avoid serving abroad, had assessments made by which, instead of producing ships, they were to pay a corresponding sum of money. The result was that the Athenian navy grew strong at their expense, and when they revolted they always found themselves inadequately armed and inexperienced in war.

In 466 Cimon led the allied fleet halfway along the southern coast of Asia Minor to smash the Phoenician navy: over 200 triremes built since the annihilation of the Persian fleet at Salamis. These were brought to battle and either destroyed or taken off the mouth of the Eurymedon river. Here indeed was a 'legitimate military objective' to ensure the security of the League – but it was followed almost at once by another punitive expedition against a reneging League member. This time the victim was Thasos in the northern Aegean. Cimon used the revolt as an

PREVIOUS PAGES: The moment of truth in one of the battles during the long fifth-century wars between the city-states of Greece – the collision of the rival shield-walls

opportunity to kill two birds with one stone. While the fleet and army were crushing the defenders of Thasos, a new Athenian colony was planted at Amphipolis near the site of Eion. This was interpreted as an act of war by the indignant Thracians, who cut the overconfident army of the colonists to pieces in a battle at Drabescus.

Before Thasos capitulated its leaders appealed to Sparta for help against the League. Sparta agreed, but almost immediately suffered the humiliation of having to turn to Athens for assistance against a mass revolt of her subject helots. Sparta and her allies managed to drive the rebels into a defensive leaguer on Mount Ithome, where they held out for over three years (463–460 BC). When the Athenian expeditionary force arrived in Sparta it displayed so much energy and inventiveness against the defenders of Ithome that the Spartans suspected it of fifth-column intentions, and brusquely informed Athens that her troops were no longer required. The Athenians took this as a grave insult, denounced the treaty of alliance with Sparta which had shakily survived ever since the Persian wars, and promptly allied themselves with Sparta's biggest enemy in the Peloponnese: Argos.

The five years since the expedition to the Eurymedon river had therefore seen Athens confidently embarking on an impressive range of overseas adventures, few of which would have been possible without her grip on the Delian League and its revenue. But these adventures were only a beginning. As well as maintaining her colonies, keeping the League thoroughly at heel and continuing to hit at the Persian Empire, Athens now began to take every opportunity of increasing the diplomatic isolation of Sparta.

THE FIRST WAR WITH SPARTA

When the rebel helots of Mount Ithome finally surrendered to Sparta and her allies in 460 they were exiled. Athens promptly welcomed the exiles and settled them at Naupactus. Such pointed hospitality for the enemies of Sparta was little more than a gesture, but it was followed by Megara dropping her alliance with Sparta and joining the Delian League to get some solid help in her current border war with Corinth. The Athenians responded with the prompt despatch to Megara of troops and engineers to build 'long walls' – a fortified causeway linking the city of Megara with its port of Nisaea, thus ensuring that the city could never be cut off from the sea by land. This move also strengthened the Athenian hold on the land link to the Peloponnese; and two of the northern Peloponnesian states, Corinth and Epidauros, declared war on Athens in retaliation.

Athens took up the challenge with gusto, even though the League had just sent out its most far-reaching expedition ever: to Egypt. The Libyan prince Inaros had revolted against the Persians, expelled them from the Nile Delta, and appealed to Athens for help in liberating the rest of the country. The Delian League obliged by diverting the fleet then deployed against the last Persian foothold in eastern Cyprus, which joined up with Inaros and his rebels, sailed up the Nile, and took Memphis (460 BC).

Nothing on this scale had ever been seen before. Not even the

Early fifth-century Athenian hoplites setting out on campaign. The long wars with Sparta saw Athens attempt the destruction of Spartan land power by Athenian supremacy at sea

Assyrians or Persians at the peak of their power had ever undertaken such a multiple stream of expansionist adventures, all of which seemed to turn to gold for Athens and the League. And this was no huge land empire, but a small city-state at the head of a widely-dispersed island confederation. Nor were the Athenians gambling all on an unbroken run of success. In 459 they were roundly defeated at Halieis by the Corinthians and Epidaurians, but this defeat was immediately cancelled out by an Athenian sea victory at Cecryphaleia. Aegina, the next island state to the south of Salamis, came in on the Peloponnesian side in 458, but another Athenian sea victory off Aegina wiped out the Peloponnesian fleet east of the Corinthian isthmus and left Aegina open to invasion by the Athenians.

The Cyprus/Egypt expedition and the Aegina landings used up the entire Athenian strength of normal military age, and the Corinthians seized the opportunity to attack Megara. They were convinced that the Athenians must pull out of Aegina in order to relieve Megara — but the Athenians did nothing of the kind. Instead they raised a scratch force of teenagers, old men, and veterans and marched against the Corinthians without withdrawing a single hoplite from Aegina. The moral effect of yet another Athenian army coming at them when such a thing had been thought impossible knocked all the heart out of the Corinthians. There was a half-hearted engagement in which both sides claimed victory and set about raising trophies of captured weapons. But the Athenians were immensely cheered by their own performance and attacked the Corinthians again. As Thucydides puts it:

The Athenians came out against them from Megara, overwhelmed the contingent that was setting up the trophy, and then engaged and defeated the rest of their enemy. As the defeated Corinthians were retreating, quite a large selection of their army, coming under severe pressure and being uncertain of its route, plunged into an enclosure on someone's estate which had a deep ditch all round it so that there was no way out. Seeing what had happened, the Athenians closed up the main entrance with their hoplites and, surrounding the rest of the enclosure with light-armed troops, stoned to death all who were inside. This was a very severe blow to the Corinthians. The main body of their army fell back on Corinth.

With this victory over Corinth the fortunes of Athens and the Delian League reached high tide. But they had taken on too much, too soon; the Athenians were at full stretch, with no reserves; and it was at this moment that Sparta finally entered the war. In 457 the Spartan army crossed the Gulf of Corinth and struck north, restoring the Boeotian League under the supremacy of Thebes as a counterweight to Athens. An Athenian/Argolid army marched against the Spartans at Boeotia but was defeated at Tanagra, whereupon the Spartan army withdrew into the Peloponnese across the Corinthian Isthmus. This limited strike was typical of the Spartans' unhappiness at having their army away from home for too long; the withdrawal of the army proved to have been premature. The Athenians concentrated on shattering the Boeotian League in battle at Oenophyta as soon as the Spartans had gone, and forced all the Boeotian cities except for Thebes to join the Delian League. The Spartan move, ineffective though it was in the short term, had underlined how precarious the Athenian power balance was — and, at the same time, how resilient the Athenians were. Their success in snapping Boeotia back on the leash induced Phocis and Ozolian Locris to join the Delian League; both regions had been powerless to stop the Spartans from marching through their territory.

In the 455 campaign the Athenians launched another amazing campaign, this time aimed at the Peloponnesian mainland instead of its offshore islands. With the forces released by the fall of Aegina, Tolmides took an Athenian fleet on a circumnavigation of the Peloponnese,

Pericles of Athens, who devised the city's ideal grand strategy against Sparta: avoid decisive land battles with the dreaded Spartan hoplites, and use sea power to hit Peloponnesian trade and coastal cities

burning the Spartan shipyard at Gytheion, entering the Gulf of Corinth and ending up with the capture of Sicyon, a Corinthian city. This *tour de force* caused Achaea, the northernmost Peloponnesian power, to break with Sparta and join the Delian League. Athens now bestrode the Gulf of Corinth and had two allies – Achaea and Argolis – in the Peloponnese. But this moment of triumph was as fleeting as the defeat of Corinth three years before. Shattering news came from Egypt. The entire Athenian expeditionary force had been cut off and destroyed by a Persian countermove from Syria, together with a relief force of fifty triremes sent out by the League. The prospect of an independent Egypt allied to the League had gone for ever, and the League came out of its most costly expedition with absolutely nothing to show for it.

As a result of this disaster the treasury of the Delian League was transferred to Athens in 454, an act which tacitly recognized the fact that the original Athenian-Ionian league had become an Athenian empire. But it was an empire which for the moment had (literally) overtaxed its resources, and which was suffering from battle fatigue. From 454 the Athenians and Peloponnesians both avoided head-on clashes and the war petered out. As the pressure of an all-demanding war effort slackened, cracks at once began to show in the Athenian power bloc.

Athens and Sparta agreed on a five-year truce in 451, and Argolis immediately returned to the Peloponnesian League to preclude a revenge attack by Sparta. Then, in 447, the Boeotians broke away from the Athenian League and defeated a significantly weak Athenian force sent against them, at Coronea. Encouraged by this example, Phocis and Locris also left the Athenian League in 447 and the following year saw the Euboeans revolt as well. Determined to stop the rot, Pericles of Athens crossed to Euboea with a powerful army – but the Peloponnesians were now convinced that the Athenian empire only needed another push to collapse completely. They marched against Megara, which immediately went over to them, and a Spartan army invaded Attica. Pericles shelved his Euboean campaign and took his army back to the mainland – but both sides shied away from another battle. Instead negotiations began for a stable peace based on the *status quo* and the Peloponnesians went home, leaving Pericles to return to Euboea and hammer it into submission.

The 'Thirty Years' Peace' was settled in 445. Megara and Argolis stayed with the Peloponnesian League; Achaea remained nominally independent. All future disputes were to be settled by arbitration. This peace endured, with increasing shakiness, until the outbreak of the second or 'Great' Peloponnesian War in 431. Neither side was happy with the compromise. Athens had had to give up most of her gains in the Peloponnese, and Peloponnesians had not broken the power of Athens outside Attica. The root cause of conflict remained. In the words of Thucydides, 'What made war inevitable was the growth of the Athenian power and the fear which this caused in Sparta.' In the first Peloponnesian war Sparta's intervention had been limited and cautious. In the second, her commitment was to be total, a relentless crusade:

Finally the point was reached when Athenian strength attained a peak plain for all to see and the Athenians began to encroach upon Sparta's allies. It was at this point that Sparta felt the position to be no longer tolerable and decided by starting this present war to employ all her energies in attacking and, if possible, destroying the power of Athens.

THE GREAT PELOPONNESIAN WAR (431–404 BC)

The extremely compressed account of the first Peloponnesian war given above shows the breadth and variety of the war zone on land and sea, with the bewildering shifts in alliances and allegiances which accompanied – and protracted – the conflict. All these features reappeared on a greater scale in the Great Peloponnesian War, which seared the Greek homeland for a whole generation. Instead of a series of successive campaigns, the conflict became a natural force – not *a* war but *the* war, going on from year to year with final victory always just around the corner. Lack of space forbids a complete account here, and Thucydides' great history of the war only suffers at second hand. The following close-ups of the war's most important campaigns have been chosen for the light they throw on Greek strategy and tactics by the end of the fifth century BC.

The Peloponnesians knew that Athens, secure behind her own 'long walls' which linked the city with its port of Piraeus, could survive any normal attack. Their policy was therefore to launch an annual 'sweep' of destruction through Attica in the hope of forcing the Athenians to come out and be destroyed in a stand-up fight. At the same time, Sparta and her allies encouraged signs of wavering and revolt amid the Athenian league and sent out expeditions to encourage defectors. The Athenian strategy, devised by Pericles, was for Athens to hold out, refuse the battle sought by the Spartans, and wear down the Peloponnesians by hitting their trade and coastal cities.

This went on for twenty-seven years and the damage it did was appalling. The general nastiness of the war is well illustrated by the fate of Plataea at the outset of the war: a little state crushed like a bug between the rival confederations.

When the Peloponnesian League declared war on the Athenian League in 432, they looked for aid from their Boeotian allies headed by Thebes. The Thebans decided to start by bringing Plataea back to the Boeotian League. Hostilities had not yet begun and the Thebans had no trouble in infiltrating over 300 armed men into Plataea. Once inside, they marched to the public assembly and issued a proclamation calling on all loyal Boeotians to join them. Instead of being paralysed by the sudden apparition of this 'fifth column' in a time of peace, the Plataeans rose in fury, closed their gates to keep the Thebans in, hunted down and killed half of them and rounded up the others. Meanwhile Theban reinforcements had arrived outside the city, but hastily retired on hearing what had happened. As soon as all Plataean territory was clear of Thebans and the citizens were safely inside the city walls, the Plataeans executed the prisoners. Caught by surprise, the Athenians had no choice but to endorse this insalubrious *fait accompli* and send the Plataeans aid.

In 427, after a two-year siege, the Plataeans surrendered to the Peloponnesians. They knew that some example would be made in revenge for the events of 431, but there was no formal trial or enquiry. Instead, on the instigation of the Thebans, the captive Plataeans were merely asked: 'Have you done anything to help the Spartans and their allies in the present war?' The Plataeans insisted on pleading their case in full; their representations were ignored, and the original question put again. The only answer was a self-condemnatory 'no'. All captive male Plataeans were thereupon executed, their womenfolk were enslaved and the city was razed to the ground.

The Pylos campaign of 425 BC was an excellent example of the complex strategies of both sides during the war, in which the involvement of Sicily was a dominant feature. The Greek colonies there faithfully reflected events in the homeland and were constantly at war with each other. Most of them, dominated by Syracuse, began the war in alliance with Sparta, thus obliging Athens to take action of her own in

Bronze head of a battering-ram from the Peloponnesian wars. Until the key reforms of Dionysus of Syracuse, the Greeks remained largely inept at siege warfare and tended to rely on blockade rather than close investment and assault

A memorial which could well commemorate disaster in Sicily: a warrior mourns on the prow of a symbolic trireme

the Sicilian theatre. The 425 campaign began with the Athenians sending out a fleet under Sophocles and Eurymedon to operate against Syracuse. It was also under orders to help the pro-Athenian faction on Corcyra (Corfu) and make itself as much of a nuisance as possible while rounding the Peloponnese on the way out. The Athenian general Demosthenes, attached to the fleet in an unofficial capacity, came up with the idea of taking and holding Pylos in Messenia, only forty-five miles from Sparta herself. This *coup* should have some effect in keeping the Spartan army from making its annual destructive foray in Attica.

The two fleet commanders were anxious to press on to Corcyra, where they knew that a strong Peloponnesian fleet had already arrived before them; they thought little of the Pylos scheme. But a timely storm obliged the Athenian fleet to shelter in the bay of Pylos. Demosthenes seized his chance and urged that a garrison should be left. In fact the northern peninsula commanding the bay needed little artificial fortification; the troops whiled away six days of bad weather and heated debate among the officers by building defences on the landward side of the peninsula. Eventually Sophocles and Eurymedon gave in and left Demosthenes to hold the place with five ships. His garrison consisted of about 50 hoplites and 20 archers, plus about 900 sailors from the ships, which he had beached and protected by a stockade. Two small Messenian ships came in to join the Athenians, adding another 40 hoplites and 50 light troops to the motley force, whose only hope of survival lay in staying where it was on the rocky headland, protected by the extremely difficult approaches from both land and sea.

Demosthenes could never have hoped that his plan could have such tremendous results. The Spartans reacted by scrapping their entire strategy for the year, withdrawing their army post-haste from Attica. Every state in the Peloponnese was ordered to send all available troops to Pylos, and the Peloponnesian fleet was withdrawn from Corcyra to blockade Demosthenes and his men in Pylos. The Athenians also brought their western fleet back to the Peloponnese, but this marked an attempt at the fulfilment – not, as in the case of the Peloponnesians, the abandonment – of Athenian war policy. Demosthenes and his tiny force, acting as bait, offered Athens the chance of defeating the massed forces of the Peloponnesian League in a campaign determined by sea power. The besiegers of Pylos were soon to find themselves the besieged.

Before the Athenian fleet came down on them, the Peloponnesians tried a combined assault by land and sea. The land attack was easily held because the only approach to the peninsula led over a narrow sandspit, which meant that the defenders met the attackers on equal terms. The Athenians' defences were weaker on the seaward side, but the approaches to this sector from the sea only allowed a few ships to reach the beach at the same time, which prevented the Peloponnesians from getting enough men ashore to overwhelm the defenders. It was a marvellous example of how to exploit the lie of the land to achieve the tactical ideal of 'imposing your will on the enemy'. This was a total reversal of the sort of battle the Spartans had hoped to fight. What had originally seemed nothing more serious than a coastal raid was now tying down the massed Peloponnesian land forces on their own territory. Matters were made even worse by the fact that it was the Spartans who were being forced to attack from the sea, while the real naval experts – the Athenians – were secure on land in a perfect defensive position. Two days of attack left the Athenian garrison virtually unscathed at the top of its cliffs, and the baffled Peloponnesians settled down for a long siege.

The Athenian fleet arrived on the scene during the second day of the assault. Instead of launching an immediate attack on the warships and transports involved in the assault, the Athenian commanders held off and made a careful reconnaissance of the Peloponnesians' overall deployment and the approaches to the harbour. Although the Peloponnesian fleet outnumbered the Athenian warships by ten, it had no intention of risking a fleet action with such a slender advantage, and stayed inside the bay. The Athenians noted that the Spartans had put a strong force of hoplites on to the island of Sphacteria, one-and-a-half miles long, lying across the mouth of the bay like a natural breakwater. Once the Athenian fleet was master of the bay, the Spartans could be blockaded on Sphacteria and the tables would be turned with a vengeance.

The Athenians attacked at dawn on the third day of the action, swarming into the bay and catching the Peloponnesian fleet before it had embarked and established battle formation. They went straight into action in a wild battle running the whole gamut of naval tactics in the age of the fighting galley: boarding, ramming, running-ashore, and towing off enemy ships abandoned in panic. Peloponnesian troops in full armour splashed into the shallows to fight cutting-out parties from the Athenian fleet; frenzied tug-of-war matches took place between Athenians trying to tow off abandoned ships and soldiers trying to haul the vessels up the beach. With about a third of their fleet captured or disabled by the triumphant Athenians and the remainder hauled above the waterline and protected by the army, the Peloponnesians yielded command of the bay of Pylos to the Athenian fleet, which wasted no time in cutting off the Spartan force on Sphacteria and joining hands with Demosthenes and his delighted force.

All Sparta's thoughts now came to bear on the trapped men on Sphacteria. An armistice was immediately settled, the Spartans recklessly handing over their entire fleet in exchange for an Athenian undertaking to allow provisions through to the men on Sphacteria. When the armistice terms had been agreed, Sparta sent a formal delegation to Athens to propose an honourable peace in exchange for the men on the island. According to Thucydides,

Their assumption was that Athens had wanted to make peace even earlier, had only been prevented from doing so by Spartan opposition, and would now gladly embrace the opportunity offered and return the men.

The plain truth was that the peace negotiations never stood a chance. There had been too many armistices and settlements of peace broken by both sides in the last fifty years. In this case the 'hawks' in the Athenian government – not the aristocracy, bankers, or merchant traders, be it noted, but the popular party headed by the demagogue Cleon – automatically saw the Spartans as negotiating from a position of weakness. They rejected the Spartan offer as totally inadequate and demanded the restitution of all territory yielded by Athens at the time of the 'Thirty Years' Peace'. When the Spartan envoys demurred and asked for a special committee to discuss each of the points at issue, Cleon's party accused them of playing for time and the talks collapsed. Hostilities were resumed at Pylos when the Athenians refused to hand back the Peloponnesian ships as agreed in the armistice.

But when the Athenians faced the task of taking Sphacteria, they found themselves up against a tactical problem quite as severe as that which Demosthenes' garrison had set the Peloponnesians. Sphacteria was a long, narrow island and densely wooded; it was uncertain precisely how many Spartans were on the island, and impossible to guess where their main base was. The Spartans therefore could very well manage to wipe out any force sent against them. While the Athenian commanders argued over the tactical problems of an assault, it became increasingly clear that the navy could not guarantee a close blockade of the island except in a flat calm. Whenever the weather grew rough the Peloponnesians managed to run food supplies through the blockade, and it was certain that no blockade at all could be kept up on that coast through the winter.

Mounting dismay in Athens at having thrown away the chance of a profitable peace induced Cleon to boast that he would direct operations

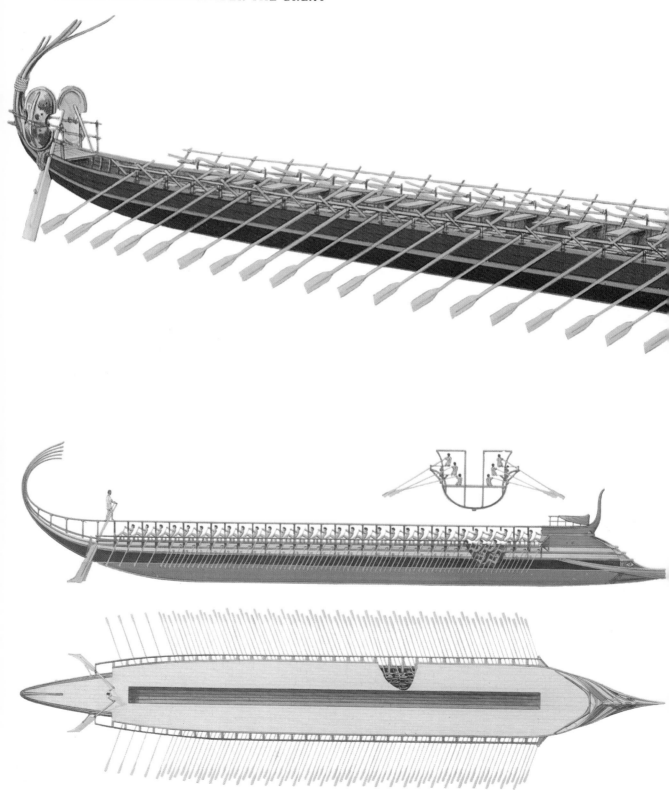

Sea power: the key to Athenian supremacy

So far from being pioneers of Greek naval power, the Athenians took awkwardly and belatedly to the idea of fighting decisive campaigns at sea. After Mycenae's collapse the Phoenicians emerged as the leading sea power, their building techniques serving as models for less prominent states seeking to expand and protect their sea trade by building oared warships. Thucydides lists the first 'navies of any importance in Hellas' before the Persian invasion as Corinthian, Ionian, Samian, and Phocaean. Even these, he claimed, 'do not seem to have possessed many triremes, but to have been still composed, as in the old days, of longboats and boats of fifty oars' (*pentekonters*). ABOVE: reconstruction of an eighth-century *pentekonter*, itself clearly

descended from the first Mediterranean war galleys: narrow dugouts propelled by oars supported on outriggers. The Phoenicians introduced the idea of increasing speed and manoeuvrability by adding a second bank of oars rowed from a higher tier of benches; the three-banked trireme followed naturally. The first Greeks to prove the worth of the trireme before 480 BC were the Sicilians and Corcyraeans. Athens, humiliated in a war with the island state of Aegina, decided to build a trireme fleet – in the nick of time to meet Xerxes' invasion. LEFT: Reconstructions of a trireme with its 170 rowers (freemen) and upper fighting deck for up to 20 archers and hoplite marines

himself. Though shaken by the alacrity with which his political enemies took him at his word and appointed him to command, Cleon chose Demosthenes as joint commander. By the time Cleon arrived at Pylos, Demosthenes had good news. There had been a big fire on the island, which had burned away most of the Spartans' cover. The Athenians now knew the strength of the opposition – 420 hoplites – and where it was deployed. Versatile as ever, Demosthenes had devised drastically new tactics to tackle the dreaded bogey of the Spartan shield wall. These amounted to a surprise attack in overwhelming strength to force the Spartans into their defensive position, then incessant pressure from light missile troops – not hoplites – to grind the Spartan formation down until it was too weak to resist further.

For his part Epitadas, the Spartan commander on Sphacteria, had no way of guessing where the Athenians would land. He kept his main force concentrated in the centre of the island, where the coastline was lowest, and picketed the ends of the island with lookout detachments. The Athenian attack plan selected the cape at the southern end of the island (furthest away from Pylos), a stealthy overnight approach from the seaward, and a massed assault by 800 hoplites just before dawn. The picket of thirty Spartan hoplites was taken completely by surprise and wiped out, allowing the Athenians to land their main force as soon as it was light. The hoplites now gave pride of place to the light troops, mostly recruited from ships' crews: 800 archers and 800 peltasts. As the massed hoplites of the Spartan main force rolled forward to push the Athenian force back into the sea, they came under a blistering fire of javelins, stones, lead slingshot-bolts, and arrows.

This barrage of missile fire was Demosthenes' answer to the specialized tactics favoured by the Spartans, whose hoplites in 425 BC were very different from those which had stood and died at Thermopylae fifty-five years before. Their weaponry had remained unchanged but they had abandoned metal helmets and armoured cuirasses in the quest for lightness, relying on robot-like precision in close formation and the shield as sole protection. This had made them specialists in fighting enemy hoplites hand-to-hand – not standing up to saturation missile-fire, which was what the Spartans had to endure on Sphacteria. For their part, the light Athenian troops were elated at having the onus passed to them and warmed to their work, keeping up their fire hot and strong as they saw that the Spartans had no effective reply.

They had been obsessed with the idea that they were actually going to attack Spartans, but now they began to despise their enemy, shouting as they charged down upon him in a mass and letting fly with stones and arrows and javelins and every weapon that came to hand.

Incessant noisy charges stirred up the ashes of the recent fire in a choking pall, while the din drowned out the words of command on which the hoplite formation depended. Casualties began to mount as the unceasing stream of missiles inevitably found chinks in the Spartan shield wall, and Epitadas decided to fall back to the high ground at the end of the island nearest to Pylos.

This move caused a temporary deadlock; for once the Spartans were in position they were in much better case to survive the Athenian fire. The Athenians tried a few head-on attacks, all of which were beaten off with heavy loss. The impasse was broken by a Messenian officer who volunteered to take a force of archers and peltasts up the cliffs behind the Spartans. Demosthenes readily agreed and the Messenian was as good as his word, appearing unexpectedly in the rear of the Spartans. This *coup* knocked the remaining heart out of the defenders, who had suffered 34 per cent losses killed since the Athenians landed and had been fighting non-stop from dawn to late afternoon without food or water. The incredible happened and a Spartan force surrendered, 292 of the 440 hoplites of the original garrison being taken to Athens in triumph.

The Athenians put a strong garrison in Pylos and held on to it for the next fourteen years, during which time it served as a base for repeated raids into the Spartan homeland. The Spartans taken on Sphacteria were held in Athens as hostages to deter the Peloponnesians from making further raids into Attica; and from 424 BC onward the war zone steadily expanded.

In 424 BC the main theatre of the war shifted to Boeotia, where the Athenians suffered a heavy defeat by the Thebans at Delium. From 423–421 it moved again, to Thrace, which the Spartans urged on to revolt against Athens. The commanders of both sides – Cleon of Athens and Brasidas of Sparta – were killed in battle at Amphipolis in 422, another Athenian defeat. Mutual exhaustion and frustration resulted in a brief peace between Athens and Sparta in 421, but not in an end to the war, which was carried on by the discontented allies of each side. The peace rapidly became a grim farce, and by the end of 419 BC Argos, Mantinea, and Elis were all at war with Sparta, busily aided by Sparta's 'ally', Athens.

The reopening of formal hostilities in 418 began with a Spartan attempt to defeat the hostile alliance which had deprived Sparta of hegemony in the Peloponnese. The Eleans dropped out of the alliance and withdrew their contingent, but Athens took the gamble of sending an army to reinforce the allies in an attempt to beat the Spartans on Peloponnesian soil. The result was the battle of Mantinea, in which Spartan discipline frustrated the wild charge of the allies and inflicted a costly defeat on them. Although this was the only head-on clash between Spartan and Athenian forces since the war had begun, it also did nothing towards ending the deadlock.

In 417 and 416 Athens sent belated expeditionary forces which failed to prevent the unbeaten Spartan army from doing what it pleased in Argos. Seeking for a 'sideshow campaign' which might point the way to victory, the Athenians demeaned their cause in 416 BC by assaulting Melos, one of the few Aegean islands which had always remained neutral. When Melos fell all its surviving menfolk were butchered and the women and children enslaved. And finally, in 415 BC, the Athenians launched their most disastrous gamble: the expedition to conquer Sicily and remove it permanently from Sparta's orbit.

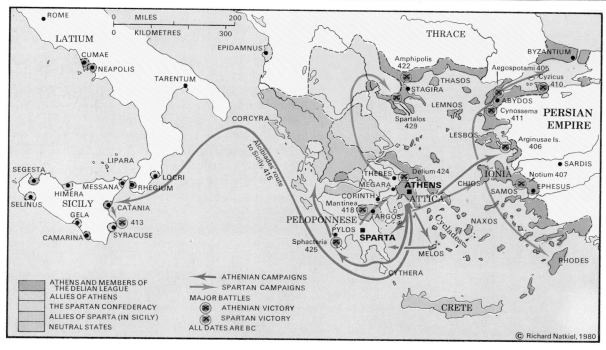

ROME

LATIUM

MILES 0 — 200
KILOMETRES 0 — 300

EPIDAMNUS

THRACE

BYZANTIUM

CUMAE
NEAPOLIS

TARENTUM

Amphipolis
422
STAGIRA
Spartalos
429

THASOS

Aegospotami 405
Cyzicus
410
ABYDOS
Cynossema
411

PERSIAN
EMPIRE

LEMNOS

CORCYRA

Alcibiades' route
to Sicily 415

LESBOS

Arginusae Is.
406

SARDIS

LIPARA

SEGESTA

LOCRI
MESSANA RHEGIUM
HIMERA
SICILY CATANIA
SELINUS
GELA
413
CAMARINA SYRACUSE

IONIA

Notium 407
CHIOS
EPHESUS
SAMOS

THEBES Delium 424
MEGARA ATHENS
CORINTH ATTICA
Mantinea
418 ARGOS
PELOPONNESE
PYLOS
Sphacteria SPARTA
425

NAXOS

Cyclades

RHODES

MELOS

CYTHERA

CRETE

ATHENS AND MEMBERS OF
THE DELIAN LEAGUE
ALLIES OF ATHENS
THE SPARTAN CONFEDERACY
ALLIES OF SPARTA (IN SICILY)
NEUTRAL STATES

ATHENIAN CAMPAIGNS
SPARTAN CAMPAIGNS
MAJOR BATTLES
ATHENIAN VICTORY
SPARTAN VICTORY
ALL DATES ARE BC

© Richard Natkiel, 1980

The long duel

Admirers of 'the glory that was Greece' can find little to say in defence of the vicious and futile struggle between Athens and Sparta known as the Great Peloponnesian War. Few cities have ever boasted more achievements in the peaceful arts than Athens in the fifth century BC, city of the goddess Athene (RIGHT), whose flawless temple of the Parthenon was built on the Acropolis (LEFT) on the very eve of the war. In theory it was hard to see how either side could ever win; the Athenian fleet was supreme at sea, the Spartan army supreme on land. But in the end it was Athens, city of the great thinkers, which made the first fatal mistake in the field of strategy. Only eighty years before, Athens had been the champion of Greek liberty, but in 415 BC she greedily over-reached herself by trying to conquer Sicily. BELOW LEFT: Main theatres of the Peloponnesian War, showing what a sideshow the Sicilian expedition was. BELOW RIGHT: Image of a squandered supremacy — carving of a war trireme from the Acropolis at Athens

THE SICILIAN EXPEDITION (415–413 BC)

In the first Peloponnesian war, the Athenians had overreached themselves in their attempt to liberate and dominate Egypt, which resulted in nothing but the fruitless squandering of men, ships and money. The Sicilian venture of 415 BC was a repetition of the same mistake: turning from a futile war 'on the doorstep' to an over-ambitious gamble far overseas. In 415 BC, however, the strategic position of Athens was far weaker than it had been back in the 460s. Thrace was in open revolt against the Athenian League and Athenian resources were again approaching exhaustion after sixteen years of war.

Attacking Sicily, whose cities had supported Sparta from the outset, was a colossal undertaking. By 415 BC the war had proved one thing, if nothing else: that Athens was incapable of marching into the Peloponnese and taking it. Sicily represented just as big a territorial objective as the Peloponnese – with the difference that Athens would have to transport and supply her entire assault force by sea. In terms of hard strategy it was a pointless venture because Sparta's war effort had never depended on assistance from Sicily. The real reasons for the expedition were as much financial as military. If Athens could take Sicily she would have what had been denied her for thirty years: a captive market for her mercantile interests. The expedition was, in modern jargon, to be 'self-financing': paid for by the wealth of Sicily, and to start with by the wealth of Egesta, the city which the Athenians were ostensibly going to help against Syracuse. It was chicken and egg: Athenian resources were so low that she could only raise a large enough force to take Sicily by hiring mercenaries, which she could only pay by taking Sicily.

The expeditionary force, assembled at Corcyra at midsummer in 415 BC, numbered 134 triremes and two 50-oared ships from Rhodes. Athens provided 100 of the triremes and the rest were furnished by allies. The attack force numbered 5,100 hoplites, of which only 2,200 were Athenian. The rest were allied or mercenary, the latter category including 500 Argives, 250 Mantineans, 80 Cretan archers (out of a total archer force of 480), and 700 Rhodian slingers. A supply fleet of 30 merchantmen carried corn stocks, plus carpenters and masons required for fortification. Following this armada like jackals were a good many merchant *entrepreneurs*, out for quick profits from the expedition's gains.

The first disappointment waiting for the expedition commanders, Lymachus and Alcibiades, was the fact that the independent Greek cities in neither Italy nor Sicily were waiting to greet the Athenian expedition with open arms; and the second was the revelation that all the rumours of the wealth of Egesta were totally unfounded. At this point, Thucydides' account reveals errors in strategic reasoning which sound like an ominous anticipation of the Franco-British decision to go ahead with invading the Crimea, 2,269 years later. 'Alcibiades said that, having sailed out in such force, they ought not to disgrace themselves by going home with nothing to show for it'. He favoured a general proclamation to all the cities of Sicily, backed up by a cruise round the island to impress the Sicilians with the might of the Athenian force. Lymachus argued for an immediate assault on Syracuse in full strength, but finally agreed to follow the scheme of Alcibiades. The absurd result

Throughout the fifth century the most obvious characteristic of hoplite equipment was the continuing tendency to lighten the body armour, which ended with the adoption of the stiffened linen cuirass seen here on a 'red-figure' vase of about 480 BC

was that the Syracusans were given a formal warning of what was in store for them by their future attackers. The Athenians were turned away at Messina, welcomed at Naxos, and finally took Catana as a base. They then wasted further time by sailing half the fleet along the south coast in a vain attempt to win over the cities of the hinterland.

Autumn was well advanced by the time that the Athenian commanders squared up to the task of moving on Syracuse. (Nicias had meanwhile replaced Alicibiades, who had been recalled to answer criminal charges.) When they did, it seemed at last that the rank amateurishness of the previous weeks had expended itself, for the Athenians used the trick that had lured the Persian fleet to its doom at Salamis – false information. They sent off a 'plant' who spun the Syracusans a splendid tale of how the Athenians were in the habit of sleeping at a distance from where their weapons were kept, and how a surprise attack would not only wipe out the invading army but offer the chance of burning the fleet as well. The Syracusans swallowed the story and marched confidently out, only to be resoundingly defeated by the waiting Athenians. But the latter had not bargained for the strong concentration of cavalry fielded by the Syracusans and their Sicilian allies, 1,200 in all. The presence of this cavalry deterred the Athenians from totally destroying the fleeing Syracusans and marching on the city. Instead they decided to play safe, sent home for cavalry of their own, went into winter quarters in Naxos — and gave the Syracusans the whole winter in which to fortify the city against attack by land and sea.

The Athenians began the 414 campaign with a burst of efficiency, as if to atone for the casual time-wasting and general ineptitude of the previous autumn. They seized the heights of Epipolae commanding the western approaches to Syracuse, established a central fort known as 'The Circle', and started building a double wall which, when completed, was intended to seal off Syracuse completely by land. The Athenian fleet would then complete the blockade from the seaward and Syracuse would be starved into submission.

Blockade was the Greeks' standard tactic in reducing fortified cities, for there was one vital military skill which they had never learned from the 'barbarians' of Asia: the art of building siege engines to batter breaches in an enemy wall. The most original piece of siege equipment seen in the Peloponnesian wars had put in a brief appearance at Delium in 424, when the Thebans had used a primitive 'flamethrower' to burn the gates which the Athenians were defending. (This consisted of a long tube with an iron pipe which led into a cauldron of coals and pitch . Giant bellows sent an air blast down the pipe into the fire which blazed up, firing all the woodwork in the immediate vicinity.) But at Syracuse the Athenians put their faith in a traditional close blockade. It was a bad mistake. To succeed in bringing the Sicilian states under exclusive Athenian patronage the Athenian expeditionary force needed a rapid string of impressive victories in the field. The last thing the Athenians should have done was sit down for a long siege, for in so doing they were repeating the mistake made by the Spartans at Pylos eleven years before: surrendering the initiative to a weaker enemy.

For their part, the Syracusans did all they could to protract the siege, while sending out appeals for help to every enemy of Athens they could think of. Abandoning sorties as being too costly, the Syracusan commander Hermocrates began the tactic of building 'counter-walls', running out from the fortifications of Syracuse to breach the Athenian circumvallation at right-angles. The Athenians bided their time before sending in an attack by 300 picked hoplites, which destroyed the Syracusan camp and counter-wall. Undeterred, the Syracusans promptly set about building another counter-wall to threaten a different sector. The Athenians repeated their earlier riposte, but this time the Syracusans counter-attacked the 300 hoplites and drove them off. A costly Athenian defeat was only averted by the intervention of Lamachus with the main body of the army, a counterattack in which Lamachus was killed.

By the end of June 414, however, the Athenians seemed set fair for victory. The southern sector of their circumvallation was fast approaching completion, and offers of help and alliance were coming in from Greek cities in Italy and western Sicily. But before the northern sector of the wall could be completed the whole picture was changed by the

Hoplites fighting off
cavalry (*below*) beneath a
rank of hoplites hurling
javelins

arrival of a Spartan relief expedition. This cheered not only the Syracusans but every ally of Sparta in Sicily who was beginning to think that nothing could stop the Athenians.

The Spartan force consisted of a small Spartan-Corinthian fleet of about thirty ships, carrying around 1,000 hoplites and 700 sailors suitable for employment as light troops. It had been sent off very much as a token gesture, in the belief that the Athenian blockade had been completed. Gylippus arrived at the Straits of Messina to find that the siege lines were still unfinished. Wisely declining to risk the total destruction of his force by making for Syracuse and running the gauntlet of the huge Athenian fleet, he put into Himera on the north coast of Sicily, raised a force of about 1,000 Sicilian hoplites and 100 cavalry, left the ships at Himera and set off on an overland relief march. The Syracusans, immensely cheered, sortied to meet him and Gylippus assumed defence of the city. He immediately planned the recovery of Epipolae and the construction of a third counter-wall up in the northern sector which would make it impossible for the Athenians to complete the circumvallation. His first move against Epipolae failed because it developed into a close-quarter fight in which the Syracusan cavalry could not get into action, but the second attack gave the cavalry full play and the Athenians were thrown off Epipolae. Simultaneously the new counter-wall crossed the head of the Athenian circumvallation, giving the defenders of Syracuse a permanent lifeline to the interior in the northern sector.

This effectively ended the Athenians' hopes of taking Syracuse. Nicias was forced to concentrate the Athenian army on the unhealthy marshy ground close to the main harbour and appeal to the government to send out strong reinforcements in a second fleet. Eurymedon was sent out at once with ten ships to say that Demosthenes, the victor of Pylos, was raising another fleet which would arrive in the spring. Before the second Athenian fleet sailed, however, the Peloponnesians sent Gylippus another 1,100 hoplites, building up the Syracusan fleet to 80. As well as attracting more useful volunteers from the Sicilian cities, he persuaded the Syracusans that there would be no beating the Athenians until they had been tackled successfully at sea.

So events drew on to the decisive campaign of 413 BC. In May the Syracusan ships attacked the Athenians in the harbour while Gylippus came overland with the army and stormed the Athenian forts at Plemmyrion. This restored both sides of the harbour mouth to Syracusan control, and had the practical effect of swinging the whole of Sicily behind the Syracusans in their fight.

The Syracusans imitated a recent trick adopted by the Corinthian navy and rebuilt their ships, sacrificing speed for strength and giving each vessel a specially reinforced prow for head-on ramming attacks. They also built up a 'mosquito armada' of javelin-throwers operating from light skiffs, their task being to get close alongside Athenian ships and kill the rowers. These refinements were a specialized answer to a specialized problem: how to tackle superior enemy numbers in a confined area. Not so long before, the Athenians had been the only Greek state which made a speciality of such ingenuity; now they were being copied, and with telling success. But the biggest Syracusan advantage was the discovery that the Athenian navy was not invulnerable. Only twelve years had passed since the Athenians had made a similar discovery about fighting Spartan hoplites, at Pylos. In July 413 the Syracusans made two more attacks on the Athenian fleet, the first being an honourable draw and the second a clear-cut victory, in which seven Athenian ships were sunk and many more disabled.

At this point, with the besiegers shaken by the new resolution shown by the defenders, Demosthenes and Eurymedon arrived with the relief fleet: 73 warships, 5,000 hoplites, and a generous complement of peltasts, slingers, and archers. Demosthenes took one look at the ruptured siege lines and realized that Epipolae must be recovered at once. The reinforced Athenians came close to success in a night attack, but when this was beaten back Athenian morale slumped. Sickness was rife in the army, thanks to its unhealthy camp down by the marsh, and the troops were clamouring to go home. Demosthenes honoured the age-old military maxim 'never reinforce failure'. He pressed for instant evacuation while the fleet could still command the sea, or a shift of the campaign to the north coast or central Sicily. But Nicias wavered, obsessed with political retribution at home rather than military reality on the spot. He ended by convincing himself that the Syracusans were approaching the limit of their resources and that just a little more pressure would make them cave in. The Athenian army, therefore, stayed where it was.

Meanwhile Gylippus was raising more forces all over Sicily, displaying his last defeat of the Athenians to good effect; and when he returned to Syracuse with a relief army Nicias agreed that the siege must be raised. But on 27 August there was an eclipse of the moon which convinced the superstitious Nicias that unknown doom was imminent, and that no move should be made for 'thrice nine days'. Gylippus was under no such inhibitions and he ordered another land and sea attack. In a full-scale battle in the harbour – 76 Syracusan ships against 86 Athenians – the Athenian right wing was destroyed, Eurymedon killed and the entire fleet driven back. This last defeat at sea broke the remaining vestiges of Athenian morale, especially when the triumphant Syracusans followed it up by beginning the closure of the harbour mouth with blockships. When a half-hearted attempt to break out by sea failed, the troops refused to re-embark.

Nothing remained but to fight their way out to the south. It was a disaster. Gylippus attacked again and the Athenian host was cut in half. Demosthenes kept some kind of rearguard together but it was totally surrounded and capitulated at Polyzelus on 19 September, 6,000 strong. On the following day Nicias and the rest of the army surrendered on the River Asinarus. The great Sicilian expedition, the biggest concentration of Greek soldiers ever seen before a single city, ended in utter humiliation and failure.

The real reason for the Sicilian disaster was that nobody in Athens had had the remotest idea of how big Sicily really was. Once the difficulties of campaigning in Sicily were realized by the Athenian commanders on the spot, concern for prestige and political expediency prevented the most sensible course: a swift and painless evacuation. The expedition could never have contributed anything like enough to the Athenian war effort to justify the cost. It was a naked attempt at conquest, not at winning more allies to help the Athenian league beat the Peloponnesians. The expeditionary force put itself beyond the pale and the Syracusans were savage in victory, penning the surviving 7,000 prisoners in the rock quarries and executing Demosthenes and Nicias. For his part, the Spartan commander Gylippus had fought a highly intelligent campaign despite being obliged, for the most part, to make bricks without straw. In this he was immensely helped by the aimlessness on the Athenian side.

THE FINAL WAR YEARS (413–404 BC)

The last nine years of the war were largely governed by a unique phenomenon: the personal influence of one man. T. E. Lawrence has argued that warfare and tactics are nine-tenths predictable and teachable, with what he calls 'the irrational tenth' being 'like the kingfisher flashing across the pool'. In the case of the later Peloponnesian War the 'irrational tenth' was a perfect description of Alcibiades of Athens, a brilliant maverick completely unfettered by any concept of loyalty or patriotism. Outlawed from Athens for crimes against the state, he went to Sparta and told her government how to win the war. When he became *persona non grata* to the Spartans (largely because he seduced the queen and made her pregnant) he intrigued with the western satraps of Persia and told them how to play off Athens against Sparta to Persia's advantage. Triumphantly returned to Athens by popular demand, he won the last great Athenian victory of the war before being expelled again. By the time the Persians finally killed him in 404 BC, Alcibiades in his tumultuous career, had transformed the whole course of the war, and there has never been anyone like him in the 2,390 years since his death.

When he was granted asylum by Sparta in 415 BC, Alcibiades was motivated by revenge. He was out to make Athens suffer and he advised the Spartans to concentrate on three essentials. The first was to raise the Ionian states, with or without the assistance of Persia, to open revolt against Athens. The second was to send whatever help could be spared to frustrate the Sicilian expedition. But the third, and by far the most important, was to seize and hold Decelea, which the Spartans finally did in 413.

Decelea was more than a vital link between Attica and Boeotia. It enabled the Spartans to cut off Athens from her main source of revenue: the Laurium silver mine. The seizure of Decelea completely prevented the Athenians from making any long-range operations on the Greek mainland. This coup was followed in 412 by the treaty of Miletus between Sparta and Persia, negotiated by Alcibiades. This ensured that the Persians would finance the maintenance of the Peloponnesian fleet in return for Sparta's recognition of the Persian king's claim to all territory liberated from the empire since the 490s.

In the following year Alcibiades transferred his allegiance from Sparta to Tissaphernes, the satrap of Sardis in Asia Minor. His policy now (for obvious personal reasons) was to persuade the Persians to prevent either the Athenians or the Spartans from winning a clear-cut victory, and this could best be done by encouraging Spartan intervention in the eastern Aegean and then denying funds. At the same time Alcibiades was angling for a recall to Athens, which was what he really wanted. By proving that he was far too dangerous an influence to be left on the loose, he achieved his aim in 411. By this time Sparta had made a new alliance with Tissaphernes and Pharnabazus, satrap of Phrygia to the north of Sardis. Claiming that he could persuade Tissaphernes to assist Athens against the Peloponnesians, Alcibiades was not only

Vividly suggestive of the defeat and humiliation of Athens in the Great Peloponnesian War: three Greek warriors from Aegina

recalled to Athens but was promoted to commander-in-chief.

The Athenian war effort in the eastern Aegean now became a matter of Alcibiades trying to reverse the consequences of the Spartan successes which his own machinations in exile had made possible. Miletus had revolted, followed by Abydos; a Peloponnesian fleet had taken Rhodes. Alcibiades began with victories over the Peloponnesian fleet at Abydos and Cynossema. He then moved through the Dardanelles to tackle the Peloponnesians and the Persians of Pharnabazus on the Sea of Marmara. In the spring of 410 he fell on the allied fleet off Cyzicus and scattered it, then raced through the fleeing enemy with twenty of the fastest Athenian ships, landed, routed the allies on shore, and took Cyzicus, wiping out the Peloponnesian garrison and gaining complete control of the Hellespont. This triumph, however, was offset in 409 by the Spartans' capture of Pylos and the failure of an Athenian assault on Ephesus. Meanwhile Decelea remained in Spartan hands.

The year 408 marked the beginning of the end. King Darius, distrusting the double-dealing of Tissaphernes, sent Prince Cyrus to take over as satrap of Sardis. Cyrus gave his backing to the Spartan admiral Lysander, offering such a high rate of pay for seamen that the Athenians found it increasingly hard to man their fleet. All Athenian hopes now reposed in Alcibiades, who had recovered Byzantium and Chalcedon but found it quite impossible to assume a general offensive in the eastern Aegean. As Plutarch puts it:

He was fighting men whose paymaster was the King of Persia, and it was this fact which repeatedly forced him to leave his headquarters and sail off to look for money and rations for his men.

When Alcibiades failed to take Chios and reduce the Ionian coast — in short, to perform miracles — his own past caught up with him. Suspected

155

A hoplite strides over his opponent (fifth century BC)

of more treachery at home, he was impeached a second time and fled to Thrace. Lysander went over to the offensive. After a string of Athenian defeats, the last Athenian fleet was annihilated by Lysander at Aegospotami in 405. In April 404 he sailed to Athens, not to negotiate peace, but to dictate it. Athens was forced to surrender her navy, demolish her 'long walls', and become an ally of Sparta, which was now the undisputed master of the Greek world. Spartan supremacy did not last long; Athens had proved herself lacking in sufficient moderation and political sense, but Sparta lacked these qualities even more. In less than fifteen years Athens' star was rising again and the Spartans were on the defensive (see pp. 165–172).

THE WAR IN RETROSPECT

Of the many changes in the nature of warfare which emerged during the Peloponnesian wars, the most important was the marriage between sea power and military power on land. Two thousand years of Mediterranean history have since been governed by the fact that no Mediterranean state can call itself fully secure unless it commands its own trade routes and approaches by sea. In land warfare there were a host of similar discoveries. Given the right circumstances, light troops could be more than a match for hoplites in phalanx, as the Athenians discovered to their advantage on Sphacteria. Cavalry, too, had acquired a potential battle-winning role, as the Athenians also discovered – this time to their cost – in Sicily. The peculiar nature of the Peloponnesian wars was the constant influence of domestic politics in both power blocs (though it was left to Clausewitz, 2,220 years later, to declare that 'war is a continuation of politics by other means'). In their protracted efforts to attain political supremacy over each other, both Athens and Sparta made one of the most painful discoveries of all: the immense cost of relying on war as the primary medium of national policy.

In the end it all came down to cost. The Greek world remained a natural recruiting-ground for excellent soldiers and sailors, and the side with the deepest pay-chest won. And it was the role of the Greek fighting man as a mercenary which contributed to the rise of Greece, in less than eighty years, to become the strongest military power in the world.

CHAPTER SEVEN

Alexander the Great and after

IN THE YEAR 400 BC the Greek world was still recovering from the ordeal of the Peloponnesian wars. It was still only thirteen years since the most powerful of all the Greek states, Athens, had failed ignominiously to take one city on the island of Sicily after putting out all her strength. Yet before another seventy-five years had passed Greece was not only subject to a single ruler: her soldiers were manning garrisons from Turkestan and India to the upper reaches of the Nile. The Persian Empire was no more, and the troops of Alexander the Great were the new arbiters of the world.

To understand how this transformation came about it is necessary to go back to the closing stage of the Peloponnesian War, when the Persian rulers decided to support the Peloponnesians and so defeat Athens by proxy. This Persian sponsorship did indeed result in Sparta's brief triumph over Athens; but it also led directly to a remarkable campaign, which paved the way for the conquest of the Persian Empire itself. This was the celebrated 'March of the Ten Thousand' (401–400 BC), which proved a long-held theory: that Greek troops were so superior to the armies of Persia that they could march through the Persian Empire as they liked.

The story of the 'Ten Thousand', one of the most famous mercenary armies of all time, has been immortalized in the *Anabasis* of Xenophon, one of its commanders. The force was raised by the ambitious younger son of Darius II, Prince Cyrus, to help him overthrow the ruling 'great king' – Cyrus' elder brother, Artaxerxes II. When satrap of Sardis, working with the Spartan admiral Lysander to administer the *coup de grâce* to Athens, Cyrus had been deeply impressed by all he had learned about the hoplites of Greece. He had no hesitation in choosing a picked force of hoplites as his master-weapon when it came to planning the military overthrow of his brother.

Cyrus was able to raise his Greek army quite openly, without arousing his brother's suspicions. Recruiting was farmed out to a number of Greek exiles, each of whom was given a thoroughly plausible task. Clearchus, a Spartan, was hired to raise a force of Greeks to fight the Thracians, ostensibly to protect Persian interests around the Bosphorus. Aristippus of Thessaly asked for the patronage of Cyrus for a *coup*

OPPOSITE: Alexander the Great, who brought to perfection the blend of cavalry mobility with the shock of the infantry phalanx advance introduced by his father Philip

d'état in Thessaly, and any new outburst of conflict in Greece was good news to Persia. Cyrus hired Proxenus of Boeotia to raise a mercenary force for service against Pisidian rebels in Cyrus' own province. Two other Peloponnesian leaders, Sophanaetus of Stymphalos and Socrates of Achaea, brought in troops to assist Cyrus in a private war against his arch-enemy Tissaphernes, the former satrap of Sardis. None of these reasons for hiring Greek troops appeared dangerous to the king. And as all the individual Greek commanders believed that they were being hired for a different job, Cyrus had no worries about security.

His troubles started when the time came to concentrate the Greek contingents and set off on the long march into Mesopotamia. Asking mercenary troops to take on a job for which they had not been hired, and thus revealing that he had not been honest with them at the outset, offered little or no chance of success. Cyrus had learned enough about mercenaries to know that they are less attracted by glory, or breathtaking challenges of fate, than in staying alive to collect their pay. He knew that if he mustered a Greek mercenary army at Sardis and told it bluntly that it was going to invade the empire and take on the king's armies, the men would simply refuse to march. He seems to have reckoned that if he could get the army as far as the Syrian frontier without any large-scale defections, he would have a good chance of persuading the men to stay with him. In any case, it was vital that the first stage of the march should look like a heavy punitive expedition confined to Asia Minor.

The force that Cyrus led out of Sardis in the spring of 401 BC consisted of 7,300 hoplites and about 800 peltasts and light infantry. Nearly all were Peloponnesians (Spartans, Arcadians, Achaeans, and Megareans) apart from contingents of Boeotians and Thessalians. The commanders of other mercenary bands whose recruitment had already been set in motion were under orders to join the main body on the march. Four days' marching from Sardis took the army as far as Colossae in Phrygia, where Cyrus halted for a week and another Thessalian contingent (1,000 hoplites and 500 peltasts) joined up. Then came another three days' march to Celaenae followed by a second wait, this time of thirty days. By the end of this time Clearchus had arrived with another 1,000 hoplites, 800 Thracian peltasts, and 200 Cretan archers. So had 300 Syracusan hoplites, and another Arcadian force of 1,000 hoplites. When the last contingents had arrived at Celaenae, Cyrus held the first joint muster of his Greek troops. The count came to 11,000 hoplites and about 2,000 peltasts.

This was not the complete army of Cyrus: he had already laid his plans to be joined along the line of march and in Asia by imperial Persian contingents whose commanders supported his cause. But the Greeks were the lead in the boxing-glove, the vital infantry shock force, on which Cyrus was counting when the day should come for decisive battle with the king's army. He needed this powerful Greek force to overawe Syennesis, King of Cilicia, about whose loyalty Cyrus had doubts. And before Cyrus headed into Cilicia he took the precaution of issuing four months' pay to the Greeks. This ensured their loyalty as far as Tarsus on the Mediterranean coast, which the army reached forty-two days after its first joint muster.

At Tarsus, however, Cyrus ran into trouble. The Greeks refused to go further. Their march through Asia Minor had involved nothing more hazardous than plundering to order in territory hostile to Cyrus. The men suspected the truth, that Cyrus was leading them on what they could only see as a suicidal rebellion against the might of Persia. Clearchus, one of Cyrus' closest friends among the Greek commanders, had been ready for this and privately advised Cyrus not to worry. In the heated debates over what the army should do, so vividly preserved by Xenophon, Clearchus played devil's advocate, backed up at crucial moments by a handful of like-minded colleagues. He reminded the resentful troops that Cyrus had been a good employer, agreed totally that Cyrus had no right to break faith with them and lead them against the king – but asked them how they proposed to get home from Tarsus without Cyrus' patronage. At the crucial moment Cyrus assured the Greek commanders that he was marching against his enemy Abrocomas (the satrap of Phoenicia) on the Euphrates, twelve days' march from Tarsus. The troops agreed to go on, in return for more pay.

At Issus, the last city in Cilicia, Cyrus halted again for three days and received his last reinforcements from Greece: another 700 Peloponnesian hoplites. Cyrus had ordered his fleet up to Issus because the next obstacle was the defile known as the Syrian Gates: only 600 yards long, but covered by a fort at each end. If Abrocomas had decided to hold the Gates, Cyrus had planned to land hoplites at either end of the defile and clear it with a pincer movement; but in fact Abrocomas was already marching to join forces with King Artaxerxes. In happy ignorance of all this the army marched through the Gates into Syria, finally arriving at Thapsacus on the Euphrates.

Once on the Euphrates Cyrus no longer had any chance – or any need – of keeping up the pretence any longer. He told the Greeks that he was marching on Babylon to seek out and fight the king, and asked them to stay with him. This seems to have caused little genuine surprise, although the troops expressed anger and predictably demanded extra pay. Cyrus promised each man a lump sum of five *minae* in silver (about £20) on arrival at Babylon, plus full pay until he had led them back to Ionia again. The troops were more than pleased with the offer and agreed to go on. Abrocomas had burned all the boats at Thapsacus to prevent Cyrus from crossing the Euphrates, but the troops forded the river breast-deep – a water-level lower, according to the locals, than at any time in living memory. It seemed the best of omens.

The Greeks were now faced with an ordeal never before faced by any of these veterans of the Peloponnesian War: 375 miles of marching through barren desert, eighteen days in all. Xenophon makes no mention of it, but the figures he gives for the muster of the army at the end of the march on Babylon indicate a decided wastage: some 1,200 fewer hoplites than had been recorded in the first joint muster back in Asia Minor. This was a fairly sizeable casualty rate and it can certainly not have been caused by excessively forced marching. The desert was crossed in two marches: a five-day march of 105 miles and a thirteen-day march of 270 miles. This meant an average pace of twenty to twenty-one miles per day, which was only slightly up on the steady eighteen-mile-per-day

average which had been maintained from Sardis to the Euphrates. It may have been fatigue sharpened by unfamiliar diet; Xenophon mentions that corn stocks ran out and the men were reduced to an all-meat diet, to which Greeks were unaccustomed.

During the march the Greeks learned to respect their Persian allies and forget the old Greek prejudices about Persians being over-dressed weaklings unable to take hardship. Once, when some wagons got bogged down in Euphrates mud, Cyrus lost his temper and ordered the exquisites of his bodyguard to haul them out. 'Then certainly one saw a bit of discipline', admits Xenophon. 'Wherever they happened to be standing, they threw off their purple cloaks and rushed forward as though it was a race — down a very steep hill, too, and wearing those expensive tunics which they have, and embroidered trousers. Some also had chains round their necks and bracelets on their wrists. But with all this on they leaped straight down into the mud and got the wagons on to dry ground quicker than anyone would have thought possible.'

Three days after the second desert march the army began to sight the hoofprints and dung of heavy numbers of cavalry, and at last the armies of Cyrus and Artaxerxes converged at Cunaxa on the Euphrates, about fifty miles north-west of Babylon. For two days before the battle, deserters came in to Cyrus with fantastic stories of the king's strength. This may have been a favourite trick used by both sides during the Peloponnesian War: the planting of false information. Nevertheless Xenophon seems to have fallen into the same trap as his fellow-countryman Herodotus as far as Persian numbers are concerned. He sets the king's strength at 900,000, against the 100,000 'native troops' of Cyrus and the Greek contingent of 10,400 hoplites and 2,500 peltasts and light troops. Working from the knowledge that the royal army

A Greek hoplite, crouching behind his shield, meets a charging Persian cavalryman

fielded four corps at Cunaxa, it is possible to estimate its strength as slightly stronger than that of Xerxes' invasion army – say 120,000, with Cyrus and his forces outnumbered by two to one. (Abrocomas and the Phoenician corps did not join the royal army until after the battle.)

Both sides formed battle lines with one flank resting on the Euphrates. Cyrus placed about 1,000 Paphlagonian cavalry on his extreme right – the Euphrates flank. Next came the Greek peltasts, then the hoplites, then Cyrus and his household cavalry, 800 strong. The Asian troops formed the remaining half of Cyrus' army and were deployed to the left rear of this array under his second-in-command Ariaeus. Cyrus seems to have hoped that his deployment would leave his household cavalry and the hoplites directly opposite his brother's position at the centre of the Persian line, but this was thwarted by the sheer size of the royal army. Cyrus rode over to Clearchus, commanding the Greeks, and pointed out the king's position which he designated as the Greeks' main objective. 'If we win there the whole thing is over.'

Xenophon describes the breathtaking deployment of the Persians as seen from the Greek lines:

In the early afternoon dust appeared, like a white cloud, and after some time a sort of blackness extending a long way over the plain. When they got nearer, then suddenly there were flashes of bronze, and the spear points and the enemy formations became visible. There were cavalry with white armour on the enemy's left and Tissaphernes was said to be in command of them. Next to them were soldiers with wicker shields, and then came hoplites with wooden shields reaching to the feet. These were said to be Egyptians. Then there were more cavalry and archers. These all marched in tribes, each tribe in a dense oblong formation. In front of them, and at considerable distances apart from each other, were what they called the scythed chariots. These had thin scythes extending at an angle and also under the driver's seat, turned towards the ground, so as to cut through everything in their way. The idea was to drive them into the Greek ranks and cut through them.

Fearsome though they looked, these scythed chariots were really a feeble and clumsy answer to trained infantry. The idea seems to have been for the drivers to 'bale out' after steering for the Greek line, but the ones which were driven into the Greek formations passed harmlessly down lanes which the Greeks coolly opened in their ranks. When the approaching royal army was within 600–800 yards, the Greeks surged forward to the attack.

The battle took the form of a 'revolving door', the Greeks carrying all before them while the Persian right flank did the same against Cyrus' Asian troops. Cyrus himself met the danger of envelopment by leading a desperate charge of his household cavalry against Artaxerxes himself. Cyrus is said to have driven close enough to wound his brother before a javelin brought him down and killed him, upon which Artaxerxes and the whole Persian right wing drove ahead and occupied Cyrus' camp. Meanwhile Clearchus and the Greeks were completing the utter rout of the Persian left flank and left centre, but they halted when they heard that the Persians were in the camp.

Clearchus faced the Greeks about, expecting that Artaxerxes would waste no time in attacking the Greeks from the rear; but instead the king gave the Greeks a wide berth, surging back round their left flank to make contact with Tissaphernes and the cavalry. The latter had charged the Greek peltasts and swept through them without killing a single man, the peltasts opening ranks to let the cavalry through. The battle came to a ragged end when Artaxerxes re-formed his men in roughly their original position, which the Greeks promptly subjected to a second charge. Once again the Persian ranks melted away instead of standing and meeting the advancing hoplites, who halted and formed a defensive position pending definite news about the fate that had befallen Cyrus.

Word came from Ariaeus at dawn on the following day. Clearchus pledged allegiance to Ariaeus before the messengers of the king arrived with a demand for the Greeks to surrender. Clearchus played his hand well, refusing anything but an armistice—'truce if we stay, and war if we go forward or backward'. The Persians had no troops who could beat the Greeks, even though the latter were totally isolated in the middle of the Persian Empire. In the end agreement was reached for a clear road home without further molestation, the ideal solution for both sides. The Greeks would be escorted home by Ariaeus and Tissaphernes.

The way home lay not up the Euphrates, where all supplies had been exhausted by the outward march, but up the Tigris, with the Greeks constantly on their guard against treachery. Three weeks after the battle, when the Greeks had marched 230 miles up the Tigris, Tissaphernes showed his true colours. At a conference called to dispel all the rumours about each side's evil intentions towards the other, all the Greek commanders were seized and Clearchus was killed. When the troops refused to surrender, the other four commanders were also executed. The troops elected five officers to replace them, one of the new commanders being Xenophon — the only Athenian to hold command.

When the retreat was resumed the army was at once subjected to damaging attacks from horsed archers and slingers. Xenophon claims that he was the man who suggested the formation eventually adopted for the retreat: a hollow box of hoplites screening the baggage and non-combatants, with counterfire provided by slingers using the Rhodian technique. Rhodian slingers hurled lead bullets which could out-range not only the bows of the Cretan archers but those carried by the Persian horsed archers. When the army left the plains and struck north into the mountains, heading for the Black Sea, the basic defensive tactic had to be modified. The problem was the endless sequence of mountain spurs, over which the army found it hard to keep formation when descending. Over this terrain the peltasts moved out to form a flank guard down on the lower ground, deterring Persian attempts to cut in from the downhill flank.

The mountains of Armenia brought respite from Persian attacks but the Greeks suffered intensely in the wind and snow of the high passes. There were repeated attacks by hostile mountain tribes. Nevertheless the army survived snow-blindness, frostbite, and ambush, reviving like a watered flower when at last the Black Sea came into sight. The northern Black Sea coast was studded with Greek colonies which helped the army on the last lap from Trapezus to Byzantium — yet, in terms of morale, the Greeks were 'home' from the moment they sighted the sea.

The 'Ten Thousand' had been reduced to 8,600 by the time they came down to the Black Sea coast — a wonderful achievement considering the odds against any of them coming through alive. They finished the march with Xenophon as their supreme commander. There is no false modesty in his epic account of the march, but it is impossible, however sceptical one might be, to read the *Anabasis* as a biased personal memoir. Told with disarming simplicity, it is the story of a professional fighting force facing and overcoming impossible circumstances, whether by improvising new tactics or relying on familiar ones. The sole bond which held the troops together was their tactical training and ever-growing *esprit de corps.* The 'Ten Thousand' were also blessed with officers who never despaired and who constantly set an example to their men. To this extent the *Anabasis* should be bedtime reading not only for every serving officer but for every civilian executive who has people looking to him for orders.

On the tactical level the 'Ten Thousand' proved that the imperial Persian army's horsed missile troops were still the most formidable soldiers in its swarming ranks, but that these could be dealt with with the right tactics. The Persian army as a whole still relied on numbers to overawe its enemies, and crumpled when attacked with energy. Not once did the 'Ten Thousand' encounter heavy infantry of the calibre of the vanished Immortals, who had fought so fiercely at Plataea in 479 but whose corps seems never to have been re-established after that defeat. All this makes intriguing food for thought as a study in military vulnerability, but perhaps Xenophon's most telling comment was on the geographical weakness of the Persian Empire:

Indeed, an intelligent observer of the King's empire would form the following estimate: it is strong in respect of extent of territory and number of inhabitants; but it is weak in respect of its lengthened communications and the dispersal of its forces, that is, if one can attack with speed.

It remained to be seen what a Greek army could do when given infantry as good as the 'Ten Thousand' and cavalry to make victory total.

FROM THE PELOPONNESIAN WARS TO THE RISE OF MACEDON (404–359 BC)

The supremacy of Sparta at the close of the Great Peloponnesian War did not last long; her arrogance and heavy-handedness proved too much for her enemies, her allies, and her former Persian sponsors. Within ten years Athens had become a client of Persia against Sparta; the Athenians rebuilt their 'long walls' in 393 BC and went on to revive their naval league against Sparta. The whole dreary cycle began again and went on until Philip of Macedon came down from the mountains of the north in the 330s and beat the southern states into submission.

The fighting force which Philip built up, and which his son Alexander led to the conquest of Asia, owed much to two vital innovations in

The new repository of military supremacy — Macedon and her kings. A gold medallion from the Aboukir hoard, tentatively identified as Philip or Alexander

Shock infantry: the pikemen of Macedon

The legendary phalanx perfected from earlier Theban models by Philip of Macedon was by no means an inflexible mass of troops. Intricate drill enabled it to advance for its decisive assault on the enemy line in oblique order with one flank leading, or in crescent, wedge, or half-square formations as well as line abreast. Basic building-block of the phalanx was the *syntagma* or battalion (OPPOSITE) of 256 men; 64 battalions made up the ideal phalanx.

Each battalion could be drawn up sixteen deep, or eight deep (with the rear sixteen half-files moving up beside the front sixteen half-files) for double the frontage. In either case the long pikes (*sarissa*) of the first five ranks formed a dense hedge before the front rank, while the raised pikes of the rear ranks helped keep off enemy missiles. BELOW· Phalangites attacking, seen from the viewpoint of a *syntagmatarch* or battalion commander

The *syntagmatarch* (1) occupied the extreme right-hand position in the front row of the battalion, with his second-in-command (2) in the centre. Each file was commanded by its leader (4) and groups of four files were commanded by a *tetrarch* (3). The second-in-command of each file was the rear man (5); and during complex manoeuvres the half-files and quarter-files could be commanded by their leaders (6 and 7)

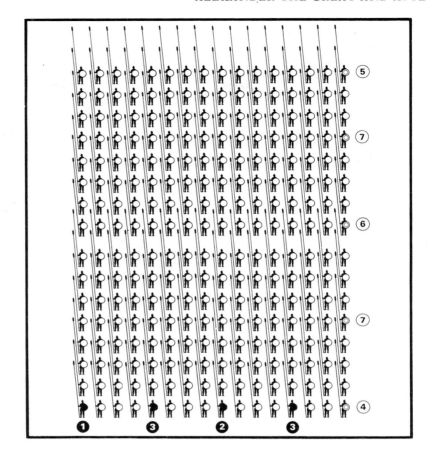

the first half of the fourth century BC. These were the development of siege weaponry to obviate the need for lengthy blockades, and the perfection of infantry/cavalry tactics.

As the lumbering Athenian performance at Syracuse proved, siege warfare had gone a long way downhill since the days of the Assyrians. One reason for this was a particularly unpleasant quirk of the Greek mentality, which regarded aggressive siege tactics against cities as barbaric. This would have made sense if the Greeks had also shunned the mass execution of prisoners and the enslavement of women and children. It was considered acceptable to condemn thousands of besieged troops and civilians to a lingering death by starvation and disease, but not to smash a way through the fortifications and take the city by storm. Close blockade became the norm for sieges, imposed by the building of encircling walls (see pp. 150–152).

The trouble with blockade was that it put as much strain on the besiegers as on the besieged; and it was no accident that a speedier alternative was first demonstrated by the city that had survived the most famous siege of the age: Syracuse. In 405 the general Dionysius made himself tyrant of Syracuse and set about reducing the Carthaginian bases in the west of Sicily. As well as using land and sea forces in the tactics made familiar since the rise of the Athenian navy, Dionysius only used blockade as an outer ring to keep his victim isolated. Within the blockade perimeter he wheeled forward siege towers, from the tops of which marksmen could fire at the troops defending the enemy wall. This provided cover for the siege engineers bringing up the battering-rams to force a breach. Dionysius also brought in the newly-developed catapult, which fired heavy javelins, to assist in keeping the enemy walls clear of defenders during the approach and assault. These tactics saved the attacker from having to sit down and wait until the enemy had consumed all their supplies, which could take months or even years. They were what we would call a 'rich man's toy', for a miniature army was needed to make them work: engineers and labourers to level the ground for the approach of the engines, carpenters and trained artillerymen to build and fire them. But the use of these tactics spread steadily through the Greek world, eventually being adopted by all the richest military powers. They meant that not even the strongest walled city in Asia could consider itself safe by the time of the Macedonian invasion in 334 BC.

All the combatant powers of the Great Peloponnesian War – even the Spartans, with their obsessive faith in the phalanx – entered the fourth century BC impressed by the demonstrations of cavalry power which that war had produced. Cavalry was able to exploit one of the phalanx's most curious weaknesses. If an attacking phalanx did not shatter the enemy line on impact and a prolonged hand-to-hand fight ensued, each phalanx tended to edge to the right: the direction of each individual soldier's weapon arm. The result was a distinctive counter-clockwise drift, giving the right flank of each army an advantage over the left flank of the enemy. At Cunaxa in 401 Cyrus had exploited this to the full by giving the 'Ten Thousand' the right-hand half of his battle line. If unchecked, the phenomenon led to a 'revolving door' of a battle, in which the side which reacted quickest and struck decisively at the enemy rear would win.

Clearly, if this 'right-hand drift' — it was never given a formal military description — could be exploited by a timely cavalry charge at the enemy's left flank, the door would revolve all the faster and the cavalry could charge deep into the enemy flank. Conversely, if cavalry put enough pressure on the enemy's *right* flank in conjunction with the attacking phalanx, the enemy line could be bent back. A good general had always needed a quick eye to judge the lie of the land and how the enemy's deployment fitted into it. With the advent of cavalry he now needed an even sharper assessment of space and time to blend the mobility of his cavalry with the mass of his infantry.

The first great exponent of cavalry/infantry tactics before the art was raised to a peak by Philip and Alexander was Epaminondas of Thebes. For some reason his name has never been recalled with the same alacrity as those of Hannibal, Julius Caesar, Alexander, or even Pyrrhus; but Epaminondas was held in the highest respect by the military writers of the Greek and Roman worlds. Making use of the traditional Theban preference for an unusually deep infantry deployment, he stood godfather, as it were, to the Macedonian phalanx/cavalry partnership perfected by Philip and Alexander. Epaminondas used the deep phalanx as a massive magnet with which to anchor the enemy infantry and deployed his supporting troops in echelon. He also showed the startling potential of an attack by a deep phalanx co-ordinated by a timely cavalry attack.

The flexibility of this technique was perfectly shown by the victory of Epaminondas over a Spartan army at Leuctra in 371 BC. Both armies were fairly equally matched — about 10,000 hoplites and 1,000 cavalry a side. The Spartans deployed their phalanx with their cavalry force out in front of the right flank, hoping to exploit the 'right-hand drift'. Epaminondas, however, put his excellent Theban cavalry squarely in front of the Spartan cavalry. His Theban hoplites, massed in a deep phalanx, lay behind the Theban cavalry with the rest of his hoplites — Boeotians — echelonned out to the right rear. Epaminondas had his army in position before the Spartan deployment was complete and launched his horsemen against the Spartan cavalry. The Thebans broke and scattered the Spartan cavalry, driving many of them back through the ranks of the Spartan hoplites. The Spartans had not recovered their formation when the Theban phalanx crashed in on them; 1,400 hoplites lost their lives in the most crushing defeat of a Spartan field army in living memory.

Epaminondas died in 362 BC, still fighting Spartans; he was killed in action at Mantinea while leading the Thebans to yet another victory. He had been a mighty fish in a very small pond, and he was irreplaceable; but his real impact on the history of warfare is to be measured by the lessons learned from his tactics by his greatest pupil and admirer: Philip of Macedon. As a young prince, Philip had been sent to Thebes to study; later, following one of the innumerable kinks in Greek city-state politics, he was a temporary hostage there. Philip's host in Thebes was the father of Epaminondas and Philip was deeply impressed by the achievements of the city's military hero.

PHILIP OF MACEDON: THE ARCHITECT OF EMPIRE

The real reason for Macedon's skyrocket rise to world predominance was the kingdom's freedom from the web of obsessive traditions entangling the other Greek states. In their eyes Macedon was a barbaric oddity, quite beyond the pale, the butt of eternal jokes. These turned to hysteria when Macedonia's juggernaut advance began. Demosthenes of Athens hurled abuse at the Macedonian king in his *Philippics*, shrilly denouncing Philip as 'a man who not only is no Greek, and in no way akin to the Greeks, but is not even a barbarian from a respectable country – no, a pestilent fellow of Macedon, a country from which we never get even a decent slave.' Macedon was so primitive that it retained its hereditary monarchy and never plunged into the whirlpool round of tyranny to oligarchy, oligarchy to democracy, democracy to oligarchy, and so on *ad infinitum*. Macedon was so sunk in dishonour that it had accepted the role of a Persian satrap and kept out of the destructive leagues, alliances, and endless wars of 'civilized' Greece. As a military nation Macedon was equally contemptible, lacking a hoplite caste and a navy. All these deficiencies were the source of Macedon's strength, and Philip was the first Macedonian ruler to see it.

He became king of Macedon in 359 BC and at once set about converting the feudal resources of the kingdom into a new army. The infantry he created was indeed primitive. It did not consist of 'all-round' spearmen and swordsmen but of massed pikemen, packed shoulder to shoulder in ranks sixteen deep. These pikemen wore helmet and greaves but no body armour; their small shields were strapped to the left arm to leave both hands free to wield the enormous *sarissa* or long pike, which seems to have had a length of about eighteen feet. The mass of spear-points presented by such a formation projected far beyond the front rank, giving the Macedonian phalanx a tremendous advantage in reach over the traditional hoplite phalanx. This was not an original idea; experiments had been made by an Athenian strategist named Iphicrates in the 390s who had been the first to arm hoplites with a longer spear and smaller shield. But Philip was the first to build a whole army which used this infantry armament.

The basic building-block, then, was the *syntagma* of 256 pikemen: sixteen men wide by sixteen deep. Four of these made up a *chiliarchy* (1,024 men); four chiliarchies made up the simple or basic phalanx of 4,096. The *Grand Phalanx* consisted of two divisions, each of two phalanxes, and was 16,384 strong.

It was an instrument relying on mass. Macedonian pikemen or phalangites could not, like hoplites, operate in small companies: they lacked the armament to do so. The performance of the Macedonian phalanx was dominated by the physical problems of wielding the *sarissa* while keeping formation. It was not a weapon which could be swung to and fro to meet attacks coming from different angles without unseaming the whole formation. The phalanx was designed for an irresistible line attack; it could not, like a hoplite force, launch a sudden charge, but advanced at a steady walk. It was in fact highly vulnerable to sudden charges from flank or rear; but it was never intended to operate on its own. The phalanx was supported by medium infantry or *hypaspists* –

virtually lightweight hoplites in armament – who screened the phalanx from such surprises. But the decisive element in Philip's army was the cavalry, for Philip had rediscovered the old Assyrian formula of using mobile troops both as strike force and as protection for the heavy infantry.

Macedonian cavalry carried lance and light sword; they were protected by an open-faced helmet and a metal corselet. The elite regiments retained the title of 'king's Companions' derived from the function of the king's mounted escort. The cavalry's primary task was to relieve the phalanx of all danger of unexpected disruption by shattering the enemy cavalry. It would then regroup for a decisive charge against the enemy light and medium infantry, invariably from the flank or rear, while the phalanx advanced to deliver the main frontal assault against the enemy heavy infantry. These tactics sufficed to beat any hostile Greek army. When the Macedonians invaded Asia, their cavalry also protected the infantry from the biggest menace encountered during the march of the 'Ten Thousand': mounted archers and missile troops.

When Philip became king in 359 BC, the Macedonian heartland was limited to an enclave around Pella at the north-western 'corner' of the Aegean. His first moves concentrated on reducing the tribes of the hinterland to subservience and expanding his domestic recruiting-area (359–357 BC). Further expansion to east or south immediately brought him into conflict with the southern states who had colonies on the southern Aegean coast, but in this he was able to use his strategic master-weapon: Macedonia's detachment from the hostile alliances which kept the south divided.

In 358 Philip made a treaty with Athens. He agreed to conquer Amphipolis; Athens agreed to surrender Pydna in exchange. Athens already had its hands full with recovering Euboea after yet another revolt and reconquering the Chersonese from Thrace, but soon refused to give up Pydna. Philip thereupon conquered and held both Pydna and Amphipolis. He then came up against a large mercenary army which Phocis had raised by seizing the sacred treasury of Delphi. The Phocian general Onomarchus inflicted two defeats on Philip in Thessaly before he himself was defeated and killed in 352, enabling Philip to unite Thessaly under Macedonian leadership. The loyal compliance of Thessaly was crucial. It permitted Philip to put direct pressure on Athens and Thebes, and secured Macedonia from any allied action from the south while Philip turned east to reduce Thrace. But when he tried to move further south he was stopped at Thermopylae in 352 by an allied army of Athenians, Achaeans, and Spartans. Instead of getting involved in a complicated series of campaigns and changing alliances in central Greece, Philip turned east again. Olynthus, in the Chalcidean peninsula, defied him with Athenian encouragement, but Philip stormed Olynthus in 348, razing the city and enslaving the inhabitants.

For the moment Athens was spent and asked for peace – the 'Peace of Philocrates' of 345, in which Athens bought her right to the Chersonese by surrendering her claim to Amphipolis. Philip immediately conquered Phocis, while continuing to profess friendship towards Athens and Thebes. Having thus secured his southern flank, Philip turned east

Gold medallion showing Alexander taming Bucephalus having wagered the price of the horse to his father Philip before attempting the feat. Bucephalus remains one of the immortal warhorses of military history, along with Napoleon's Marengo, Wellington's Copenhagen, and Robert E. Lee's Traveller

to conquer Thrace. This he achieved in two campaigns: 342–341 and 340–339 BC. In the second of these campaigns, which carried Macedonian power east as far as the Dardanelles and Sea of Marmara, Athens sent help which enabled Perinthus and Byzantium to hold out against the besieging Macedonians. During this campaign, too, Philip's sixteen-year-old son Alexander was given his first taste of power as regent in Macedonia while the king was away on campaign. He also showed his quality by leading a strike force to crush a rebel Thracian tribe which made the mistake of seeking to profit by Philip's preoccupation with Byzantium.

The showdown with the Athenians and Thebans came in 338, with the battle of Chaeronea in Boeotia. This was the battle which completed Alexander's military education. He led the great cavalry charge which scattered the Boeotian right wing and opened up the allied centre and left to destruction by the phalanx. After Chaeronea there was no choice open to the autonomous Greek states than to submit to Philip or go under one by one. They accepted his proposals for an all-embracing Hellenic League, promulgated at Corinth in 338, which spared the member states from Macedonian garrisons and exactions of tribute – the normal results of defeat. (Thebes was the only important exception.) And as joint League policy for the immediate future Philip announced his plans for the invasion of Asia. War was declared in 337 and in the following year Philip's second-in-command, Parmenio, crossed the straits into Asia Minor with an army of 10,000. The Greek cities of Asia Minor rose in support and the occupation of Ionia was well under way when Philip was assassinated.

THE CAMPAIGNS OF ALEXANDER

The convolutions of Macedonian court politics which led to Philip's murder were matched only by those of the Persian court and are too

The battlefield of Chaeronea, where the young Alexander led the great Macedonian cavalry charge, winning the battle and making his father master of an all-embracing Hellenic League

complex to trace here. Alexander had been estranged from his father: his first task was to get himself accepted as king by the Macedonian army, which he did. But as the news of the murder spread, the Greek states revolted *en masse* from the condition of subservience which Philip had forced upon them. Thebes, Athens, and the Peloponnesian states of the Hellenic League repudiated Macedonian rule, and most of Philip's generals advised Alexander to let them go. This he refused to do. There had been too many examples, over the previous 150 years, of individual and joint subversion clipping the power of dominant states, and Alexander was determined not to have it happen to him.

The most urgent priority was to make sure of Thessaly. Before the southern states had had time to get over their orgy of public celebration over Philip's death Alexander had swept into Thessaly and had himself proclaimed *archon* in succession to Philip. He then marched straight on Thebes and encamped outside its walls. The message was plain, if the Athenians and Thebans wanted another Chaeronea they would get it. They made the wise decision to send envoys to apologize for the delay in recognizing Alexander as the supremo of the Hellenic League, and repeated the joint resolution to press the war in Asia, under Alexander's leadership.

Alexander then showed that he had mastered the basics of strategy by taking a year to campaign against the tribesmen of northern Thrace, where he had first cut his teeth on an independent command. Before he crossed into Asia he wanted to make certain that there would be no threat to the army's lifeline across the Straits. In his first campaign as king of Macedon he pushed his borders north to the Danube in a series of brilliant successes over the elusive Triballians, making effective use of mercenary archers and slingers where the terrain forbade the use of cavalry and phalanx. Having crushed the tribesmen, Alexander was immediately faced with another crisis on Macedon's north-west frontier: an invasion by the Illyrian tribes under Glaucias and Cleitus. Alexander force-marched his army west to prevent the Illyrian leaders from joining forces, but succeeded only too well, becoming encircled at Pellion. In the fighting which first shattered the Illyrian ring and then defeated its components, Alexander made the first known use of siege machines as field artillery to cover the advance of the phalanx. This victory at Pellion kept the Illyrians subservient for the rest of Alexander's reign.

Meanwhile the Greek states had broken out again, encouraged by a rumour that Alexander had been killed while campaigning on the Danube. Darius of Persia, who, like Alexander, was a born survivor (he had become 'great king' in 356 by poisoning the man who was trying to poison him), was bribing Greek politicians to resist Macedon. Demosthenes of Athens, indomitable in his crusade against the northern barbarians, pledged Athenian support for Thebes, which was still held by a Macedonian garrison. The Thebans had risen and the Macedonian garrison was penned inside a close siege perimeter within the city when Alexander and his army suddenly appeared outside the city after another forced march of thirteen days.

He had 30,000 infantry and 3,000 cavalry and was confidently expecting the Thebans to see sense and capitulate, but the Thebans were

determined to hold out. They had been promised help by Athens and the Peloponnesian states and were unfortunate enough to take the promises at face value. They defied Alexander and invited the Macedonians to join them in overthrowing the tyrant of Greece. What happened next was to be repeated several times before Alexander died. The king saw red. He put out his entire strength to destroy Thebes. Left in the lurch by the cowardice and hesitation of their allies, the Thebans fought magnificently, repelling assault after assault. This only increased the temper of the attacking troops and Alexander's rage. By the time the Macedonians forced the walls and broke into the city, with the besieged Macedonian garrison breaking out to make the rout complete, the attackers were out of control. No quarter was given or taken; 6,000 defenders died and the entire population, 20,000 strong, was sold into slavery. To complete his vengeance Alexander had Thebes razed to the ground.

The carnage at Thebes was supremely effective. Athens caved in at once, in abject terror. Sad things had happened to the Athenians since the Persian invasions. Alexander was not left an empty city, with the Athenians taking to the islands and putting their faith in sea power. Instead the Athenians drove Demosthenes from office in disgrace and grovelled to Alexander for mercy, and the Peloponnesian members of the League did likewise. It only remained to dot the i's and cross the t's. The Hellenic League reassembled at Corinth, pledged their loyalty to Alexander and elected him their generalissimo for the invasion of Asia, the date of which was set for the spring of 334 BC. Parmenio and Antipater (who was to remain in Macedon as regent with 15,000 infantry and 1,500 cavalry) begged Alexander to wait until he had married and produced an heir. But they were thinking of Macedon. Alexander was impatient to see what he could do with his talents and his troops.

The army which Alexander led across the Dardanelles in 334 was not an all-Macedonian force: it was a composite army representing all Greece except for Sparta. Macedonian infantry (phalangites and hypaspists) made up 50 per cent of the army; Macedonian companion cavalry another 10 per cent. The light cavalry was Thessalian and Thracian — javelin-throwers and lancers. Small hoplite contingents from the Greek states fought with the hypaspists, and the light infantry consisted of Thracian and Greek peltasts. These troops gave the army all the mobility that the 'Ten Thousand' had lacked. It also had impressive hitting-power in the form of missile troops: Cretan archers, Rhodian slingers with their deadly lead bullets, and Agrianian javelin-throwers from Thrace, all troops on whom Alexander placed a specially high value. Few of these types of soldier had been in existence when Cyrus had recruited his Greek mercenary army, only sixty-seven years earlier, proof of the military revolution which had followed in the wake of the Peloponnesian Wars.

Alexander's army was not, like the 'Ten Thousand', a purely mercenary force, though it did include mercenaries. But he was just as concerned with seeing that his men were furnished with regular loot, if not pay, as Cyrus had been. No money would come out of Macedon: he had exhausted the kingdom's treasury to pay for this expedition. He had no fixed objective and no plan of campaign other than to march in search of the richest cities and treasuries in Asia, crushing whatever armies got in the way.

It is significant that Alexander's first destination across the Hellespont was the site of Troy and the grave of Achilles, where appropriate sacrifices and homage were paid. Apart from Alexander's personal hero-worship of Achilles, this was the first time a composite army of Greeks had invaded Asia Minor since Agamemnon's time.

If Alexander seems to have read his Xenophon as well as his *Iliad*, so does Darius. The armies of the western satrapies had been stiffened by 20,000 Greek mercenaries under a shrewd commander, Memnon of Rhodes. Memnon advised the satraps not to give premature battle but to fall back and wait for Darius to come up with the main army, but the satraps refused indignantly. Memnon therefore prepared to hold the east bank of the River Granicus with the Greek mercenaries and another 20,000 Persian cavalry. The Granicus was running high after the spring rains and the Persian bank was steep; it was a most formidable position, and Parmenio played the wise second-in-command. He advised Alexander, as it was late afternoon when the armies made contact, to wait until morning and spend the night in reconnaissance. Alexander would have none of it. He noted that the Persians had, in their usual manner, insisted on their cavalry being deployed in the place of honour in front of the Greek infantry; and he plunged straight into the river at the head of thirteen squadrons of Companion cavalry.

This was a tremendous gamble. If the horsemen had hit a deep patch on the way over, Alexander could well have lost his most important

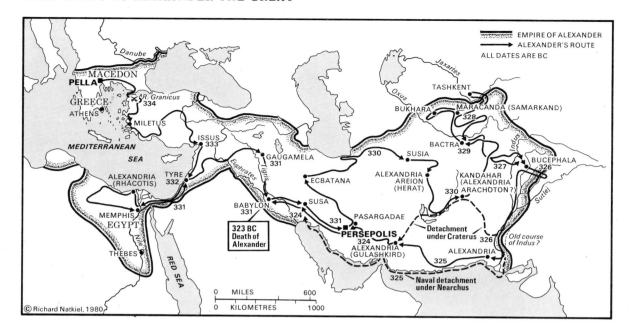

troops before they had even come to blows. As it was the horses fought the current with the greatest difficulty, their riders coming under heavy javelin and arrow fire as they neared the far bank, which fortunately caved in as the first horses struggled to land, and made life easier for those following. The Persian cavalry swarmed up to the landing-place and a hectic *mêlée* ensued, with Alexander himself in the thick of the action. He marked down a senior officer and charged with the lance, which broke on impact. As Alexander drew his sword another Persian officer loomed up and gave him a stunning blow with a battleaxe, but the Persian was killed before he could get in another blow, by a lance-thrust from Clitus, one of Alexander's closest Companions.

As the Companions fought and won the battle of the bridgehead the first elements of the phalanx came struggling across the river, and when they formed up on dry land the Persians broke and fled. The Greek mercenaries withdrew to a hill in battle formation and asked for mercy. Alexander refused — a stupid decision, because destroying a hoplite phalanx of 20,000 was a bloody and costly business. Only 2,000 prisoners were taken; these were sent back to hard labour in Macedonia. Casualty figures for this, as for all Alexander's victories, are particularly suspect, being inflated on the Persian side and written down on Alexander's. He almost certainly lost more than 100 (Plutarch gives the absurd figure of 34 killed, of which 12 were infantry). But the figure of 20,000 killed on the Persian side was very probably correct. There was plenty of loot for the troops, gold and silver plate to send back to Macedon, and battle trophies to distribute round the cities of Greece. Alexander deliberately refrained from announcing a Macedonian victory: this was a *Greek* victory (Sparta excepted) over 'the barbarians of Asia'.

Victory on the Granicus destroyed the only Persian army defending Asia Minor, which fell effortlessly to Alexander. Memnon, however, had

The campaigns of Alexander hammered the Persian empire into submission — but the fusion of East and West remained a mirage. After Alexander's early death his generals warred between themselves to seize and hold the most important provinces

escaped from the Granicus and organized the resistance of Miletus, which Alexander besieged with the aid of the Athenian fleet. His siege engines, hurling incendiaries, set fire to the defences and this time Alexander pardoned the 300 Greek mercenary survivors who joined his army. Halicarnassus was also defended on Memnon's orders and here Alexander had to cope with 2,000 Greek mercenaries and additional Persian troops. The garrison fought tenaciously, launching sortie after sortie, before the triple ring of defences was cracked and the blazing city fell. Even then Memnon refused to give up. He took advantage of Alexander's early dispersal of the Athenian fleet after the capture of Miletus and organized the defence of the Ionian islands with the support of the Persian fleet, which effectively regained control of the eastern Aegean.

Alexander had meanwhile received the submission of Caria in south-west Asia Minor, which for most of the army marked the end of the 334 campaign. All troops who had been married just before the invasion were given home leave, and officers were sent back to recruit more troops. Alexander himself spent the winter of 334–333 BC leading a small force along the southern coast of Asia Minor to take out the ports used by the Persian fleet and thus hasten its withdrawal from the Aegean.

As the time drew on for the 333 spring campaign Alexander was contemplating a move against the main body of the Persian army, inhibited by the continuing successes of Memnon in the eastern Aegean. Memnon had taken Chios and was directing the battle for Lesbos when he was killed – the worthiest and most dangerous opponent Alexander ever had. His death transformed the course of the war. Memnon had advised Darius to lure Alexander as far east as he could and only to give battle when his strongest possible forces had been assembled; but now Darius decided to fight in Syria. He left the Cilician and Syrian Gates undefended, as Memnon had advised, to encourage Alexander east – but in blundering forward to meet Alexander he was caught with his back to the sea at Issus.

Alexander's army of no more than 30,000 was facing odds of over two to one at Issus, but certainly not the 600,000 of the usual Greek estimates. As at the Granicus, the Persian army included a hard core of Greek mercenary infantry, about 20,000 of them. It is hard to see how Darius could have had more than 85,000 at Issus; this was the army of Syria/Palestine/Egypt, without the masses still waiting in Mesopotamia/Babylonia/Persia/Media. Despite his eagerness to force a decisive action, Alexander took the time for a careful reconnaissance and deployed with care, sending the Thessalian horse to support Parmenio, who was holding the seaward flank and faced with the heaviest concentration of Persian cavalry. Alexander led the charge on the right flank, consisting of the massed Companion cavalry. But in extending his right-flank infantry to prevent any Persian encircling move, Alexander could not prevent a gap from developing through which the Greek mercenaries charged, lapping round the Macedonian phalanx and pressing it hard before Alexander could afford to send his cavalry to the rescue.

All accounts agree that Darius' army was doing very well until the 'great king' panicked and fled in his chariot. Greek sources claim that Alexander and his companions drove close enough to Darius for blows to be exchanged, Alexander collecting a light sword wound in the thigh. This could well have panicked Darius and his 'headquarters staff' into a hasty withdrawal which then proved impossible to control. After a vain cavalry chase, Alexander returned to count the immense spoils of Darius' travelling palace and treasury.

After Issus, Alexander did not pursue Darius into Mesopotamia: he turned south to make sure of the Mediterranean coast and his sea link with Greece. All Phoenicia and the port of Sidon capitulated but Tyre, an island fortress-city, defied him. Alexander was forced to undertake the most difficult siege of his career, starting with the building of a gigantic half-mile causeway which, like the Roman ramp at Masada (see p. 231), is still there. Fighting magnificently, the Tyrians held out for seven months; but their resistance, long after it was obvious that no help would be coming from Darius, provoked another vicious burst of 'frightfulness' from Alexander. As well as enslaving the civilian population of 30,000, he crucified 2,000 men of military age. The same fate was reserved for Gaza, which blocked the only road leading into Egypt and was stoutly defended by the satrap Batis. Sources say Alexander hitched Batis to a chariot and dragged him alive round the walls of Gaza.

ABOVE: A detail from the 'Alexander mosaic' shows Darius III in his chariot at Issus, at the moment he turned and fled from the charge of Alexander's Companion cavalry

OPPOSITE: This colossal statue at Luxor depicts Alexander as pharaoh of Egypt. The dynasty established by Alexander's general Ptolemy endured to the Roman conquest, Cleopatra being the last of the line

Egypt welcomed Alexander with open arms. The Persian troops stationed in Egypt had been accounted for at Issus and the Greeks, whose earlier attempts to 'liberate' Egypt were gratefully remembered, were hailed as liberators. Having paid his famous visit to the shrine of Amon at Siwah (in which the Egyptian equivalent of Zeus hailed Alexander as his son) and marked out the site of his future city of Alexandria, Alexander returned to Tyre to plan his next campaign.

Alexander's army was much stronger when it left Tyre than when it had crossed the Dardanelles three years earlier, thanks to reinforcements from home and the recruitment of Darius' former mercenaries. He now had 40,000 infantry and 7,000 cavalry, all of which would be needed, as he well knew, for the coming trial of strength with the main army of Darius in Mesopotamia. Alexander opened the campaign by making Darius do some marching. Instead of taking the direct route to Babylon down the Euphrates, Alexander crossed both the Euphrates and the Tigris as if to outflank Darius from the east. Darius came north to meet him, failed to stop the Greeks from crossing the Tigris, and halted to deploy his immense army on the plain of Gaugamela.

The troops deployed by the Persians at Gaugamela showed that they were learning at last, if far too late. Darius was putting his faith in his cavalry, 35,000 strong; but his best infantry had been wiped out at Issus and he had not been able to replace it. He hoped that 200 scythed chariots would go some way towards remedying the deficiency and would perform better than they had done for Artaxerxes against the 'Ten Thousand' at Cunaxa. All told, his army totalled something like 100,000 men.

This time the Persian numbers were so huge that there could be no question of a whirlwind flank attack. After keeping the Persians standing to arms all night in expectation of a night attack that never came, Alexander deployed his forces on the same plan used at Issus. He then began pushing his light cavalry further and further out to the right as if to outflank Darius. The Persian king fell into the trap and began sending out stronger and stronger cavalry detachments to eliminate the Greek light cavalry until 1,100 of the latter had successfully drawn off 11,000 Persian cavalry. Thinking that he had engulfed Alexander's entire right flank, Darius sent in the chariots against the Macedonian infantry, who avoided them with ease. Despite increasingly urgent requests for help from Parmenio over on the left, Alexander kept his Companion cavalry poised until Darius had sent off so much heavy cavalry that the right flank of the Persian centre was exposed. Alexander then swept into this gap with the Companion cavalry and ordered the phalanx to attack in the centre.

The effect of this stroke was the slicing in half of the Persian army. For Alexander and the Companions the battle now followed the pattern of Issus: a relentless drive through the enemy centre towards the king's command post and the distinctive figure of Darius himself. As at Issus, Darius panicked and fled from the battle on horseback, but there could be no question of pursuit.

Mazaeus, satrap of Babylon, had forced Parmenio to detach the left-flank division of the advancing phalanx as emergency reinforcements.

This opened a gap through which Mazaeus poured his Indian and Persian cavalry, which flooded enthusiastically through the left centre of the Macedonian line. Instead of wheeling either to complete the ruin of Parmenio or to counter-attack Alexander and the Companions, the Persians and Indians charged right ahead to plunder Alexander's camp. They were driven out by the rearmost units of the phalanx, which faced about and counter-attacked, forcing the Indians and Persians into the arms of Alexander and the Companions advancing from the centre. The battle ended in a gigantic *mêlée* from which the now leaderless Persians eventually fled in their thousands.

Gaugamela was the decisive victory of Alexander's career. He won it largely through the Persian belief that superior numbers *must* prevail, which tempted Darius into committing his cavalry against the Greek light horse. The battle was also the result of Alexander's marvellous sense of timing, judging precisely the right moment for his own counterstroke. He took immense liberties with the tenacity of his own troops and was extremely lucky that the Persian and Indian cavalry breakthrough was not headed by a competent commander. All these factors, combined with the hopeless deficiencies of Darius as a commander-in-chief, enabled Alexander to rout the only army capable of defending Babylonia, Persia, and Media.

Alexander marched on to Babylon where his troops, glutted with the wealth of Darius' war chest, enjoyed a thoroughly splendid month of feasting, sports, and general recreation. He imitated Cyrus of Persia 200 years earlier and won over the Babylonians by respecting their gods and traditions, and appointing Mazaeus as their new satrap. He had no intention of changing the Persian Empire's infrastructure, merely of taking it over. Before resuming the pursuit of Darius he took ceremonial possession of the imperial capitals, Susa and Persepolis. He gave the latter city over to plunder by his troops, which his generals and advisers considered stupid because it was now his own property. But there was method in all the thieving and destruction. Persepolis was the city of Xerxes, the would-be conqueror of the Greeks, whose colossal statue was now overthrown by Greek soldiers, and whose palace was now burned to the ground by the master of the Greek world.

In the spring of 330 BC Alexander headed north for Ecbatana, the old Median capital, where Darius had come to rest after Gaugamela and was frantically trying to raise a new army. As the pursuit got under way, Alexander heard from deserters that Darius was a prisoner of the satrap Bessus. Fearing that Darius would pass the Persian crown to Bessus, Alexander raced ahead of the army with sixty light cavalrymen and eventually discovered the abandoned wagons of the king's train, in one of which lay the body of Darius in chains. Bessus not only escaped into the eastern provinces: he assumed the title of king, leaving Alexander with no choice but to pursue. As he did so he was obliged to take countermeasures against Persian satraps whom he had appointed but who now supported Bessus, revolting as soon as Alexander's army was elsewhere. The chase led the army through Parthia, Drangiana, Bactria, and Sogdiana before Bessus was captured and tortured to death north of the Oxus.

A ten-drachma piece, struck at Babylon, shows Alexander on horseback attacking King Porus on his war elephant. The momentous Indian campaign introduced the war elephant to the Western world, where these hapless beasts served for the next two centuries

After reducing the wild mountain tribes of Afghanistan, Alexander was asked for help by Taxiles, an Indian king at war with a neighbouring monarch, Porus. The invitation was superfluous: Alexander never had any intention of staying within the traditional eastern frontiers of the Persian Empire. He proved this by conquering every tribe on his line of march to the Indus, beyond which lay the warring kingdoms. Taxiles became a client-king, contributing 700 Indian cavalry and giving Alexander a dubious excuse for campaigning indefinitely in India on his client's behalf.

Like the battle on the Granicus seven years before (and an unbelievable 2,500 miles away), the decisive battle with King Porus hinged on a contested river-crossing. But this was like no battle ever fought: it brought European troops into contact with war elephants for the first time. The animal itself was phenomenon enough to any fourth-century Greek; used as a weapon of war it was pure science fiction. The biggest problem was that Alexander's most important arm – the cavalry – was reduced to an uncertain quantity because the horses were terrified of the elephants. He was not worried about the infantry; they could see that the elephants were managed by 'savages', and the word was spread that the right place to hit an elephant was in the trunk.

Alexander, therefore, could not force a sudden crossing and open the kind of whirlwind attack which was his speciality. Instead he delayed on the west bank of the Jhelum river long enough for Porus to feel secure, then divided his army of 10,000 infantry and 3,000 cavalry into three detachments. Porus had 200 elephants, 30,000 infantry, 6,000 cavalry, and 420 chariots massed on the far bank; when Alexander began to string his detachments upstream, leaving a rearguard force facing Porus, the latter was in a quandary. If he stayed where he was, Alexander would be able to cross. If he moved upstream the rearguard would come across and encircle him. In the end Porus stayed where he was and sent off his son, with 2,000 cavalry and 120 chariots, to cover Alexander. Having crossed and beaten this force, Alexander brought the rest of the army across to tackle Porus and his elephants. He now had a decisive superiority in cavalry, which he used in attacks on both ends of Porus' line. This spared the Macedonian horses from any head-on confrontations with the elephants and herded the frightened monsters into the centre. All that was then needed was to move in the phalanx and let the elephants stampede Porus' infantry into a disorganized wreck.

After beating Porus and making him a client-king on terms of uneasy equality with Taxiles, Alexander announced his plans to advance further into India. The troops refused point-blank, and it is impossible to feel anything but sympathy for them. Conquering Persia had been a finite challenge. Persia was the old enemy, familiar on that account: Greeks had fought in her armies and visited her capitals. But India offered nothing but infinite campaigning far beyond the horizons of the known world, and Alexander's troops recoiled from the prospect.

Ten years after Alexander had crossed the Dardanelles into Asia Minor, he led his army back to Susa. No other commander and no other army has ever accomplished so much in so short a time. Whether Alexander would have escaped assassination if he had not died at

Babylon in 323 BC is extremely uncertain. His lunatic outbursts were becoming more frequent, as were the judicial murders of old comrades; his policy of integration with the Persian ruling class was not only misunderstood but actively resented by his Macedonian officers. But his early death proved that he had built an empire only in name. It was too big for one man to rule, and the wars of the Macedonian generals which followed Alexander's death proved it.

AFTERMATH: THE WARS OF THE GENERALS (323–283 BC)

Alexander had made warfare an epic way of life; his successors reduced it to the level of a deadly board-game, with the original stake of each player being the forces he commanded at the time of Alexander's death. The object of the game was to gain control over the whole of Alexander's conquests by eliminating all rivals. No holds were barred with regard to insincere alliances, broken treaties, or opportunist dynastic marriages. The basic trouble was that there were too many generals in the game: Perdiccas, Antipater, Cassander, Seleucus, Ptolemy, Antigonus, Lysimachus. The older players had ambitious sons who carried the war into the second generation. The most colourful of these was Demetrius Poliorcetes ('Besieger of Cities'), the son of Antigonus, who earned his nickname by his inventiveness in siege warfare but ended up dying in captivity as a prisoner of Seleucus.

The most fascinating aspect of these wars was the spectacle of battles which set phalanx against phalanx and introduced the war elephant to the Middle East and Africa. These battles usually involved only the minimal destruction of good troops, with the rank and file of the losing side usually going over to fight for the better man. Certainly the most spectacular collision occurred at Ipsus (Asia Minor) in 301, when Antigonus and Demetrius fought Seleucus and Lysimachus. The rival armies were virtually equal in foot and horse, each fielding about 70,000 infantry and 10,000 cavalry. Seleucus, however, who had gained control of Mesopotamia, Persia, and the eastern provinces, had brought west 420 elephants. He used them to shield the flank and rear of his phalanx, which they did to telling effect. The cavalry of Demetrius demolished the facing Seleucid cavalry, but found themselves blocked out of play when their horses refused to attack the line of elephants. By the time Demetrius and his cavalry were ready to re-enter battle, Antigonus had been killed when his unsupported phalanx was broken by the advance of Seleucus.

In the end, as with the Peloponnesian Wars, there was no clear-cut decision other than general acceptance of the fact that no one was big enough to fill Alexander's shoes. The wars petered out in the 280s with Seleucus controlling Asia Minor and the bulk of the old Persian Empire, Ptolemy Pharaoh of Egypt, and Demetrius' son Antigonus King of Macedon.

PART THREE

From Bandit Stockade to World Empire

CHAPTER EIGHT

The Roman Republic

O UT OF ALL THE MILITARY SUPREMACIES of the ancient world,
Rome's rise to imperial power was the most uncertain and prolonged. Rome produced no Sargon, Tiglathpileser, Cyrus, or Alexander
who set off to conquer the world in his lifetime. In this she was
exceptional. Her control extended step by step – sometimes hesitantly,
sometimes in desperation – with far more accident than method. It took
her over 700 years to rise from a primitive fighting community hungry
for womenfolk and farming land to the mistress of the Mediterranean
world and western Europe.

Only one other empire of the ancient world – Egypt – lasted for
longer than Rome, and that was because of its geographical isolation.
Rome, by contrast, was geographically committed from birth, situated
in the middle of a peninsula commanding the middle of the Mediterranean. First surviving, then asserting her superiority over her immediate
neighbours brought her into conflict with the Etruscans to the north and
Greek colonies to the south. Gaining control of the Italian peninsula
forced Rome into conflict with Carthage, the great sea power of the
western Mediterranean. Beating Carthage left Rome with new territory
in Africa, Spain, and southern France. Inevitable conflict with the
leading Greek states on her eastern doorstep made her the overlord of
Greece. So it went on, one war leading to the next. Until the entire
Mediterranean coast was controlled by Rome there was never a moment
when the Republic could sit back, secure in the knowledge that its
interests were secure on all fronts.

Imperial security produced the inevitable propagandists who set out
to justify the system. Borrowing heavily from Homer, the Roman poet
Virgil codified the legends of how Rome had been founded by the
descendants of Aeneas, the leading refugee from the fall of Troy. The
importance of the *Aeneid* in the Roman world was due to the fact that it
magnificently answered all the questions about the phenomenon which
was Rome. The long feud with Carthage was the inevitable result of
Aeneas' ill-fated jilting of Queen Dido, founder of Carthage; the conquest of Greece was the delayed revenge of the heirs of the Trojans for
the conquest of Troy, and so on. As for a detailed history of the origins of
Rome and its rise to power, this was provided by the historian Livy who,

OPPOSITE: Bas-reliefs on
the *Ara Casali* at Rome
depict scenes from the
founding of the city –
according to tradition by
Romulus, son of the war
god Mars and the Vestal
Virgin Rhea Silvia

serenely composing speeches and motives for the heroes of old, gave the Romans what Homer had given the Greeks: a written shrine for the heroic past.

Romans were left in no doubt of what that past had been. The city had been founded in 753 BC by Romulus, the first king of Rome, son of the war-god Mars and the Vestal Virgin Rhea Silvia. The line of the kings had been ended in 510 BC by the expulsion of the tyrannical Tarquinius Superbus and the establishment of a republic. Warring valiantly against its neighbours, the city set out to fulfil its destiny, for destiny it surely was.

'I must believe,' wrote Livy, 'that it was written in the book of fate that this great city of ours should arise, and the first steps be taken to the founding of the mightiest empire the world has known – next to God's.' In the *Aeneid* Virgil added his own exhortation: 'But you, Roman, must remember that you have to guide the nations by your authority, for this is to be your skill, to graft tradition onto peace, to show mercy to the conquered, and to wage war until the haughty are brought low.'

Both Virgil and Livy wrote their eulogies to the Roman past in the days of Augustus Caesar, who had become 'first citizen of the Republic' in 27 BC after a crippling century of gory civil wars. From its traditional foundation in 510 BC, therefore, the Roman Republic can be said to have lasted 483 years – but despite all the literary skill of Livy only the latter 285 years enjoy a clear-cut history, unobscured by myth and legend. And this period begins at the close of the fourth century BC, during the great reorganization of the Roman state under the censor Appius Claudius. Before his reforms the Romans had fought their wars from hand to mouth; after Claudius the state had the framework of a military machine.

The earliest Roman armies can only be reconstructed from the reforms which superseded them. These early armies were basically no more than a muster of every able-bodied man of military age: a militia of spearmen. In Roman tradition King Romulus got the city off to a flying start by attracting the service of all neighbouring warriors who owed no allegiance to anyone else – outlaws and bandits included. They put up with his leadership because he led them to victory, most notably against the more settled Sabines from whom the Romans plundered their first womenfolk. Military service to the state was therefore one of the earliest functions of its citizens, who turned out in times of national emergency at his own expense and providing his own equipment and weapons. This system survived well into the Republic, with the spearmen muster being led into battle by a pair of elected consuls – the supreme magistrates – instead of a single king. It enabled Rome to fight and beat the other cities in the immediate neighbourhood, and to survive attacks from the Etruscan cities north and west of the Tiber.

Rome's position on the Tiber enabled her to call on military aid from the cities to the south and west for which she acted as a frontier-guard against the Etruscans. These were the cities of Latium, the region delineated by the Tiber, the Apennines and the Auruncian hills to the south-east. They formed the 'Latin League', an extremely loose association over which Rome claimed and eventually won supremacy after

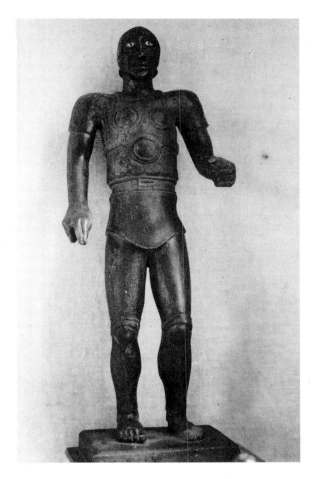

Early enemies of the Roman state. ABOVE: An Etruscan statue of a Samnite warrior. ABOVE RIGHT: An Etruscan warrior of the middle fifth century

repeated challenges and revolts throughout the fifth and fourth centuries BC. At the same time Rome was seeking to break the spearhead of Etruscan pressure: the fortified city of Veii, only 12 miles away from Rome across the Tiber.

The constant threat of war had induced the Romans to build a special emergency measure into their constitution. This was the office of *dictator*: the entrusting of supreme power into the hands of a generalissimo in times of acute national crisis. It was a strictly constitutional post; the dictator only held power for six months at the outside, and was required to resign when the task for which he had been appointed was completed. It was a way of ensuring that supreme military command went to the right man at the right moment, if the right man did not happen to have been elected one of the consuls for that year. Such a man was the dictator Marcus Furius Camillus, who finally took Veii in 396 after an alleged ten years of blockade and siege. The parallel with the ten years' siege of Troy is obvious and is indeed significant. It did for the Romans what Marathon did for the Athenians: act as a psychological trigger, a demonstration of heroic tradition in a concrete achievement of arms.

Further stimulus was provided six years later by a mass invasion from the north by the Celts, to whom the cities of Italy offered ideal plunder. The Celts or 'Gauls' who fell on Rome in 390 BC were out for loot, not conquest, and even Livy admits that Rome was willing to buy them off with 1,000 pounds of gold. The Gauls of 390 BC scattered the troops sent against them by Rome with their solitary tactic: a wild, screaming charge, swinging their long swords. Whether or not the Romans helped the invaders on their way back to the Po valley, the need for a disciplined fighting force capable of holding similar attacks in the future was obvious.

Subsequent wars against raiding Gauls and rebelling Latin cities throughout the fourth century BC continued the steady evolution of the Roman army. It had come a long way from the early days when the richest citizens provided horsed troops, the middle classes provided the heavy infantry, and poorest classes provided light infantry. The troops were now paid in time of war, both from state funds and from plunder taken from the enemy. The old triple distinction in troop types had survived, but had been modified tactically. The youngest troops now formed the front line or *hastati*, and were javelin-throwers. The second line, also javelin throwers, was the main infantry force or *principes*, and

A magnificent study of an Etruscan warrior, wide open to a death-blow after having his shield-arm swept aside by his enemy

the third line was manned by the veterans or *triarii*, armed, like the *principes*, with thrusting-spears.

The troops were massed in *legiones* or legions of 5,000 men, each legion having 300 cavalry in support. Even when the short sword was adopted as the legionary's side-arm he still cut a poor figure compared with a Greek hoplite – but in the wars with the Samnites, a southern people whose territory stretched across the Apennines and involved the Romans in their first serious mountain fighting, Rome adopted a new sub-division for the legion which greatly improved tactical efficiency. This was the *maniple* or company of 120 men, a small, handy unit which enabled the legion to operate in difficult terrain without losing cohesion. As events were soon to prove, the maniple was an inspired invention, simple though it was; it enabled far less experienced Roman troops to tackle professional Greek infantry massed in phalanx.

It was during the Second Samnite War (326–304 BC) that all these trends were rationalized in the reforms of Appius Claudius referred to above. By far the most important new reform was Rome's formal adoption of strategic warfare in the decision to build military roads. The first of these, the *Via Appia*, justly bore the name of its sponsor. The *Via Appia* was begun for the sole purpose of speeding the flow of troops and supplies from Rome, using the shortest possible route, to the war zone in southern Italy. This enabled the Romans to keep the coastal plain of Campania permanently occupied, so depriving the western Samnites of their winter pastures. The *Via Appia* was the vital prototype; the next two roads, *Via Flaminia* and *Via Valeria*, both reached east across the Italian peninsula, connecting Rome to the summit of the Apennines.

All these developments – the improved troops, the military roads, and the swifter deployment of units to where they were needed – enabled Rome to fight the confederations of Italian peoples which the Samnites raised against Rome – Etruscans, Umbrians, and the Picentini of the Adriatic coast. From 310 Rome also began to make tentative experiments in sea power against the ports and shipping of her enemies on both sides of the peninsula. She came out of the Samnite wars in control of the Apennines and the Adriatic coast from Ariminum to Bari.

Victory over the Samnites led directly to conflict with the Greek colonies of southern Italy: the cities of Hydrus (Hydruntum), Taras (Tarentum), Metapontion (Metapontum), Heracleia (Heraclea), and Rhegion (Rhegium). These cities naturally viewed the steady advance from the north of Roman power with the gravest suspicion, particularly as it was accompanied by the planting of outlying Roman colonies. They turned for aid to King Pyrrhus of Epirus, the most celebrated fighting monarch in mainland Greece, who crossed to Italy in 280 BC eager to found a new empire in the west at the expense of Rome. This was by far the biggest challenge which the Roman army had yet faced, eclipsing even the trauma of the Gallic irruption 120 years before. Pyrrhus was confronting the legions not only with the phalanx but with elephants as well.

On paper it should have been a runaway victory for Pyrrhus. With elephants to panic the skimpy cavalry forces of the Romans and their Italian allies, he had more than enough cavalry to trigger the rout of

unsupported infantry fighting in line. But he was unable to destroy the Roman and Italian armies, which came against him 24,000 strong at Heraclea (280 BC) and 40,000 strong at Ausculum (279 BC). Pyrrhus' army consisted of 20,000 infantry, 3,000 cavalry, 2,000 archers, and 20 elephants — but in each battle the yielding Roman line took immense punishment from the phalanx without breaking, and harried it furiously. At Ausculum, moreover, Pyrrhus had the help of the Samnites, Lucanians, and Bruttians, who had deserted Rome after Heraclea. But his losses spelled plain disaster. At Heraclea Pyrrhus lost 4,000 men to the Romans' 7,000; at Ausculum he lost 3,500 to the Romans' 6,000.

A fanciful study of one of the most dramatic encounters in ancient history: the clash between the Hellenic expeditionary force and elephants of Pyrrhus and the legions of the Roman Republic.

Aghast at 32 per cent losses in two battles, Pyrrhus crossed to Sicily in search of easier meat, but the Romans promptly made an alliance against him with the Carthaginian cities in the west of the island. He returned to Italy in 275 BC and this time was beaten squarely at Beneventum, after which he withdrew from Italy for good. An Epirot garrison was left at Tarentum but this surrendered in 272 BC, after which Rome completed her triumph by occupying the entire 'heel and toe' of southern Italy.

The Samnite Wars and their sequel, the Pyrrhic Wars, mark Rome's coming of age as a military nation. By 272 BC the Roman Republic had routed one of the legendary Hellenic armies which had completely dominated the military scene for the past eighty years, and Rome's grip on central and southern Italy was secure. But this was only the beginning of new entanglements. Without knowing it, Rome had already taken the first step on the path to world empire. Before another ten years were out she was battling with Carthage for control of the central Mediterranean.

THE FIRST WAR WITH CARTHAGE (264–241 BC)

It is safe to say that when Rome went to war with Carthage in 264 BC, championing the doubtful cause of a band of Campanian mercenaries in Messana, she had no idea what she was taking on. Carthage had been founded a century before Rome and by the middle of the third century had grown into the biggest sea empire the world had ever seen, dwarfing the Athenian League at its zenith. Carthaginian ports, colonies, and the friendly territory of allies stretched east to the Gulf of Sirte and west through the Straits of Gibraltar to extend down the Moroccan coast; inside the Straits the Carthaginians also controlled half the coast of Spain. Carthage held the Balearic Islands, Corsica, Sardinia, and the western half of Sicily. With her immense merchant and shipping fleets she could sail where she liked and hit where she liked – and nine-tenths of Rome's frontier was vulnerable coastline. As for land warfare, Carthage blended her Phoenician origins with a healthy respect for Greek civilization, the latest refinements in military tactics included. Her long sea lanes, covering the entire Mediterranean, enabled her to recruit and ship mercenary forces at will.

But the amazing feature of the First Punic War ('Punic' being the convenient Latin corruption for 'Phoenician', or Carthaginian) was the gusto and inventiveness with which the Romans took to naval warfare. No other sea power in history has ever learned its trade so quickly. Improving on Greek models, the Romans introduced a novel feature into their warships, the *corvus*, a weighted boarding-bridge for dropping onto enemy ships. After only four years of initial reverses a Roman consul, Caius Duillius Nepos, beat a Carthaginian fleet at Mylae off eastern Sicily and took fifty ships. This encouraged Rome to send an expedition against Carthage – a fatal piece of overconfidence. Regulus, the Roman commander, landed near Carthage with 15,000 infantry and 500 cavalry; his arrogant demands for the instant surrender of Carthage were rejected and he found himself isolated, unable to take the city with this insufficient force. The mercenary leader Xanthippus, a Spartan,

191

crushed the Roman force on the Bagradas river in 255, attacking frontally with 100 elephants and enveloping the Roman flanks with attacks by a cavalry force of 2,000. This was about the only victory ever won by using elephants in an initial frontal attack instead of as a defensive screen.

After the failure of the expedition to Carthage the war centered on Sicily. The Romans lost another fleet at Drepana and failed to eject Hamilcar Barca from his stronghold at Eryx. Peace was finally settled after another Roman sea victory at Lilybaeum in 241. Rome came out of the war with Sicily as her first province, but in 238, with Carthage wracked in civil war against the rebel mercenaries of Hamilcar Barca, Rome seized Sardinia and Corsica and demanded double the war indemnity of 3,200 talents. Carthage had no choice but to yield in order to avoid another war – a humiliation which she never forgot. In 235 an extremely rare event occurred: the doors of the temple of Janus were closed in Rome, indicating that the city was at peace with all nations – for the first time on record since the temple's foundation in the eighth century. But Rome was soon obliged to move down into the Po valley to deal with more trouble from the Gauls, beating them at Clastidium in 222 BC leaving Lombardy studded with fortress colonies.

This Carthaginian coin from Spain shows Hannibal (*far left*) and an elephant. Despite the propaganda value of taking elephants across the Alps, none of Hannibal's three great victories in Italy were won by elephants

HANNIBAL'S WAR: THE SECOND PUNIC WAR (218–201 BC)

War was resumed with Carthage in 218 BC ostensibly as a result of Carthaginian expansion in Spain, forcing Saguntum to apply to Rome for aid. This time, however, the Carthaginians were planning to take the offensive under Hannibal, the son of Hamilcar. Hannibal was planning to invade Italy from the landward, crossing the Alps and detaching Rome's Italian allies by marching on Rome. It was a strategic *tour de force* but it entailed leaving as many troops to cover the eastern Pyrenees and Rhône valley as Hannibal actually led into Italy, quite apart from losses due to tribal ambushes, exposure, and the other intense hardships of the march. Hannibal set off from 'New Carthage' (Cartagena) with some 102,000 Carthaginian and allied troops; he passed the Pyrenees and Rhône with no more than 60,000 and arrived in Italy with only 23,000. (Most of the elephants succumbed on the way.)

Hannibal was the immediate successor to Alexander the Great as military 'grand master', and in Italy he proved himself the greatest living tactician; but it must be admitted that he was not nearly so successful as a strategist. The invasion of Italy did not make the Romans concentrate their forces at home; it did not lead to a mass desertion of Rome by her Italian allies; it was intensely difficult to support and reinforce. His biggest tactical mistake, and the most notorious, was deciding not to stake all on a march on Rome after Cannae in 216. Hannibal's greatest talent was perhaps as a leader of men. He managed to inspire a polyglot army of allies, mercenaries, and native Carthaginian troops so that it stayed in being for fifteen years, a constant menace to Roman Italy — but for all that unable to prevent Rome from executing her own strategic *coups*.

Hannibal won his empty battles over the Romans in Italy largely by exploiting their weakness in mobile troops. He was strong in cavalry — Numidian and Spanish javelin-throwers and lancers, plus Gallic volunteers from northern Italy. The first clash in Italy, on the River Ticinus, confirmed this superiority and Hannibal used it, together with the eagerness of the consul Sempronius to force a battle, to win his first victory on the Trebia. He posted 1,000 infantry and 1,000 cavalry in ambush under his brother Mago, then lured out the Roman main body by an assault on the outposts by Numidian light infantry, which reached the Roman camp before falling back. The Roman and Italian infantry mass advanced against Hannibal's light and medium infantry, but was soon left unsupported by the rout of its flanking cavalry. To increase the effectiveness of his cavalry wings (each 5,000 strong), Hannibal deployed his last surviving elephants — probably no more than half a dozen on each flank. The elephants had their usual effect of panicking enemy horses which had never encountered elephants before; but the Roman infantry used anti-elephant tactics presumably learned against Pyrrhus. (These consisted of infuriating the beast by determined jabbing at trunk and tail with spears and javelins.) Hannibal shrewdly withdrew the elephants before they stampeded, and left the cavalry wings with the job of enveloping the Roman infantry. At precisely the right psychological moment Mago sprang his ambush and charged deep into the rear of the labouring Roman infantry, which soon broke. No small part was played in this victory by the care Hannibal took beforehand, in seeing that his men had breakfasted and had been issued with oil with which to rub themselves down. As a result the Carthaginian army went into battle fed, warm, and supple, while Sempronius' men were cold and hungry, already tired after slogging through the mud and rain of the appalling Italian winter, and practically frozen after having to ford the icy waters of the Trebia.

At the Trebia, Hannibal had faced a frontal attack. In his next battle, at Lake Trasimene in 217, he attacked from the flank while his victim was still in column of march. Hannibal opened the 217 campaign by moving across the Apennines into Tuscany, leaving a trail of destruction to lure the Romans into precipitate action and keep their allies loyal. In this he succeeded, drawing the army of Gaius Flaminius in full cry along the north shore of Lake Trasimene, lured on by what he thought was Hannibal's retreating rearguard. Hannibal had meanwhile deployed his army on the low hills above the lake, screened by the night

The early republican army had four types of legionary who were recruited from all citizens as and when required. *Hastati* (RIGHT) and *principes* were the younger recruits who formed the first two lines of battle. They wore some armour and carried a sword and two long javelins (*pila*). *Triarii* (BELOW) were the veterans in full armour who carried a sword and a long heavy spear. They formed the third line and were rarely brought into battle except in an emergency. The *velites* were lightly-armed skirmishers. The organization of the early legion is shown in page 198

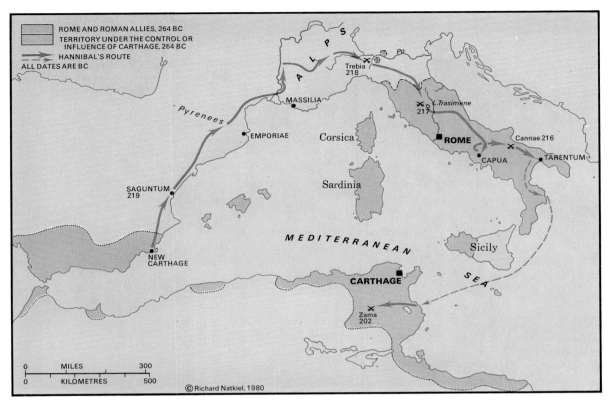

ROME AND ROMAN ALLIES, 264 BC
TERRITORY UNDER THE CONTROL OR
INFLUENCE OF CARTHAGE, 264 BC
HANNIBAL'S ROUTE
ALL DATES ARE BC

ALPS

Po

Trebia
218

Pyrenees

MASSILIA

EMPORIAE

Corsica

L. Trasimene
217

ROME

Cannae 216

CAPUA

TARENTUM

SAGUNTUM
219

Sardinia

MEDITERRANEAN

Sicily

NEW
CARTHAGE

CARTHAGE

SEA

Zama
202

0   MILES   300
0   KILOMETRES   500

©Richard Natkiel, 1980

ABOVE: The main theatres of combat in the Second Punic War between Rome and Carthage (218–201 BC)

mists rising from the waters and marshland. From the moment his forces charged the passing Roman columns and trapped them against the lake, the only serious question was how many Romans would cut themselves out of the trap. Flaminius was not one of them; he died with his men. Altogether 15,000 Romans died out of a strength of 25,000.

It took a third defeat, in 216 BC, for the Romans to realize that Hannibal's speciality was hoodwinking and enveloping armies motivated by the desire to force a battle. This third battle was the first time that Hannibal had been confronted by the combined armies of both consuls, and the defeat annihilated them both. The basic tactics of Cannae are well-known: allowing the Romans to roll deep into the Carthaginian centre, then closing in behind the Roman infantry. It all sounds so simple that one wonders why the Romans ever fell for it at all. But the essence of Cannae was its simplicity. At the Trebia Hannibal had tempted Sempronius with what looked like a premature attack; at Lake Trasimene Flaminius had been reaching out to snatch at what looked like the Carthaginian rearguard. At Cannae Hannibal drew up his forces quite deliberately on an open plain where there could be no possibility of Carthaginian forces lurking in ambush. This time his whole army was the bait. Nor was the battle an easy one. If the legions had pushed too hard on the yielding Carthaginian line and broken through, or if the Roman cavalry had feigned flight and drawn off the Carthaginian cavalry, Hannibal would have faced disaster instead of Lucius Aemilius and Terentius Varro.

Cannae has been legendary for the past 2,000 years, lauded as the 'model battle of annihilation', the 'battle without a morrow', even as the 'perfect battle'. But it was a most perfect demonstration of the uselessness of good tactics if they fail to fulfil a strategy. Hannibal's strategy was aimed at the destruction of Rome as a military power, not the repeated slaughter of Roman armies by the use of elegant tactics. At Cannae he beat the combined armies of the Republic in a single stroke – and failed to follow it up by marching on Rome. This error of Hannibal's shows how inferior he was as a war leader compared to Alexander the Great, who knew how to exploit every battle to the full. Alexander would never have paused for a council of war after Cannae: he would have been riding for Rome as soon as the battle was won. Certainly he would never have stayed on the battlefield to haggle over the ransoms he wanted for the 4,500 prisoners taken at Cannae.

After 70,000 of her best troops had been killed in a single day, Rome's decision to fight on when all seemed lost stands out as the Republic's 'finest hour'. What is not generally remembered is the hideous trauma suffered by the city when the news of Cannae arrived. Special prayers and rites to appease the obvious wrath of the gods have always been a natural accompaniment to military disaster (as witness Britain's National Day of Prayer at the time of Dunkirk in 1940); but after Cannae the Romans desperately resorted to human sacrifice. Ancient rites of atonement were dug up and brutally performed. A Vestal Virgin who had broken her vow of chastity was buried alive, while her lover was publicly flogged to death by the Supreme Pontiff. Two Gauls, a man and a woman, together with two Greeks, were also buried alive in an ancient walled enclosure in the cattle market. Seldom has a lost battle unleashed such dark excesses, which even Livy was bound to describe primly as 'most un-Roman'.

This tortuous feeling of national guilt was no blind reaction to fate: it was all the keener because the disaster had been self-inflicted. After Trasimene and the death of Flaminius, Fabius Maximus had been appointed 'acting dictator' pending the next consular elections. Fabius had come up with the only tactic guaranteed to deprive Hannibal of victory: to refuse any more pitched battles and shadow Hannibal wherever he went, recapturing any city or port he took as soon as the Carthaginian army moved on. These patient but inglorious 'Fabian tactics' had caused grave dissatisfaction in Rome. The new consuls, Varro and Aemilius, had been elected amid popular clamour to end the war with an early victory – and the slaughter of Cannae was the result. After Cannae, Roman strategy against Hannibal in Italy reverted to using these 'Fabian tactics' and sticking to them. By 209 BC the Romans had successfully recovered Hannibal's two most important acquisitions after Cannae: Capua and Tarentum. Unable to win over the central Italians, Hannibal was forced to operate more and more in the south.

By far the most important aspect of the Roman revival after Cannae was the way in which Roman grand strategy remained intact. This had been agreed at the outbreak of hostilities in 218: to open a 'second front' against the Carthaginian empire in Spain, and build up Sicily as a base for an amphibious assault on Carthage herself. The Spanish front was kept in being throughout the opening years of the war, despite all the disasters in Italy. For six years the Scipio brothers, Gnaeus and Publius, operated in Spain with great success from advanced bases at Emporiae and Tarraco, supported by the Roman fleet. The Scipios not only prevented Carthage from supporting Hannibal by land, but advanced across the Ebro river. There they overreached themselves, and both were killed in a Carthaginian offensive led by Hasdrubal, Hannibal's brother, in 212. The survivors fell back on Tarraco which, so far from being evacuated, was reinforced. When they appointed a new commander for Spain the Romans took a tremendous gamble: they chose another Scipio, Publius' son, twenty-six years old and without any experience in independent command. The war was entering an extraordinary new phase: what amounted to a blood feud between the sons of Hamilcar Barca and the Scipio family.

Young Scipio soon showed that he was far more than the bearer of a famous name. Supported by the fleet under Gaius Laelius (with whom Scipio forged a military partnership fit to rank with that between Marlborough and Prince Eugene, or Robert E. Lee and 'Stonewall' Jackson), he embarked on the most audacious Roman venture of the war: an amphibious assault against New Carthage. The essence of the plan was a forced march direct from Tarraco, to arrive under the walls of New Carthage before the Carthaginian armies in Spain could react and march to intercept. He force-marched his army from Tarraco to the Ebro in a week (an average pace of nearly 43 miles a day) and stormed New Carthage from land and sea in two days — an incredible feat. The capture of New Carthage was a strategic masterpiece; the Carthaginians could

Roman war galley going into action, with soldiers on the central gangway poised to deliver a volley of *pila* (javelins)

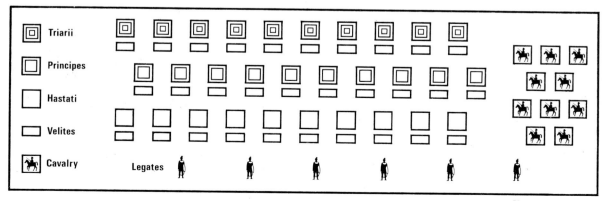

	Triarii													
	Principes													
	Hastati													
	Velites													
	Cavalry		Legates											

The evolution of the Roman legion

An imperial legion of the first century AD on parade (ABOVE). This developed from the early Republican legion (OPPOSITE BELOW) which had thirty maniples — ten of 120–150 *hastati*; ten of 120–150 principes; and ten of 60 *triarii*, plus *velites* and ten *turmae* of cavalry each with 30 horsemen (see page 194). In the reforms of Marius all legionaries were given the same equipment and the maniples were combined into ten cohorts. The original legions were commanded by six tribunes, but by Caesar's time these were often inexperienced young aristocrats gaining sufficient military service to qualify for a magistracy and legions were frequently put under the command of a *legatus* appointed by the consuls.

The basic structure of the imperial legion remained unchanged with one significant innovation — the first cohort (on the left) was increased in strength from about 480 men organized in six centuries to 800 in five centuries. The legion also had about 120 cavalry (on the right) who acted as scouts and despatch riders.

The legion was now commanded by a legate (1) appointed by the emperor, with a staff of six tribunes (2). The senior centurion was the *primus pilus* (3) commanding the first century of the first cohort. He held rank for one year only and might go on to be *praefectus castrorum* (4), who commanded the legion in the absence of the legate and senior tribune. Each legion had its eagle borne by the *aquilifer* (5); and each century had its standard bearer, trumpeter, and orderly (6). The centuries were commanded by centurions (7) — who were usually selected from the ranks — with a deputy (8). The legions — recruited only from Roman citizens — were the backbone of the Roman army and usually used for offensive actions, putting down revolts, or repelling invasions. Frontier patrol and garrison work was left to locally recruited auxiliary regiments which were usually organized in a similar fashion. All auxiliaries received Roman citizenship when they retired.

not recapture it without gaining command of the sea, and if the Carthaginian land armies sat down in front of New Carthage for a long siege they would be completely taken out of play. In fact, Scipio's achievement was the turning-point of the war: it persuaded the Spanish tribes, on whom both Romans and Carthaginians depended for their military operations in Spain, to transfer their support from Carthage to Rome.

In 208 Scipio marched against Hasdrubal Barca and defeated him at Baecula on the upper Guadalquivir, after which the remaining Carthaginian armies in Spain joined forces. But they did not attempt to crush Scipio. Instead Hasdrubal set off on a bold new flanking march – to Italy. As Scipio blocked the eastern gate of the Pyrenees, which Hannibal had passed in 218, Hasdrubal left Spain by way of the western Pyrenees, then headed for the Rhône and repeated Hannibal's crossing of the Alps. The Roman reaction to this phenomenal march was simply to raise two home armies instead of one for the crucial campaign of 207 BC, the twelfth year of the war. Rome's war effort was now surpassing itself with every year: in 207 BC, with 137,108 Roman citizens of military age recorded by census, 75,000 of them were under arms together with an equal number of Italian and foreign allies. There were now fifteen legions serving in Italy, four under Scipio in Spain, two in Sicily, and two in Sardinia.

To meet Hasdrubal in the north, Rome originally deployed the consular army of Marcus Livius, whose colleague Claudius Nero went south to help contain Hannibal. Nero, however, realized that it was vital to stop Hasdrubal from getting too far south, and that Livius was probably not strong enough to hold Hasdrubal. Nero therefore weeded out 7,000 picked men from the armies screening Hannibal, and force-marched them north to join Livius. With these reinforcements Hasdrubal's army was smashed on the River Metaurus, ending the only serious threat that Hannibal might receive sufficient aid to break out from the south.

As if all these exertions were not enough, Rome had also managed to maintain a third front in Sicily, where Syracuse rebelled in 214 BC and declared for Carthage. Thanks to its immensely strong fortifications and the ingenuity of the philosopher Archimedes, who contrived the siege artillery, Syracuse held out for two and a half years. (Archimedes' most startling invention was a giant grapnel for snatching up ships which came too close to the harbour walls, up-ending the victim and letting it crash back into the water to sink.) Syracuse was eventually retaken in 211 BC. By this time Rome was involved on a fourth front, against Philip V of Macedonia. In 215 BC Rome had the luck to intercept the envoys sent by Hannibal to ratify an alliance between Macedon and Carthage. The spectre of a Macedonian army landing in Italy to join hands with Hannibal was dispelled by the fleet of Marcus Laevinus, who crossed the Adriatic with a single legion and broke up Philip's invasion fleet at Apollonia in 214 BC. The troops were withdrawn and the eastern Roman fleet supported the confederated Greek states in their war against Macedon until peace was settled in 205.

Scipio had meanwhile added to his laurels by defeating the combined Carthaginian field armies in Spain – those of Hasdrubal Gisgo and Mago – at Ilipa in 206. This was at once a victory of veteran troops over the untried allies serving with the Carthaginian army, and the result of out-thinking his opponents. Based on their camps, the armies eyed each other for days, and Scipio accustomed Hasdrubal to seeing the Romans form up with their allied troops on the flanks. He then confounded Hasdrubal by bringing on the battle with the *Roman* troops on the flanks, then reversing this surprise deployment with great skill as the Carthaginian wings fell back in confusion. Hasdrubal fought a costly retreat back to his camp, but his allies deserted in the night, leaving him with no course but retreat. Scipio followed hard on his heels and eventually 6,000 exhausted and half-armed men, hopelessly trapped on a hilltop, surrendered. They were the survivors of what had been an army of 55,000. It was the effective end of the war in Spain.

By the end of the same year Scipio had completed the occupation of the Spanish coast with the exception of Gades (Cadiz). He was already at work on the next stage of his 'private war' with Carthage: winning over the African allies of Carthage in preparation for the Roman invasion of Africa. In this he was only half successful, gaining the friendship and support of Masinissa of the Maesulii, but losing Masinissa's rival Syphax to Carthage. These negotiations involved several 'cloak-and-dagger' diplomatic missions to North Africa, in a manner strongly reminiscent of the preparations for the Anglo-American 'Torch' landings in the Second World War. Against heated protests from opponents, Scipio's strategy prevailed and he led a Roman expeditionary force of no more than 20,000 to Africa in 204. He landed near Utica, planning to take the port and use it as a beachhead, but was only able to put it under siege. Hasdrubal Gisgo, the Carthaginian commander in Africa whom Scipio had repeatedly beaten in Spain, advanced with Syphax to raise the siege of Utica with a joint army of nearly 80,000 infantry and 13,000 cavalry.

Scipio was now in much the same position as Hannibal had been in ever since his invasion of Italy fourteen years back, only with the advantage of sea communications. He built a secure base camp, the Castra Cornelia, on a narrow coastal peninsula – and then worked out a plan for the destruction of Hasdrubal, when any other commander facing such odds would have been more than content to remain on the defensive. Scipio's eventual attack was one of the most horrible events in military history. So far the world has been spared a demonstration of what tactical nuclear missiles might do to troop concentrations, but this attack in 204 BC gives one a very good idea. It featured a stealthy night approach and the sudden firing of the camps of Syphax and Hasdrubal, in which the troops were sleeping jammed together amid makeshift partitions of reed matting. Scipio supervised the firing of Hasrubal's camp while his old lieutenant Laelius, aided by Masinissa, dealt with Syphax. The camps went up in flames like twin brush-fires in which 40,000 men roasted to death. Hasdrubal's army was destroyed as a fighting force, although he and Syphax escaped. The siege of Utica was resumed, and when a Carthaginian attempt to raise the siege from the sea was beaten off, Carthage asked Scipio for an armistice.

Peace negotiations began with both sides fully aware that the last act was yet to be played: Hannibal's recall from Italy for a decisive confrontation with Scipio. He and his army sailed for Africa in the autumn of 203 BC and landed at Leptis. While Hannibal was still at sea the Carthaginians broke the truce, attacking a fleet of some 200 transports bringing much-needed supplies and reinforcements to Scipio. Both Scipio and Hannibal, therefore, played for as much time as possible before their inevitable battle, each of them raising as many troops as possible — particularly the superb Numidians, experts with the javelin on foot or on horse-back. All the accounts (and not just those of Livy, the master of melodrama) agree that Hannibal and Scipio met for a brief parley before the battle, one of the most poignant encounters of all time. The only point of agreement between these two great men was that they had no choice but to fight it out to a finish.

Hannibal had about 50,000 men, Scipio slightly less, but what mattered in this battle was quality, not numbers. Scipio had the advantage in trained infantry; he had his trusted lieutenant Laelius (one of the very few officers in military history who have been as comfortable commanding a fleet as a brigade of cavalry) commanding the left-flank cavalry; he had Masinissa, now a king recognized with full honours by the Roman state, commanding 4,000 crack Numidians on the right. Hannibal's trump card, apart from himself, was his army of Italian veterans, 24,000 strong. These he deployed in line as his rear formation. In the van he had 80 elephants — more than he had ever commanded before. His light infantry was deployed in absorbent layers in front of the Italian veterans. Hannibal's greatest weakness was in cavalry, in which he may have been outnumbered by as much as two to one. For this reason he deployed on as wide a front as possible to make it harder for Scipio to outflank him.

Scipio took unusual care in his deployment, because the last time Roman infantry had faced an elephant charge on African soil (see p. 192) it had been wiped out. He used the normal deployment — hastati/principes/triarii — but instead of placing the maniples checkerboard-fashion he aligned them in straight files with clear lanes between each file. The few elephants which did get through to the Roman infantry mass headed naturally down these lanes and were urged out to the rear, playing no further part after their initial charge. Masinissa and Laelius then charged on the flanks and a furious cavalry battle developed while the infantry of the two sides clashed. Hannibal's 'shock-absorber' deployment very nearly worked. Scipio's legionaries were slowing nicely when they came up against Hannibal's main defence line, the Italian veterans. According to past form, the Romans should have battered blindly onward, allowing the outer Carthaginian units to work round the flanks, but at this point Scipio 'threw the book away'. He sounded the recall, pulling back the legionaries and dividing the second and third lines into portions which moved out on either side of the hastati. Then he advanced again, and this time Hannibal's flanks were in danger. The infantry battle was still hanging in the balance when Laelius and Masinissa, having driven off Hannibal's cavalry, came thundering back to complete the ruin of his army. Zama ended like

Cannae, with the hemmed-in foot soldiers of the losing side struggling in vain to break out. Percentage losses were not so murderous as at Cannae – the Carthaginians lost about 20,000 killed, or under 50 per cent compared to the Roman 87.5 per cent killed at Cannae – but the last army of Carthage had been destroyed as a fighting force. Zama, not Cannae, was the battle that ended the war.

Though possibly tying for first place with Xerxes' invasion of Greece, the Second Punic War is probably the best-remembered conflict in ancient history. It is easy to see why: it was a gripping human drama with a star-studded cast. It had Hannibal, Scipio, Fabius 'The Delayer'; it had the beaten Varro formally thanked, after Cannae, because 'he had not despaired of the Republic'; it had Hasdrubal's head flung into Hannibal's camp; it had Archimedes cut down at Syracuse while engrossed in his calculations, and a host of other *memorabilia*. But the splendid stories tend to outshine the war's darker side. By 205 BC Rome was fighting with a savage intensity which she had never known before and would never really know again. The Republic was no longer trying to survive, or even to emerge with equal honours. Rome was hell-bent on triumph and *punishment*. This vindictiveness against Carthage was not dispelled in the years after Zama. The refugee Hannibal was hounded by Roman agents for nineteen years after his last defeat, until he committed suicide rather than be handed over to Rome. But at least he had been entertained by enemies of Rome and had given advice to their rulers. Carthage herself had been reduced to impotence after Zama, but she continued to be treated by extremist Roman politicians as the source of all Rome's troubles. So far from being a former enemy to be treated generously in defeat, Carthage, like Hannibal himself, was eventually hounded to destruction.

Of course there was a positive side, with plenty to be proud of: Rome's victory over Carthage remains, for all its grimmer features, a shining example of joint national effort in the face of all adversity. In the struggle to beat Carthage the Republic had grown into a military power able to send powerful expeditionary forces anywhere it chose, and whose protection was to be constantly requested far from Italy. By this criterion alone, Rome emerged from the Second Punic War with what today would be called 'super-power status'.

Military supremacy had, however, thrust on Rome a role for which the institutions of the old Republic were almost totally unsuited. The constitution of the Roman Republic aimed at investing its leaders with power for as brief a period as possible, and keeping its troops under arms for as little time as possible. But the new provinces – Sicily, Corsica/Sardinia, 'Nearer Spain', and 'Farther Spain' – could not be accommodated within this simple framework. They needed governors, tax collectors, port officials, and customs officers. Above all they needed permanent garrisons of troops, if only for defence against marauding inland tribes. To defend the trading empire which she had wrested from Carthage, Rome needed fleets to be kept on a war footing for operations against pirates – not individual buccaneers, but genuine rogue fleets able to give any regular navy a run for its money. Long before Hannibal even left Italy, the old Rome, which called on its citizens to arm and march out to defend the Republic, had gone for ever. For a while the old traditions would still be strong enough to make successful generals loyally resign their commands and retire to private life when their work in the field was done. But within 150 years of Zama the generals were jockeying for supreme power. Victory over Carthage was the invisible foundation-stone of the Roman Empire.

CONQUEST OF GREECE (200–146 BC)

That Rome had her hands full with regard to her new western provinces is shown by her reluctance to take on any permanent commitments in the east for thirty-five years after Zama. Reconstruction in Italy involved a ten-year running campaign against Hannibal's most loyal allies, the Gauls of the Po valley (200–191 BC), whose territory was subsequently reorganized as the province of 'Nearer Gaul'. While this was going on Rome was dragged into the Second Macedonian War (200–197 BC) to fight Philip V of Macedon in alliance with the troops of the Aetolian and Achaean Leagues. At Cynoscephalae (197 BC) Quinctius Flaminius won the first decisive victory of a Roman army over a Macedonian phalanx. The speedier Roman legionaries, fighting in maniples rather than line, fell on the phalanx as it was struggling up a ridge with its downhill flank still in marching formation and tore it apart. After proclaiming the independence of the Greek cities and enforcing a humiliating peace treaty on Philip, the Romans withdrew – but four years later they were back to champion the Greeks against another persecutor. This time the aggressor was the Seleucid king, Antiochus III, 'The Great', who sought to profit by the discomfiture of Macedon by taking Greece. Acilius Glabrio and Porcius Cato ejected Antiochus' army from the Thermopylae Pass by using precisely the same tactics as the Persians 289 years before (see p. 121). In the following year the Romans took their first steps in Asia, led by Scipio 'Africanus', the victor of Zama, and his brother. For the first time, a Roman army crossed the Dardanelles.

At Magnesia, near Smyrna, the Roman army of 24,000 and its 6,000 Greek allies came up with Antiochus' main army, 70,000 strong. The confrontation was a tableau of the old and the new in combat troops, for the Seleucid forces were a throwback to the days not only of Alexander the Great but of the Persian army that had failed to stand up to Xenophon's 'Ten Thousand'. They were an extraordinary mixture. Antiochus had scythed chariots, light infantry, Cretan archers, slingers, a phalanx of 10,000, Median cavalry, 3,000 *cataphracts* (heavy armoured cavalry with the horses fitted with armoured breastplates), and 54 elephants. It was a military museum, not a balanced fighting army. Scipio had 16 elephants on his side, which he kept stationed *behind* his infantry; having seen what little use they had been to Hannibal at Zama he wanted to keep them safely in hand for as long as possible.

The battle of Magnesia, 189 BC, was a grim caricature of a glorious past. On Antiochus' side everything went wrong that could go wrong. The opening charge of the scythed chariots was as useless as it had ever been, the chariots being repelled and sent careering off in all directions by massed javelin volleys. They caused havoc among Antiochus' light infantry and scattered the *cataphracts*, which in turn charged blindly into

LEFT: Roman *denarius* celebrating the victory of the Republic in the Mecedonian wars

BELOW: Roman legionaries in their defensive *testudo* ('tortoise') formation, first recorded during the Third Macedonian War

the phalanx and made it lose cohesion. Greek and Roman cavalry charges against the flanks, and a legionary assault against the wavering phalanx, completed the rout of Antiochus' army — a defeat due as much to its inherent lack of structure as to Roman efficiency. The most significant aspect of Magnesia was the utter failure of the Seleucid mounted and infantry missile troops, because of the chaos on their side, to make any impression at all on the legionaries. After the fiasco of Magnesia Antiochus had to accept the enforced surrender of all Asia Minor west of the Taurus Mountains, the surrendered territory being shared out between Rhodes and Pergamon, the allies of Rome.

From 171–166 BC Rome was hauled back into Greek affairs with the Third Macedonian War, in which Perseus of Macedon sought to avenge the humiliation of his father, Philip V. This war produced the first recorded instance of legionaries fighting in close *testudo* ('tortoise')

formation behind linked shields to keep off missiles, which they did at the siege of Heracleum during the invasion of Macedon from Thessaly. Livy makes the interesting comment that the *testudo* was adopted by the army from a popular showpiece in gladiatorial contests, but Livy's understanding of military matters was extremely patchy. (He thought that the Macedonian phalangite order to 'lower pikes' was an order to abandon pikes and draw swords.) When Perseus finally accepted battle at Pydna (168 BC) there came the long-awaited stand-up fight between the legion and the phalanx. Perseus' phalanx failed to break the Roman line at Pydna, and was soon forced onto the defensive. Paullus threw it into confusion by a scatter of attacks by maniples coming in from different directions. In vain attempts to cover all these attacks by swinging their pikes to and fro, the phalangites found it impossible to hold formation and were broken up with surprising ease. The aftermath of Pydna was the final dismemberment of Macedon, with Rome annexing Illyricum, across the strait from Brundisium, as a permanent foothold in the Balkans.

Rome's permanent hold on Greece dated from 149 BC, when she crushed an attempt to reunite Macedon and annexed all four of the client-states into which the country had been divided after Pydna. Three years later, after a war between Achaea and Sparta, a Roman army under Lucius Mummius smashed the Achaeans and took Corinth with great brutality, looting and burning the city and enslaving the inhabitants. The former territory of Corinth became the core of the province of Achaea, which Rome finally annexed in 127 BC. Two years before that date Rome had made good her claim to the territory of Pergamon, which had been bequeathed to the Republic by the last King of Pergamon, Attalus III, in 133 BC. Rome's territory now stretched unbroken from the Adriatic coast across northern Greece to the far shore of the Dardanelles.

In the same year as the final assimilation of Macedon, 149 BC, Rome at last gave the death-stroke to the old enemy, Carthage. The pretext was Carthaginian 'aggression' against Rome's ally in Africa, the elderly King Masinissa of Numidia. Scipio Aemilianus, grandson of the great Scipio, took Carthage after a ferocious siege in 146 BC, the year Corinth fell. Carthage was treated with even greater severity than Corinth. It was levelled to the ground and its territory sown with salt, a formal curse being pronounced on all who might dare rebuild the city. After destroying Carthage, Rome took her first African province, a narrow slice of territory around Carthage, but left the rest to the heirs of Masinissa, who had died in 149.

In the latter part of second century BC, the Romans had their first real taste of guerrilla warfare on the frontiers of the Spanish provinces, against the tribesmen of the central peninsula who refused to accept domination from the Roman-controlled coastal strip. Rome had particular trouble with the tribal leader Viriathus in Portugal or Lusitania, where a third province was eventually established. Other persistent trouble-makers for Rome were the Celtiberians of central Spain, from whom the Carthaginians had recruited some of the best of their infantry for their wars against Rome. The speciality of the Celtiberians was the building of massive hill-forts, one of which, at Numantia, held out for eight months against the conqueror of Carthage, Scipio Aemilianus. Experience gained in reducing these hill-forts was to bear useful fruit when the Roman army began its campaigns against the Celts of north-west Europe from the middle of the first century BC.

MARIUS AND THE NEW ROMAN ARMY

In 107 BC Rome was in the fifth year of an inconclusive desert war with the African King Jugurtha when a fateful event took place. Gaius Marius, son of a peasant, a soldier risen from the ranks, was elected consul. His rise to this supreme office was the direct result of the vicious polarization of Roman politics between the *populares* or 'people's party' and the *optimates* or 'establishment party' (for want of a better translation). Marius was the first military champion of the *populares* and he was feared and distrusted by all conservatives from the moment he took office. Denied an army by the senate, he raised his own — a volunteer force recruited from the urban poor and footloose veterans — trained it and led it to victory over Jugurtha in 105 BC. Then, in his third consulship, he set about the total overhaul of the Roman army.

The Marian reforms not only opened the army to the poorest citizen volunteer: they transformed the weaponry and equipment, for the new recruits could not be expected to pay for them. The short Spanish stabbing sword, increasingly popular in the Roman army since the close of the Second Punic War, was now made standard; the old distinctions between *hastati*, *principes*, and *triarii* were also abolished. All legionaries were now armed with light and heavy *pila*, javelins with short heads and shafts of soft iron, weighted at the junction with the wooden butt to make for extra range. Making every legionary a combined javelin-thrower and stabbing swordsman added considerably to the firepower of the legion as it advanced to the attack. As many an excavated skeleton has shown, the *pilum* had impressive penetration and made a neat hole in bone. A *pilum* head was just as efficient if stopped by shield or armour, for it tended to go in deep enough to be held firmly and make extraction difficult. The light *pila* introduced by Marius were riveted with a wooden dowel, making the wooden shaft break off on impact and preventing the weapon from being thrown back.

Other standardized equipment following in the wake of the Marian reforms included a bronze helmet with neck-protecting flange and cheek-pieces, and a mail shirt.

The Second Punic War had also emphasized the need for constant security on campaign, and the new legionary was trained to be his own field engineer. No unit bedded down for the night before the men had dug an encircling ditch, raised an earth rampart and crowned it with a palisade of stakes. As well as his weapons, the legionary now had to carry necessary tools for field engineering, which together weighed about eighty pounds. No wonder the legionaries called themselves the 'mules of Marius' — and with all this deadweight to carry they were trained to march at 20 miles a day. Bridge-building, siegeworks, and the construction of forts were all part of the legionary's job.

Unit reorganization made for tighter structure within the army and

A Roman coin shows the swearing-in of a new recruit for the army

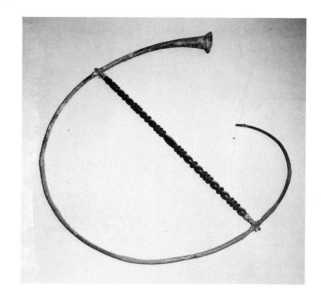

LEFT: A bronze statuette of a Roman legionary.
ABOVE: A *cornu* — the curved war-horn of the Roman army

a closer sense of identification between the legionary and his unit. Marius strengthened the legion to a paper strength of 6,000 men composed of ten cohorts, each of three maniples. The legionary commander or *legatus* was appointed by the general; the *centurions* or commanders of maniples were promoted on merit and service record. The length of service was sixteen years.

These army reforms, expanded and extended to the subject and allied peoples of Rome, would in time produce *auxiliary* regiments with quite as much combat efficiency as a Roman legion. The auxiliaries spoke their own languages, were officered by their own countrymen and used the type of weapon to which they were traditionally accustomed. By the middle of the first century AD they were an integral part of the Roman war machine, and it was quite possible for a general to win a battle with his auxiliaries alone, as Gaius Agricola showed in his victory over the Caledonians in Britain.

In 105 BC, however, there was barely enough time to institute the basics of the Marian army reforms before Rome was facing the biggest threat since Hannibal's invasion. This took the form of massive irruptions by two northern tribal confederations: the Teutones, who approached Italy from southern Gaul, and the Cimbri, coming from the north-east. They turned on Italy because their passage west across the

Rhine was blocked by the Celts of northern Gaul. The Teutones and Cimbri were not operating in close collaboration. Their approach did not constitute a military invasion but their numbers were huge; each group could field about 100,000 warriors. Marius took the field against them with his new legions in 102 and 101 BC. His 'secret weapons' were legionary discipline, volleys of javelins, and above all the deadly stabbing swordplay against which wild slashes with long cutting weapons lost every time. Once the warriors had been broken and scattered, the women, children, and old folk were slaughtered, the legionaries feeling few qualms about butchering barbarians. Marius turned back the Teutones from the Little St Bernard Pass and annihilated them at Aquae Sextiae (Aix-en-Provence) in 102; in the following year he shattered the Cimbri, who had come over the Brenner, at Vercellae on the upper Po. The threat from the north had been lifted at a stroke, and Marius was the hero of the hour.

Unfortunately for Rome, Marius was not content with being the hero of the hour. At the beginning of the first century BC, Marius and the ruthless demagogues who backed him were scheming how to exploit his aura as the saviour of the nation and turn it to political advantage at home. The imminent entry of the army into politics not only cast a heavy shadow over the Roman Republic: it was the Republic's death sentence.

CHAPTER NINE

The Roman Empire

FOR THE BEST PART OF SEVENTY YEARS – from Marius' defeat of the Cimbri in 101 BC to Octavius Caesar's defeat of Marcus Antonius and Cleopatra in 31 BC – the fate of the Republic was decided by the commanders-in-chief of the provincial armies. Without their acquiescence and support, no political regime could survive in Rome for long. But the extraordinary feature of the fall of the Republic was the underlying strength of the ancient Republican ideal. There never was so much lip-service paid to the best interests of the Republic and the good of the state as in the seven decades which encompassed the Republic's death as a political reality. Even the most hardened realist, whether civilian or soldier, who knew in his heart that the interests of the state would best be served by a monarchy, never dared come out in the open and say so. Only one of the provincial commanders-in-chief, Julius Caesar, ventured to beat his rivals, come to Rome, and try to rule as an imperial wolf in republican sheep's clothing. His efforts fooled no one and he lasted barely six months before his rivals assassinated him – in the name of liberty and the Republic.

PRELUDE TO EMPIRE: THE ARMY AND THE CIVIL WARS

The mad power game which destroyed the Republic therefore possessed a powerful set of unwritten rules, the listing of which began with the first consulship of Marius. To get to the top it was essential to secure one of the plum provincial commands and gain control of an army. The next step was to secure the loyalty of that army, so that even if it were demobilized its veterans would flock to their former commander when he called. Nobody mattered who did not command the loyalty of an army – but it was vital to go through the constitutional motions and receive the appointment in the traditional form, no matter how much bribery and bullying was used to secure the right number of votes. Anyone who tried to cut corners and operate outside the constitutional framework instantly branded himself as a public enemy, with every man's hand against him. The most notorious example of this infringement of the rules was the 'Catiline Conspiracy' of 64–63 BC, when Lucius Sergius Catilina resorted to subversion after two unsuccessful runs for a consulship.

Having gained command of an army, the next requirement was a successful campaign or two to win the respect of the troops and at least a token vote of thanks from the Senate in Rome. There were plenty of opportunities for military glory in the first century BC, both in Italy and the provinces. Some were comparatively cheap, like the crushing of the Italian rebels and the slave revolt of Spartacus; other campaigns, deliberately undertaken to boost the political prestige of the commander concerned, were desperately hard-fought, like Caesar's conquest of Gaul. And one of these politically-motivated campaigns, Crassus' invasion of Parthia, produced the greatest Roman military disaster since Cannae (see p. 195). For this reason the steady dissolution of the Roman Republic proceeded against an unprecedented spate of military campaigns and conquests, all of them ostentatiously undertaken for the security or glory of the Roman Republic.

But the *leitmotiv* of the political turmoil at home and the military activity in the provinces was the power-struggle between the *populares* and the *optimates*: the radicals and the conservatives. It was virtually impossible for an ambitious general to be neutral: he had to side with one or the other. This produced three distinct collisions between rival generals in the seventy years after Vercellae: Marius and Sulla; Julius Caesar, Pompeius, and Crassus; Lepidus, Marcus Antonius, and Octavius Caesar.

Marius was the first army commander to throw his hat into the political ring: as the saviour of the Republic after the defeat of the Teutones and Cimbri, he stood forth as the hero of the *populares*. The first chance for the *optimates* to establish a military champion of their own persuasion came with the Italian revolt of 91–88 BC, generally known as the 'Social War', which should be translated as the 'war against the allies' (*socii*). Marius took the field and crushed the northern rebels; the *optimate* Lucius Cornelius Sulla finished off the southern rebels in 88. At this moment Rome was faced with a formidable new challenge in Asia Minor: Mithridates IV of Pontus, who seized on Rome's troubles at home as the ideal chance to expel the Romans from Asia. A new command was decreed for the war against Mithridates: Sulla, elected consul for the year 88, received this Asian command, and moved south to prepare for the crossing to Greece.

The demagogues of the *populares* reacted to this by a decree of their own which gave the command to Marius. Sulla marched his army to Rome and drove Marius out of Italy, but as soon as Sulla went to Asia Minor in 87 BC Marius returned. He and the *populares* indulged in a gory 'proscription' or purge of the *optimates*. Marius was elected consul for 86 BC but he died – old, mad, and bloody-minded to the last – just after taking up his seventh consulship. His successor, Flaccus, went out to Asia with a new army to take over from Sulla in 84 BC. Meanwhile Sulla had beaten Mithridates and pushed him out of Roman Asia, ably seconded by Lucius Lucullus. He was dictating peace terms when Flaccus arrived in Asia only to be murdered and replaced as commander by the legate Fimbria. Sulla won over the whole of Fimbria's army, leaving Fimbria with no choice but to commit suicide. He was now free to return to Italy as the glorious conqueror of Mithridates and, with the

OPPOSITE: A coin celebrating the triumph of Sulla; he was the only Roman soldier-statesman of the Civil Wars to die in his bed

PREVIOUS PAGE: Roman legionaries, holding close formation, carve their way into the enemy ranks.

approval of the *optimate*-dominated Senate, to exact revenge on the *populares*.

Sulla landed at Brundisium in 83 BC and began a cautious advance on Rome. The *populares* had enlisted the help of a Samnite army which Sulla repulsed from Rome in the battle of the Colline Gate in 82 BC. He and his army were now absolute masters of Rome, but he contrived to stay within a hair's breadth of constitutional precedent in securing the legal authority for the punishment of the *populares*. He revived the old office of dictator, appointment to which had always involved an acute national crisis. This Sulla respected: he had himself appointed 'dictator for the purpose of restoring the State', and announced another terrible proscription. The money and property from this proscription was, of course, used for rewarding his veterans and political supporters. Sulla had no intention of holding onto his extremely precarious eminence for a moment longer than necessary. He announced a series of constitutional reforms to restore the old style of Republican government, of which the most important was the banning of successive consulships to prevent another Marius from coming to power. Then, in 79 BC, Sulla retired to enjoy life and write his memoirs, dying in the following year at the age of sixty.

Sulla's dictatorship put the *optimates* firmly in the saddle in Rome but leaders of the *populares* continued to cause trouble in Italy and the provinces. One of Sulla's *protégés*, Gnaeus Pompeius, crushed the *populares* in Spain and northern Italy in 77–72 BC. Then came the great slave revolt under Spartacus in 73–71 BC. This was tackled by another of Sulla's men, Marcus Crassus, a singularly unpleasant character who had made himself a millionaire by buying up the property left by victims of the proscription. Pompeius joined forces with Crassus to stamp out the revolt and the two of them earned the consulship for 70 BC. Meanwhile their only serious rival, Lucullus, was doing brilliantly in Asia Minor in a resumption of the war with Mithridates. He beat Mithridates and his ally Tigranes of Armenia and planned the conquest of Armenia. This started well in 69 BC with victory over Tigranes at Tigranocerta, but Lucullus made one fatal mistake. He failed to obtain fresh troops for his command and made his bid for glory in Armenia with soldiers who had first gone out to Asia Minor twenty years before, under Flaccus. They mutinied and forced Lucullus to pull back to the province of Asia, which had been bled white by the Mithridatic wars. Lucullus' attempts to relieve the financial burden on the citizens of Asia earned him no thanks at Rome and he was replaced by Pompeius.

Pompeius took over the programme of Lucullus and pursued it with extraordinary success. In 66–65 BC he hounded Mithridates to exile and suicide in the Crimea, took Syria, pushed southward and took Jerusalem in 64 BC, then set about reorganizing the territories east of the Dardanelles to Rome's advantage. He added three new provinces (Bithynia-Pontus, Cilicia, and Syria) and left the rest (eastern Pontus, Cappadocia, Galatia, Lycia, and Judea) as client-kingdoms of Rome. In 61 he returned home with his army. There was the greatest alarm in Rome, and memories of the return of Sulla were keen. But Pompeius chose to observe the rules. He dismissed his army and returned to Rome

as a private citizen. By this time both Pompeius and Crassus were estranged from the Senate. Their candidature for the consulship in 70 had shown how empty Sulla's settlement really was (neither man had been eligible) and both now began to court the *populares*' support.

In this they were first helped, then reconciled one with the other, by Gaius Julius Caesar, a protégé of Crassus as Crassus had been a protégé of Sulla. Caesar was the man of the age *par excellence*. His aunt Julia was Marius' widow, an accident of birth which brought Caesar to within an inch of proscription by Sulla. Born in 102 BC, he grew up a natural supporter of the *populares*, entering politics in 68 BC first as *quaestor* and then (66 BC) as *aedile*. These city magistracies gave him excellent chances of improving his reputation with the *populares*, though he ran deep into debt and only kept his head above water thanks to the financial backing of Crassus. It was Caesar who urged Crassus to reach agreement with Pompeius for a tripartite division of power. He himself was desperate for a military command with prestige; Pompeius wanted his settlement of the east ratified by the Senate and a generous land settlement for his veterans; Crassus wanted tax reductions to swell his immense personal fortune. The result was the First Triumvirate of 60 BC, which, like Sulla's dictatorship, stopped just short of being a flagrant breach of the constitution.

The Senate gave way to the demands of the Triumvirs largely from fears of what Pompeius could do if he chose to exploit his popularity with the army. The appointment of Caesar as *proconsul* of Gaul, with an extraordinary tenure of five years, was an excellent way of getting rid of Caesar for five years. Caesar's ties with Pompeius were strengthened by the marriage of Pompeius to Caesar's daughter Julia.

THE CONQUEST OF GAUL

Caesar was forty-four years old when he took up his command in Gaul in 59 BC. There was no reason to believe that he would accomplish anything worthy of note, for apart from the normal scraps of military service as a young man he had never even commanded a single legion. Faced with the martial but woefully disunited Celts of Gaul, plus the political necessity of conquering them as quickly as possible, he based his strategy on speed and mobility. The latter qualities he sought and found in the Gallic cavalry which he recruited in his province together with the famous 10th Legion, which he made uniquely his own.

It took him four years to defeat the tribes of central and northern Gaul, and he had to start by eliminating a twin threat to the province of 'Gaul-beyond-the-Alps': the enclave of Roman-controlled territory on the lower Rhône. First he beat the Helvetii, who had moved out of Switzerland, at Bibracte (Autun), then the Germans under Ariovistus who had crossed the Rhine in great strength. His campaign in 57 BC temporarily broke the Belgae and Nervii in the north-west, then (in 56 BC) the Veneti of Brittany and the Aquitani of the south-west. He rounded out his operations in Gaul with two demonstrations of Roman versatility: a fortnight's campaign on the east bank of the Rhine, which he spanned with his famous bridge; and two forays across the Channel to Britain. The first British expedition was hardly more than a reconnaissance in force; the second, in 54 BC, broke the tribal confederation dominating the south-east of the island and pushed across the Thames.

The Triumvirate began to break up in 54 BC – despite an attempt to keep it in being by a meeting of the three men at Luca in 56 – when Julia died. Caesar's run of victories in Gaul stung Crassus into requesting command of an eastern expedition to conquer the Parthians, who had moved into the vacuum created by the destruction of Mithridates and the Seleucid Empire. He marched east with seven legions in 53 BC.

The Parthian expedition was contemptible as an example of political expediency and personal greed (Crassus was hoping to gain the sole monopoly of Rome's eastern trade-routes). As a military proposition it was a most salutary reminder that the legion had severe limitations as an all-conquering weapon. The auxiliary cavalry attached to the legions was wiped out in its first clash with the Parthian *cataphracts* and the legions were left wholly unprotected against the fire of the Parthian mounted archers. The army was cut off when it was already in full retreat to the west, trapped and shot to pieces in the open desert near the frontier-town of Carrhae. Crassus and 20,000 of his men were killed and another 10,000 surrendered. In the long term there was to be repeated pressure for a war of revenge against Parthia; in the short term the disaster only hastened the clash between Caesar and Pompeius.

By the end of 53 BC Pompeius' supremacy seemed assured. Crassus had met with disaster in Syria and Caesar was fighting desperately against a massive revolt by the tribes of Gaul. Caesar's scattered forces all came under attack in their forts, attacks made all the more dangerous because the Gauls had learned from the first conquest and copied the Romans' siege tactics. Caesar spent 53 BC in relieving the garrisons beleaguered by the revolt and in putting down the Belgae of the north. During the winter of 53–52 BC Caesar was in northern Italy, raising two more legions in 'Nearer Gaul'; and he was still on the wrong side of the Alps when he heard that the whole of occupied Gaul had broken out under a national leader, Vercingetorix.

The story of Caesar's campaign against Vercingetorix, as told in Caesar's own commentary *The Gallic War*, makes many of the campaigns of the Second Punic War look tame by comparison. It was the hardest-fought of all Caesar's campaigns. Vercingetorix was no mere tribal leader but a gifted strategist. Realizing that Gallic tribesmen could never match the discipline of the legions in pitched battles, he set out to wear the Romans down in prolonged sieges of the huge Celtic hill forts. Repelled at Gergovia in the *Massif Central*, Caesar tried again when Vercingetorix withdrew to the heights of Alesia (Mont Auxois). This was one of the most extraordinary battles ever fought by a Roman army. Caesar refused to waste his strength in assaulting Vercingetorix's positions; but he knew that by maintaining the siege he had put himself on the defensive against the huge Gallic masses summoned by Vercingetorix. The Gallic leader, in short, had made the besieging Romans the meat in the sandwich.

Caesar made full use of his time before the relieving forces arrived. He tightened the ring round Vercingetorix with massive siege-works, and defended the outer perimeter with belts of concealed defences which

were the direct ancestors of the modern anti-personnel mine. There were trenches filled with sharpened stakes ('Tombstones'), concealed pits each containing a sharpened stake ('Lilies'), and buried blocks of wood with iron hooks in them ('Spurs' or 'Goads'). This enabled the besiegers to beat the relieving force while containing Vercingetorix's attempts to break out.

The crux of the battle was the inability of the Gauls to achieve split-second timing in their attacks, which left Caesar with just enough leeway to fight on both 'fronts' – inner and outer – without being overwhelmed. Alesia was the supreme effort of the Gauls. When the relief army had been savaged and dispersed, and it was obvious that he would never get out, Vercingetorix surrendered to Caesar with the ironic comment: 'I hand myself over to you to deal with as you think best. You can either win the favour of the Romans by putting me to death, or you can surrender me to them alive'. Caesar chose the latter course, which came to the same end: Vercingetorix was kept alive until Caesar's triumph six years later, then killed in a dungeon of the Capitol.

Alesia ranks as one of the greatest of all Roman victories. With 65,000 men, Caesar had pinned down 80,000 Gauls and fought off 250,000 more. He had also captured the one man who had proved himself capable of giving the Gauls effective leadership. With Vercingetorix in Roman hands the great revolt collapsed. Eighteen months of implacable mopping-up followed, but by the time Caesar left Gaul in

ABOVE LEFT: Julius Caesar, the great exemplar of the excellence of the Roman war machine by the middle first century BC. When Caesar first received an independent command he was a middle-aged maverick politician with little military experience.
ABOVE RIGHT: One of Caesar's Gallic captives, from the triumphant arch at Carpentras

51 the fighting spirit of the Gauls had been broken. The conquest of Gaul could never have been achieved in so short a time if the Gauls themselves (on both sides of the Alps) had not been such magnificent fighters, highly suitable for recruitment and training in Roman tactics. Caesar had proved himself to be as great a military organizer of troops as Marius had been. Between 59–52 BC he had raised five new legions and trained them to become magnificent fighting units.

Looked at in general terms, the conquest of Gaul had kept honours even in the propaganda war between Caesar and Pompeius. The latter had conquered Syria and Palestine in the east; Caesar had conquered Gaul in the west. Pompeius had marched as far as the Caspian Sea; Caesar had crossed the Channel to 'conquer' Britain. But there had been a price to pay: while Caesar had been fighting in Gaul, Pompeius had been in Rome, putting down the bully-boys of the *populares* and consolidating his position as the champion of the Senate. In 52 Pompeius reached the zenith of his power: the Senate named him sole consul. When the appointed span of Caesar's command in Gaul ran out at the end of 50 BC, the Senate tried to browbeat Caesar into submission by naming him a public enemy unless he immediately disbanded his forces. To this Caesar reacted by crossing the Rubicon brook, the boundary between 'Nearer Gaul' and Italy, and marching on Rome with his army in January 49 BC.

The Senate and their military figurehead now found themselves acutely embarrassed for the want of troops, which were now the only way of imposing the *optimates'* will on Caesar. The government fled from Rome, with Pompeius heading for Greece to assemble an army there. Caesar arrived in Rome with no more authority than that of Supreme Pontiff, which post he had held since 62 BC. But he secured the appointment as dictator by an emergency government convened by the city *praetor* Marcus Lepidus, whose family had a strong tradition of support for the *populares*. Even at this supreme opportunity, the obsession with constitutional etiquette prevailed, Caesar was made dictator with the task of making possible the regular holding of elections and keeping the state intact, which meant free from civil war. In this his two weapons were what was already being called *Caesarina celeritas* – 'Caesar-speed' – and disarming friendliness towards all opponents. The former quality was made possible by the network of military roads spanning the provinces; the latter, by avoiding the horror of another proscription and the perpetuating of blood-feuds, aimed at a general reconciliation.

Caesar did not rush headlong after Pompeius; instead he disbanded or won over the cadres of the ten Italian legions which could have been formed by the Pompeians. He then headed for Spain to 'take out' the Pompeian forces, which he outmanoeuvred and blockaded at Ilerda. By the end of 49 BC he was master of Italy, Gaul, Spain, Sicily, Sardinia, and Corsica. Pompeius meanwhile had assembled a powerful army in Greece; he also controlled the Adriatic and planned an invasion of Italy in the spring. This was anticipated by Caesar, who scraped up enough ships to cross to Epirus. But when Caesar tried to blockade Pompeius' 50,000, wintering in Dyrrhachium, with his own 20,000, he found that

Makers and guardians of the empire

BELOW: The growth of the Roman Empire with a list of the major opponents which the legions had to contend with. In military terms Britain proved a costly investment, requiring three legions for a province which was not — as with the Rhine or Danube — vital to the security of the empire. The legions did not patrol the frontiers: this was left to auxiliary units organized in cohorts. While the auxiliaries manned the border forts and handled frontier skirmishes, the men of the legions were stationed in permanent garrison towns, which they left only in new campaigns of conquest or to repel full-scale barbarian irruptions. Many auxiliary units, however, became formidable fighting units in their own right. When Agricola invaded Scotland in 84 AD, his decisive victory at Mons Grapius was won by the auxiliary cohorts — Batavians and Tungrians from the Low Countries, not native-born hillsmen — without the legions getting into action at all.

The illustrations on the right show the evolution of the legionary from the Civil Wars of the first century BC to Trajan's Dacian campaign, with the introduction of segmented plate armour, the straight-sided shield, and the lead-weighted *pilum* or javelin to give the latter additional range. The levy of citizens which had formed the early republican armies proved inadequate to meet the demands of long foreign campaigns, and it was the consul Marius at the end of the second century BC who introduced the idea of a permanent professional army.

The early legionaries had had to supply their own equipment, and this was reflected in the different types of legionary with varying levels of armament. One of Marius' reforms was that the new professional legionaries who served for twenty-five years should receive a level of pay sufficient to equip themselves identically with body-armour, a helmet, shield, short sword, and two javelins.

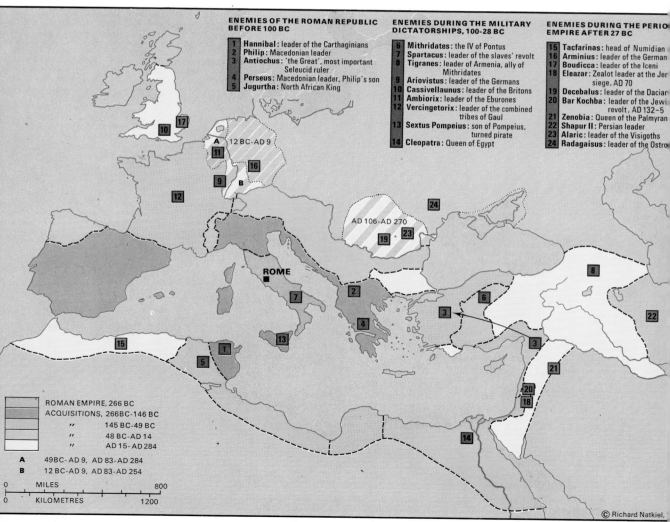

ENEMIES OF THE ROMAN REPUBLIC BEFORE 100 BC
1. **Hannibal**: leader of the Carthaginians
2. **Philip**: Macedonian leader
3. **Antiochus**: 'the Great', most important Seleucid ruler
4. **Perseus**: Macedonian leader, Philip's son
5. **Jugurtha**: North African King

ENEMIES DURING THE MILITARY DICTATORSHIPS, 100-28 BC
6. **Mithridates**: the IV of Pontus
7. **Spartacus**: leader of the slaves' revolt
8. **Tigranes**: leader of Armenia, ally of Mithridates
9. **Ariovistus**: leader of the Germans
10. **Cassivellaunus**: leader of the Britons
11. **Ambiorix**: leader of the Eburones
12. **Vercingetorix**: leader of the combined tribes of Gaul
13. **Sextus Pompeius**: son of Pompeius, turned pirate
14. **Cleopatra**: Queen of Egypt

ENEMIES DURING THE PERIO[D] EMPIRE AFTER 27 BC
15. **Tacfarinas**: head of Numidian
16. **Arminius**: leader of the German
17. **Boudicca**: leader of the Iceni
18. **Eleazar**: Zealot leader at the Jer[usalem] siege, AD 70
19. **Decebalus**: leader of the Dacian
20. **Bar Kochba**: leader of the Jewi[sh] revolt, AD 132-5
21. **Zenobia**: Queen of the Palmyran
22. **Shapur II**: Persian leader
23. **Alaric**: leader of the Visigoths
24. **Radagaisus**: leader of the Ostro[goths]

ROMAN EMPIRE, 266 BC
ACQUISITIONS, 266BC-146 BC
" 145 BC-49 BC
" 48 BC-AD 14
" AD 15-AD 284

A 49BC- AD 9, AD 83-AD 284
B 12BC-AD 9, AD 83-AD 254

MILES 0 — 800
KILOMETRES 0 — 1200

© Richard Natkiel,

RIGHT: Mail-shirted Civil War legionary in battle order. FAR RIGHT: The formidable weight of kit carried by a legionary on the march – hence the famous nickname 'mules of Marius'. Each man had three days' rations, plus a saw, pickaxe, sickle, and bucket. This is a legionary of the first century AD with segmented plate armour. BELOW: Legionary hurling his lead-weighted *pilum*; with a charging auxiliary in foreground. Both are of Trajan's time

what had worked at Alesia against Gallic warriors did not work against trained troops, and was driven off. The initiative passed to Pompeius, who tried clumsily to manoeuvre Caesar into a corner in Greece. There is now general agreement that the story told by Caesar in *The Civil War* is misleading, and that at the end Pompeius managed to surprise Caesar at Pharsalus. The decisive battle fought there in August 48 BC was a classic example of a smaller army depriving a larger army, with all the advantages in cavalry and missile troops, of the tactical initiative. Caesar deployed for reserves in depth rather than make an attempt to match the breadth of the Pompeian front. He defended his right flank with a stack of infantry cohorts who used their *pila* as stabbing-spears to repel Pompeius' cavalry, charged the Pompeian centre before it could charge him, and tipped the scale by throwing in his rearmost troops at the crucial moment. The Pompeian army at Pharsalus was certainly not a disorganized shambles, relying purely on the weight of numbers; but it had been promised an easy time by its lack-lustre supreme commander and was certainly thrown off balance by the fierce confidence displayed by Caesar's troops.

Pompeius soon abandoned hopes of raising a fresh army in Syria and took ship for Egypt. He was not so much hoping for political asylum as for the return of a favour which the Triumvirate had done King Ptolemy XI, sending a Roman army to restore Ptolemy to his throne in 55 BC. A token Roman 'army of occupation' had remained, and this was Pompeius' real objective in Egypt. It was his misfortune that he arrived at a moment when young Ptolemy XII had driven out his sister and co-ruler, Cleopatra. Ptolemy's advisers decided to curry more favour with Rome by killing Pompeius, the news of which greeted Caesar when he arrived at Alexandria in hot pursuit of his beaten enemy, with only two legions and 800 cavalry. This tiny force was blockaded in Alexandria throughout the winter of 48–47 until relieved by the army of Mithridates of Pergamon, whose support Caesar had taken the precaution of enlisting. His romance with Cleopatra caused him to establish her as the new ruler of Egypt: a new client-kingdom for Rome. A lightning campaign in Syria removed the last threat to stability in the east, with Caesar defeating Pharnaces, son of Mithridates of Pontus, at Zela in August 47 BC.

Caesar's last campaigns crushed the last pockets of Pompeian resistance in the west. In the first six months of 46 BC he smashed the army of Pompeius' son Sextus at Thapsus in Africa and reduced the kingdom of Numidia, which had supported Pompeius, as a new province. Sextus Pompeius escaped to Spain and raised an army which Caesar crushed with immense slaughter in March 45 BC.

After Munda, Caesar was, in effect, sole ruler of a world empire, for which he now had to contrive a new form of government with the institutions of the old. He might have got away with it if he had settled for a periodic renewal either of the consulship or dictatorship, but he made the fatal mistake of taking the title of dictator for life in 44 BC. This was the direct cause of his assassination on 15 March of that year, when he was planning a great rallying war against Parthia to avenge the destruction of Crassus' army. Comments on his generalship are almost superfluous, but the speed and versatility of his operations certainly rank

ABOVE RIGHT: Golden *aureus* of Marcus Antonius, with a warship on the reverse. With Cleopatra of Egypt (*above*) supplying the financial sinews of war, Antonius relied heavily on his formidable eastern Mediterranean fleet until this was neatly blockaded at Actium by Agrippa

him with Alexander. Caesar took much the same risks, and the few mistakes he made were the result of taking on odds which were too great – mistakes which his resilience enabled him to recoup. As a trainer and inspirer of troops he was second to none.

The assassination of Caesar set the power game in motion again. The conspirators had nothing but a vague cause, and abandoned first Rome and then Italy to the Caesarians under Marcus Antonius and Lepidus. Caesar's eighteen-year-old son, Gaius Octavius, played his first masterstroke by adopting the name of Caesar and made the third element of the Second Triumvirate of 43 BC. He and Antonius eliminated the army which the conspirators Brutus and Cassius had managed to assemble in Thrace, defeating it at Philippi in 42 BC. Then the politics began. By 39 BC Lepidus had been manoeuvred into subservience in Africa and Octavius and Antonius were lining up as rivals for a final struggle. An inhibiting factor to all parties was Sextus Pompeius, who had lived as an increasingly successful pirate since Munda, and had seized control of Sicily by 39 BC. This enabled him to threaten Rome's overseas grain supplies and intrigue with all three of the Triumvirs.

The last act began in 36 BC when Octavius' new fleet, commanded by Marcus Agrippa, broke the assembled fleet of Sextus Pompeius, and left Sicily lying like a bone between two dogs. Lepidus came across from Africa and was bidding fair for the conquest of Sicily until his legions came into contact with those of Octavius, when they deserted *en masse* to the magic name of Caesar. Antonius meanwhile, hopelessly infatuated with Cleopatra, tried to revive an increasingly tarnished reputation by invading Parthia. Although humiliatingly defeated, he managed to withdraw to Armenia and returned to Egypt. A savage campaign of propaganda preceded the final clash between Octavius and Antonius, though Octavius finally took the field in 31 BC in a war declared only against Cleopatra.

The last great battle of the civil wars was fought off the Bay of Actium on 2 December 31 BC, between fleets of over 200 warships a side. It was decided by the defection of the Egyptian squadron under Cleopatra, whom Antonius immediately followed. This gave Agrippa, commanding the Caesarian fleet, a decisive advantage in numbers after

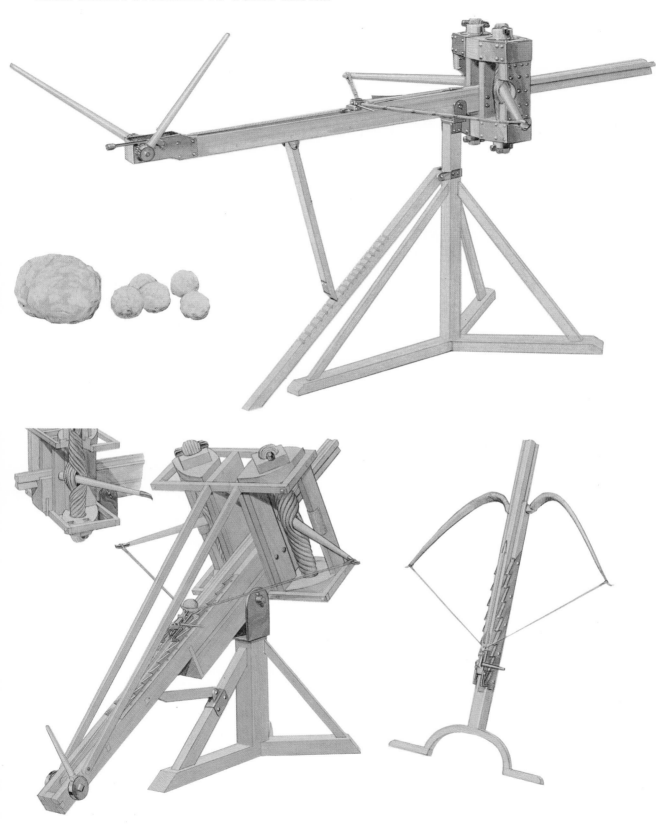

The deadly arts of siege warfare

Though the Assyrians were the first masters of siege warfare it was the Greeks who introduced field and siege artillery, using catapults. One of the earliest known catapults was the fourth-century belly-bow (BOTTOM LEFT). This ancestor of the medieval crossbow was cocked by the marksman placing the stock end on the ground, resting his stomach on the curved bar, and leaning on the bar with all his weight. The Macedonians perfected larger catapults whose separate arms were mounted in springs of twisted sinew or hair (BOTTOM FAR LEFT). Weapons like this were used throughout the Roman period to throw either rocks or heavy bolts (ABOVE LEFT) – either at or from walls, or against enemy troop concentrations. By the time of Caesar the Romans were adept at siege tactics as was shown in Titus' siege of Jerusalem (ABOVE) which lasted six months and demanded the efforts of four legions – X which camped on the Mount of Olives (1), and the V, XII and XV which camped at first to the north-east (2) and then moved closer as the outer walls were breached (3 and 4) and a siege line established (A). The arrows show the successive Roman assaults into the citadel (B) and the temple area (C)

223

an extremely hard-fought opening engagement. The Antonian ships fought gallantly after being deserted by their commander but were progressively captured or burned. Actium gave Octavius the complete control of the Mediterranean. After a brief campaign in Egypt early in 30 BC, both Antony and Cleopatra committed suicide and left Octavius where Julius Caesar had been after Munda, fifteen years before: master of the Roman world.

THE SETTLEMENT OF AUGUSTUS (27 BC–AD 14)

Though mediocre in most ways in comparison to Julius Caesar, Octavius (who accepted the title of 'Augustus' in 27 BC) had one priceless advantage: political caution. Surviving, then dominating after the assassination of Julius had made him determined never to accept the extravagant honours which had cut down his adoptive father. Ostensible reluctance and caution were the keynotes of the political settlement of 27 BC, which brought the Roman Empire into existence as a monarchy in all but name.

Augustus operated by claiming to be the instrument and servant of the Senate. He took personal control of the provinces in which the permanent presence of troops was required: the Senate ran the others. The provinces with the troops were of course the only ones that mattered: Syria on the Parthian frontier, Egypt, Galatia in the middle of Asia Minor, Illyricum, Gaul, and Spain. Augustus refused to embark on further grandiose conquests: he concentrated on trying to find a stable set of frontiers behind which the unified Roman world could live in peace. He made a treaty with Parthia in 20 BC which recovered the standards lost by Crassus at Carrhae. This added immensely to his reputation; but his attempt to set up a stable frontier in the north-west led to a military disaster on the same scale as Carrhae.

This was the attempt to conquer Germany as far as the Elbe and so set up a buffer against future pressure on the western empire from the east. Unfortunately the German tribes found themselves a leader, Arminius, of the same quality as Vercingetorix in Gaul. He trapped and annihilated three legions under Quinctilius Varus, who tried to march through the *Teutoburgerwald* in AD 9. After this disaster Augustus contented himself with the frontiers of the Atlantic, the Rhine, the Danube, and the Euphrates, and advised his successors to do the same.

For the army, the ultimate source of his power, Augustus put through far-reaching reforms. Its main task now became the defence of the frontiers and the policing of the provinces, which enabled Augustus to reduce it by over half. From seventy legions he had cut it down to under thirty by his death. The army became a professional long-service force, with discharged veterans receiving a pension from a state fund financed by death duties. The troops took an oath of allegiance to Augustus as commander-in-chief and the renewal of this oath became one of the first acts of Augustus' successors. Far more important was the new position of the auxiliary forces which were recruited in the imperial provinces in the cohorts of 500 for the infantry and *alae* ('wings') of 500 for the cavalry. These not only made up half of the empire's defence forces: they were one of the most potent instruments of Romanization

Three Roman memorials acknowledging the blessings of seapower. Being soldiers rather than sailors, the Romans developed their warships as large, heavy platforms designed to carry about 120 troops, with the oars arranged in bireme or trireme fashion (see page 143). Their basic tactic was to come alongside an opponent and drop a gangplank with a spike (the *corvus*) in one end to hold it in the enemy's deck so that the marines could charge across supported by missiles thrown or fired from towers at bow and stern. These methods worked well against the Carthaginians and Philip of Macedon, but as Roman control over the Mediterranean was consolidated, lighter faster vessels had to be developed to deal with the pirates who had flourished during the civil wars. Two of these *Liburnians* can be seen in the right-hand illustration on page 233

throughout the empire. The standing rule for auxiliary units was that they were never to serve in the country of their origin, an obvious and enduring precaution against provincial revolts.

The most fateful institution of Augustus was a hangover from the civil wars, when the candidates for supreme power learned the importance of offering the troops the highest incentives for loyalty. This was the Praetorian Guard, nine cohorts of 1,000 men each, commanded by a prefect appointed by the head of state. An elite corps for the defence of Italy and the capital, the Praetorian Guard inevitably became a deadly instrument in time of disputed succession. The Guard 'made' its first emperor, Claudius, as early as AD 41. It reached rock bottom in AD 193 when it murdered the new emperor Pertinax and put the empire up to auction, promising to support the candidate who came up with the biggest cash payment. The dissolution of the corps by Constantine (who reigned from AD 306–337) was long overdue.

All in all, the reorganized and redeployed Roman army at the death of Augustus numbered some 300,000 men – a diminutive force with which to defend the long frontiers of the civilized world. But the civil wars of the previous century had made the army a superb fighting instrument, although they had also shown that the legions of the provinces could, under ambitious and selfish leadership, be the central government's biggest enemy. The acid test of an efficient Roman emperor was the quality of the men whom he appointed to be provincial commanders-in-chief with two or more legions under their command. After Augustus the emperor depended on the army, but the army also depended on the emperor to look after its interests by giving it

LEFT and RIGHT: The Roman fort at Chesters on Hadrian's Wall is typical of the permanent garrison forts which were established all over the empire. The playing-card shape of the simple Roman marching-camp has been expanded to accommodate a permanent garrison.

BELOW: The Roman base at Richborough, Kent, shows the impact of nearly four centuries of Roman occupation. Inside the original fort the cross-shaped foundation of the monument built to commemorate the conquest of Britain stands out clearly. The massive outer walls with their projecting bastions were built when Richborough became a key link in the 'Saxon Shore' defence system in the third and fourth centuries AD

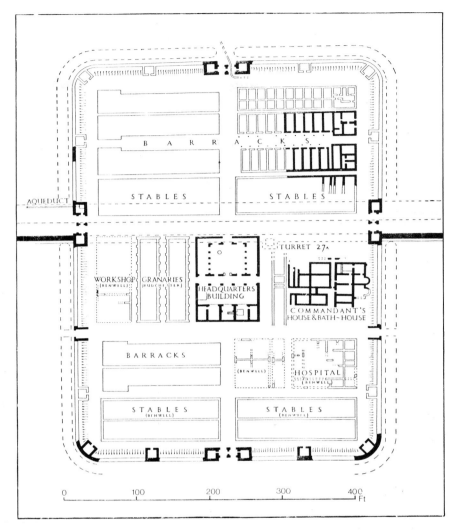

commanders of a sufficiently high calibre. Nothing less than the stability and survival of the empire depended on the observance of this vital unwritten contract.

The tremendous upheavals caused by imperial civil wars in the third and fourth centuries AD obscure the fact that for the first 224 years of the empire – 27 BC–AD 197 – this unwritten contract was observed. In that period the Praetorians only set up two emperors – Claudius in AD 41 and Didius Julianus in AD 193 – and there were only two sets of civil wars between rival generals (AD 68 and AD 193–197). It was also during those 224 years that the last two provinces, Britain and Dacia, were added to the empire, the fixed military frontiers or *limes* were first planned and constructed, and that the empire reached its most defensible condition.

This long period of comparative tranquillity was due in no small measure to the lack of serious pressure on the frontiers of the empire. In the east the old enemy, the kingdom of Parthia, was in decline, and there were no massed barbarian movements on the Rhine or Danube fronts until the middle of the second century AD. Had this not been the case it would never have been possible for Claudius to send four legions into Britain in AD 43.

The conquest of Britain – or, to put it more accurately, the *partial* conquest of Britain – is of the highest interest as far as the evolution of the Roman army was concerned. For a start, the four legions of the conquest can be identified, and it is clear that by the middle of the first century the legions of Rome now had that essential attribute of any professional army: the living traditions and *esprit de corps* of famous regiments. The legions of the invasion were the 9th *Hispana* ('Spanish'), transferred from its previous station on the lower Danube; the 2nd *Augusta* ('Majestic') from Strasbourg; the 14th *Gemina* ('Twin') from Mainz, and the 20th *Victrix* ('Victorious') from Cologne. These crossed the Channel from Boulogne under the supreme command of Aulus Plautius and established a secure base camp at Richborough in Kent.

The motive for the invasion has always been a topic of debate. Britain certainly posed no military threat to the Romans in Gaul, and can have been no more than a diplomatic nuisance: a natural refuge for trouble-makers and criminals who would have been hunted down anywhere else in the empire. The petty kingdom of Verica in Sussex had appealed for Roman protection against the Catuvellauni, the dominant British tribal confederation in the south-east of the island, but that was hardly sufficient motive for the invasion. It does seem, however, that Claudius was acutely aware of his non-military reputation and embarrassing status as the 'soldiers' emperor', the creature of the Praetorians. He was not a general of proven ability, as Augustus and Tiberius (AD 14–37) had been; nor had he been taken on campaign in his boyhood by a famous father and been adopted as the mascot of the legions of the Rhine, as in the case of the third emperor, Gaius 'Caligula' (AD 37–41), whose very nickname meant 'little army boot'. Claudius was a civilian nonentity in the most vulnerable position in the world and he must have been very keen to gain the respect of the army by waging a new campaign of conquest. He had the sense not to lead the invasion in

An ornate cavalry helmet, with vizor contoured to fit the face, from the first century AD

person, but to 'leave it to the professionals' – though he did make one mistake on the eve of the invasion, which shows how touchy the legionaries could be. He sent his freed slave Narcissus to give the 14th *Gemina* their marching orders at Mainz, and the troops took it as an insult when Narcissus tried to harangue them. A mutiny threatened until some nameless joker in the crowd bellowed 'Up the Saturnalia!' (the Roman festival of misrule when slaves dressed in their masters' robes and gave orders); and the resentment of the troops evaporated in a roar of laughter.

Though the real motive for the invasion remains a mystery the military objective does not. This was to establish a permanent military presence in the south-east of Britain, with Rome conferring client status on all former enemies of the Catuvellauni. The expeditionary force was therefore able to cross the Thames with its left flank safeguarded by the compliance of Cogidumnus, the new client-king of Sussex who was given the unusually exalted status of 'king and emperor's representative'. Claudius is said to have crossed to Britain for the decisive battle which broke the Catuvellauni in Essex, taking at least nominal command and becoming entitled, at last, to a public triumph. The subsequent advance to the north, west, and north-west proceeded after the Iceni and Trinovantes of East Anglia had confirmed their allegiance to Rome.

The most interesting sector of this second phase – exploitation – is that of the 2nd *Augusta*, which undertook the reduction of the south and west under the command of the future emperor Vespasian.

The *Augusta's* line of march took it from the Home Counties through Wiltshire, Dorset, and Devon, angling back to the north-east to establish a tentative frontier base at Gloucester. The biggest problem Vespasian had to tackle was the innumerable fortified strongholds (misleadingly termed 'hill-forts') which menaced his line of communications. The biggest of these, Maiden Castle, is still one of the most breathtaking historical sites in Britain. It is not a fortress: it is a converted hill, two-thirds of a mile long and one-third of a mile across, sculpted into three concentric ramparts 100 feet high and separated by cavernous ditches. Excavations have shown where the men of the *Augusta* broke in, braving dense missile-fire from the crests of the ramparts (at one point a British 'dump' of over 20,000 sling-stones was unearthed). Once the legionaries were inside the ramparts and the grip of the tribesmen on the heights had been broken, the survivors were steadily herded back amid progressive slaughter which did not spare the non-combatants huddled at the centre. The dead were found in shallow graves and they included women, children, and old men. This was the biggest, but by no means the only stronghold stormed by the *Augusta* during its march into the west, which was easily the most ambitious programme undertaken by a single legion during the conquest. And by AD 49 – only six years from the first landings in Kent – the Mendip lead mines were turning out pigs of lead stamped with the *Augusta's* crest.

But the ease of the invasion and initial reduction of Britain was deceptive. The attempt to draw a stable frontier from the Bristol Channel to the Humber proved ineffective against hostile tribes beyond;

Bronze legionary helmet of the first century AD, showing the horizontal plate to protect the neck. The rivet to support the cheek-piece can be seen on the left-hand side

and in the eighteenth year of the occupation the revolt of the Iceni led by Queen Boudicca came very close to throwing the Romans out of the island. The 9th Legion was badly mauled in East Anglia, the 2nd was isolated at Gloucester. Colchester, St Albans, and London were razed amid hideous slaughter; and the governor, Suetonius Paulinus, barely saved the day by abandoning his campaign against the Druids of Anglesey and racing back with the 20th and 14th Legions. The decisive battle (fought on an unknown site) was one of the greatest triumphs of legionary troops over odds of nearly ten to one. If Roman sources are to be believed, nearly 80,000 British tribesmen fell, making the battle as deadly as Cannae. But the crushing of the revolt did not solve the problem of finding a stable frontier. The province was reluctantly expanded to take in the Silures and Ordovices of south and north Wales, then the Brigantes of Yorkshire. Finally, under the governor Gaius Agricola in the early 80s, an attempt was made to solve the running problem of Britain by conquering the whole of the north: the Caledonian Highlands.

Agricola came tantalizingly close to success. He advanced methodically into Caledonia, planting forts as he went, with his fleet in close support along the coast. The fleet circumnavigated the Scottish coast and Agricola reckoned that a single legion would suffice for the conquest and retention of Ireland. At Mons Graupius in AD 84, Agricola shattered the last army of the confederated Caledonian tribes, a victory remarkable for the fact that it was achieved by the auxiliary forces alone, without any intervention by the waiting legions. But Agricola was recalled by the emperor Domitian (AD 81–96) before the decisive occupation of Caledonia could be completed.

Britain was certainly not the only theatre of imperial military activity in the first century, though it saw the most prolonged campaigning. In the late 60s the stabilizing line of succession provided by the Julio-Claudian house finally broke down in the increasingly unpopular reign of Nero (AD 54–68). In AD 68–69 the empire suffered the first civil war caused by generals fighting for the imperial dignity: the 'year of the four emperors'. Servius Galba marched from Spain to oust Nero; Marcus Otho overthrew Galba with the support of the Praetorian Guard; Otho committed suicide in the face of Aulus Vitellius' advance on Rome with the support of the legions of Lower Germany. The eventual victor, however, was Vespasian, commander-in-chief in Judea, who enlisted the aid of the legions of Pannonia on the middle Danube. Unlike the three unsuccessful candidates for the throne, Vespasian was hampered in entering the power game because he had been originally sent out to Judea to crush a most formidable revolt by the Zealot nationalists.

The Jewish revolt of AD 66 crowned a disastrous series of events during the latter reign of Nero, following the Boudiccan revolt in Britain and the devastation of Rome in the Great Fire of AD 64. What the Zealots lacked in troops and weaponry they more than compensated for in fanaticism, seizing Jerusalem and the rock of Masada and defending both places in the teeth of two appalling sieges. Sent to Judea with three legions to crush the revolt, Vespasian started by reducing the

In honour of a terrible victory: a *sestertius* of Vespasian commemorating the sack of Jerusalem by the emperor's son Titus (afterwards emperor himself)

country and the siege of Jerusalem was not fairly begun when he was proclaimed emperor; Vespasian turned the siege over to his son Titus, who carried it through to its terrible conclusion in September AD 70.

The siege of Jerusalem was made all the more appalling because the city was crammed with Jews, mostly non-combatants, who had assembled for the Passover only to find themselves trapped when the siege began. The count of prisoners captured during the siege was 97,000 – but 600,000 died in Jerusalem, where famine and disease were the Romans' main allies. To root out the last defenders the Romans tore the city apart and fired it, amid scenes destined to be hideously re-enacted during the destruction of the Warsaw Ghetto by the Germans in 1943. According to Josephus, the historian of the revolt:

Every man who showed himself was either killed or captured by the Romans, and then those in the sewers were ferreted out, the ground torn up, and all who were trapped were killed. There too were found the bodies of more than 2,000, some killed by their own hand, some by one another's but most by starvation. So foul a stench of human flesh greeted those who charged in that many turned back at once.

But even after Jerusalem fell the horrors of the revolt were not over. The Zealot leader Eleazar and a garrison of 1,000 held out on the rock of Masada until Flavius Silva, governor of Judea, decided to make an end in AD 73. His problem was how to close with the fortifications on top of the rock, for all the approaches were easily defensible. Silva finally decided on an assault plan which stands out as one of the great feats of Roman military engineering, starting with an enormous earth and masonry ramp up the side of the Masada *massif*, the ramp being crowned with a stone causeway to take the weight of siege towers. These were 90 feet tall and covered with iron plates, and just reached to the Zealot defences on the summit. When the outer wall of stone was battered down another wall was found inside, specially designed to stand up to the Roman rams, of huge wooden timbers interspersed with loose earth. After great exertions the Romans managed to set fire to this inner wall, but there was no final battle on the summit. The men of the Zealot garrison had killed their wives and children, and finally themselves, rather than run the risk of capture.

Vespasian and his second son Domitian were the first emperors to plan for the improved defence of the northern frontiers. In AD 73–74 Vespasian began the conquest of the lands forming the acute angle between the headwaters of the Rhine and Danube (*agri decumates*), a process completed by Domitian ten years later. Unlike the costly detachment of four legions in Britain (which Domitian reduced to three legions when he recalled Agricola in AD 85), this new territorial expansion shortened the Roman frontier instead of expanding it, and vastly improved communications between the upper Rhine and Danube. From Domitian's reign the drawing of military frontiers or *limes* continued without a break until the middle of the second century AD. The *limes* network basically consisted of a line of frontier forts connected by a road, shielded by an outer rampart and palisade. Hadrian's Wall in Britain is the enduring example of the *limes* network. This did not seek to

A selection of details from the finest and most comprehensive memorial to the imperial Roman army of the first and second centuries AD: Trajan's Column (LEFT). The Column was built to commemorate Trajan's conquest of Dacia, the last province to be added to the Roman Empire. ABOVE LEFT: Massed standard-bearers tramp across the pontoon bridge over the Danube. Each standard is thickly clustered with its unit's battle honours

TOP CENTRE: After a clash
with the enemy,
legionaries take time out
to erect a battle trophy
featuring Dacian heads
impaled on stakes.
Auxiliaries can be seen on
the right. ABOVE: Two
auxiliaries (*left foreground*)
watch legionaries display
their skills as masons,
building a fort. ABOVE
RIGHT: Troop reinforce-
ments cross the Danube.
In the lower spiral,
Dacians surrender to an
auxiliary unit, watched by
their conquerors

surround the entire empire with an impregnable fortress-wall: there
were never enough troops to man such defences. They have been
described as a 'military tripwire' to prevent hostile forces from suddenly
breaching the frontier without warning, so enabling the legions, lying
behind the *limes* in permanent fortress-towns, to be rushed to the point
of danger. But the building of *limes* was only part of the process of
improving the frontier defences. It was still vital that the Roman army
should, at any given time, be able to dominate a deep belt of territory on
the far side of the frontier, and Domitian failed to prevent the rise of a
hostile new power north of the Danube. This was the kingdom of the
Dacians (modern-day Romania) which, if it were ever to make common
cause with the Marcomanni, Quadi, and Iazyges (in modern Hungary
and Czechoslovakia), would create a highly dangerous hostile combination.

   This was averted by Domitian's successor Trajan (AD 96–117).
After repeated failures to come to a peaceful settlement with the Dacian
king, Decebalus, Trajan conquered Dacia and annexed it as a province,
the final territorial expansion of the Roman Empire. The strategic
function of Dacia was that of a deep bastion on the eastern flank of the
Marcomanni, Iazyges, and Quadi; and the conquest of Dacia was
recorded by 'Trajan's Column' in Rome, a unique monument to the
excellence and versatility of the Roman army at its peak. The graphic
bas-reliefs, ascending the column in a slow spiral, show the Roman

legionaries and auxilaries performing a multitude of tasks of which disciplined tenacity in battle was only one. The most famous of a host of details of the army's equipment is the final stage in the development of legionary armour: the overlapping plate armour or *lorica segmentata*, giving the legionary maximum protection against heavy cutting weapons in hand-to-hand fighting. The Column remains the best visual guide to the Roman army's field equipment and weaponry, both legionary and auxiliary, before the demands of the third century made the heavy armoured cavalryman the most important element in the army.

The Column also shows the troops which Trajan led on the last serious attempt at Roman expansion east of the Euphrates: the Parthian War of AD 116–17. Here at last was the campaign of which Roman generals had dreamed since the days of Crassus. Trajan marched through Armenia and Mesopotamia as far as the Persian Gulf, delineating the new provinces of Mesopotamia and Assyria with the Tigris as the new eastern frontier of the empire. But this splendid vision soon faded. Trajan had not even turned for home when the first revolts broke out and he abandoned his eastern conquests, keeping only Armenia as a bastion against further encroachment from the east. This policy was confirmed by his successor Hadrian (AD 117–38), who toured the empire and personally supervised the improvement of its amenities, both civil and military.

The zenith of the Roman Empire was attained under the long and peaceful reign of Hadrian's successor Antoninius Pius (AD 138–61), but in fact Antoninus was a disastrous steward of the empire's military preparedness. He never left Rome, let alone improved the frontier defences or took action to break up the growing power of the Marcomanni and Quadi north of the Danube. Rome's security by the middle of the second century no longer depended on long periods of peace on the frontiers, but on ceaseless vigilance and the judicious launching of 'pre-emptive strikes' against the barbarian peoples beyond the *limes*. Gibbon, in his *Decline and Fall of the Roman Empire*, waxed lyrical over the felicity of the Roman world under Antoninus, but he failed to see that Antoninus' reign amounted to twenty-three wasted years. It may have been a golden summer, but the harvest reaped by the next emperor, Marcus Aurelius (AD 161–80) was a bitter one. Marcus was obliged to spend the bulk of his reign in constant campaigns on the Danube frontier with the Marcomanni and Quadi. If sufficient action had been taken in the last ten years of Antoninus, the problem could have been scotched at birth and Marcus would have had little trouble in completing the process begun by Vespasian's advance into the *agri decumates* in the previous century. A huge glacis of Roman-controlled territory could have been set up, running along the Elbe to the mountains of Bohemia and finally connecting with the bastion of Dacia. Marcus Aurelius seems to have been working towards this aim when he died in AD 180, still leading the army on the Danube.

Marcus Aurelius let the empire down almost as badly as his predecessor by breaking the pattern of the imperial succession which had been maintained for the past ninety years. This had consisted of each emperor selecting the most suitable man as his successor and adopting

Witness to the weary years of campaigning north of the Danube under Marcus Aurelius: a detail from the Antonine Column in Rome shows the emperor's legions crossing the river

him as his son, thus ensuring a trouble-free transference of power into the right hands. Marcus, however, selected his own son, Commodus, a pleasure-loving, vicious incompetent who lasted for twelve years before being murdered in a palace *coup*. Helvius Pertinax was chosen by the Senate as the next emperor, but in March 193 he was murdered by the Praetorian Guard, who cynically offered the imperial title to the highest bidder. When the millionaire Didius Julianus bought his way on to the throne, the only question was which of the three military contenders would pull him down first. As in the 'year of the four emperors', the challengers came from the western, Danubian, and eastern provinces: Clodius Abinus from Britain, Septimus Severus from Pannonia, and Pescennius Niger from Syria. This time the eventual victor reached Rome first. Severus ousted Julianus after a lightning march on Rome from the Danube, then headed first east to eliminate Niger and west to eliminate Albinus. But it took four gruelling years for Severus to make good his claim to the empire, in which time Britain, emptied of troops by Albinus' march on Rome, was ravaged by the unrestrained tribes of Caledonia.

From the moment the news of the Praetorians' election of Julianus reached the provinces and set the armies marching into civil war, Rome was never to enjoy genuine security again. From time to time a strong emperor emerged – Aurelian (AD 270–75), Diocletian (AD 284–305), Constantine (AD 306–37), and Theodosius (AD 379–95) – but each attempt to create a stable settlement and line of succession was soon ruined by a fresh spate of assassinations, provincial mutinies, and civil wars. After Severus died at York in 211 while restoring the province of Britain, the empire had nine emperors in thirty-three years, not one of whom died of natural causes. The emperor who celebrated the millenial anniversary of Rome with the great Secular Games of AD 248, Philippus Arabus, was an Arabian Praetorian prefect who had murdered his emperor in AD 244, and who was himself killed in battle the year after the Games while fighting his commander in Dacia. This permanent threat to the stability of the imperial government would have proved sufficiently crippling without the simultaneous rise of formidable new enemies beyond the frontiers: the Franks and Alemanni on the Rhine frontier, the Goths on the Danube, and the aggressive Sassanid Persian Empire in the east. By the 260s the legions had been proved totally inadequate to guarantee the security of the frontiers when all three sectors came under attack simultaneously. As the archaeologist knows, the third century was the time when the cities and towns of the empire suddenly began to build walls for their own protection.

The empire's nadir in the third century was reached in the reign of Gallienus (AD 259–68). The Goths broke through to the Aegean and ravaged Asia Minor. The legate Postumus set himself up as emperor in Gaul. King Odenathus and Queen Zenobia of Palmyra in Syria repelled a Persian attack on the eastern provinces, but when Odenathus died in AD 267 the whole of the east broke away from the impotent rule of Rome under the inspiring and above all efficient rule of Zenobia. Gallienus was finally killed by his own men while trying to capture Milan and eliminate the usurper Aureolus. The empire was saved from near-certain dissolution by a splendid succession of rulers from the Danubian provinces. The first of these was Claudius Gothicus (268–70) who owed his nickname to his destruction of the invading Goths at Nish in the Balkans (AD 269). Claudius' deputy, Aurelian (270–75), repelled an invasion of Italy by the Alamanni in 271 and gave Rome a splendid new set of walls – the ultimate proof, if any were needed, of how vulnerable the empire had become. He then embarked on one of the most difficult campaigns ever undertaken by an imperial Roman army: the reduction of the Palmyran Empire of Zenobia, which took from AD 271–73. Easily the most dangerous element in the Palmyran army was the use in mass of *cataphracts*, completely armoured in segmented plate and mail, riding armoured horses and carrying the long lance or *kontos*; and the siege of Palmyra itself was exceptionally difficult. The irony was that the Palmyran army was modelled on the best traditional Roman lines; but the effectiveness of its armoured cavalry was a revelation, and played a major part in the reconstruction of the Roman army in the fourth century. Aurelian's final achievement was the destruction of the short-lived 'empire' of Gaul in 274. But there was a price to pay for his

Diocletian (AD 284–305), one of the greatest of the later Roman soldier-emperors. He did his best to bequeath stability to the empire, dividing it into East and West, each ruled by an 'Augustus' with a trainee 'Caesar' as heir-apparent. But human nature and the selfishness of his successors proved too strong for his best intentions

reconstitution of the empire, and that price was the abandonment of Dacia as a Roman province. By the time Aurelian died in AD 275, the continental frontiers of the empire were once again those of Augustus: the Rhine and the Danube. In retrospect, given the baneful role played by the British pretenders of the fourth century, it would have been better if Aurelian had evacuated Britain as well, but this does not seem to have been considered even in passing. In any event, Britain was one of the few provinces of the western empire to have led a virtually trouble-free existence since the reconstruction carried out by Septimius Severus.

The emperor Diocletian (AD 284–305) made the last serious attempt to solve the empire's biggest weaknesses at the end of the third century AD: the succession and the excess weight of the imperial administration. The succession problem remained the old one: any successful general could oust a weak emperor. Diocletian divided the empire into east and west, each half ruled by an 'Augustus'. Each Augustus chose his own successor, or 'Caesar', and involved the Caesar in the work of running his half of the empire. This only worked once. Diocletian and his fellow Augustus, Maximian, dutifully abdicated in AD 305 and their Caesars (Galerius and Constantius) took over as Augusti. But the old problem only reappeared in a new form: nobody was content to be a Caesar. Eventually, under Constantine, the empire was reunited under a clinging bureaucracy and entered its last century of existence.

In the fourth century the last vestiges of the original provincial defence network vanished from sight. The frontiers were no longer defended by legions operating from fortified bases. Instead there were now light troops settled in the frontier regions, the *limitanei*, and the powerful field army under the emperor's command, the *palatini*, consisting of five cavalry regiments (*vexillationes palatinae*) and five infantry regiments (*legiones palatinae*). The emperor appointed his commanders-in-chief, or *magistri militum* – 'masters of the soldiers'. These held either cavalry command (*magister equitum*) or infantry command (*magister peditum*). Generals appointed to command both horse and foot were styled *magistri utriusque militae*. The magistri had under them about thirty-five *duces* or 'dukes', who commanded the frontier armies. The legions were never formally abolished but their manpower was halved in the efforts to create faster and more mobile infantry units. The dominant soldier of the fourth century AD was, however, the armoured or heavy cavalryman, for only the heavy cavalry units could now combine mass with mobility in moving from crisis-point to crisis-point with sufficient speed. The best of them were *cataphracts* on the Persian and Palmyran model. Auxiliary units were still recruited, as in the heyday of the empire two centuries before, but the auxiliaries of the late fourth century AD were very different from the efficient professionals who had won the battle of Mons Graupius for Agricola in AD 84. They were now, increasingly, no more than mercenary masses of barbarian warriors in Roman pay.

The concept of the mobile field army as the best guarantor of the empire's survival was perfectly sound, as was proved by the military achievements won under the last effective rulers of Constantine's line:

Constantius II (337–61) and Julianus (361–63). In the twenty-five years separating the death of Constantine in AD 337 from that of Julianus in 363, imperial troops were switched repeatedly between east and west, with Roman troops from the west joining in Rome's last serious venture in Mesopotamia. But most of those twenty-five years were spent in civil wars between the heirs and Constantine, with mutual frontier defence taking second place.

By the time Constantine died it had been obvious for nearly a century that the imperial frontiers had three permanent pressure-points: the Rhine and upper Danube (Franks and Alemanni), the lower Danube (Goths), and the east (Persians). Diocletian's division of the empire into east and west had not matched this triple threat, and neither did the cumbersome family share-out prescribed by Constantine. Even King Lear did better. The east went to Constantius II; Illyricum, Italy, and Africa to Constans; and the west to Constantinus II. But the lower Danube was carved off as a portion for Constantine's nephew Delmatius, while another nephew, Hanniballianus, was to rule north-eastern Asia Minor as 'King of Kings'.

Constantine's failure to accept military reality first proved fatal for his nephews. Both Delmatius and Hanniballianus were murdered by troops of the resentful army of the east within a year of Constantine's death by indignant troops of the army of the east. This left only two of Constantine's nephews alive: Gallus and Julianus. The west was then caught in the time-honoured cycle of futile waste. Constantinus tried to oust his brother Constans from the central provinces, only to be killed in battle at Aquileia in AD 340. Constans then took over as ruler of a temporarily united west until he perished in a mutiny ten years later. Magnentius, a German-born soldier, was elected to replace Constans, but Vetranio, commander in Illyria, refused to recognize Magnentius and proclaimed himself temporary emperor with the agreement of Constantius. Finally a lull in the sporadic frontier war with Persia allowed Constantius to come west with the pick of the eastern army and shatter Magnentius in battle at Mursa in AD 351.

The victorious army at Mursa represented the late imperial Roman army at its zenith. Constantius had diligently reconstructed the eastern army to incorporate the best ideas the east had to offer, foremost among them being large cataphract units and horsed archers. At Mursa, Constantius deployed his infantry legions in the centre and infantry missile troops behind the legions. Cataphracts held the inner flanks and horsed archers the outer flanks, with conventional light shield-and-javelin cavalry behind. The keynotes were armoured protection for horse and foot shock troops, missile power, and the mobility enjoyed by a strong cavalry element. But Mursa was a tragedy. Constantius was facing the best Gallic units from the west and the battle was a protracted killing-match, the most damaging misfortune possible for the imperial Roman army. The battle was dominated by the defeat of Magnentius' right wing and the successive erosion of his infantry centre by alternating cataphract charges and horsed archer attacks. Even after his victory – it cost 54,000 men, all of them prime troops – Constantius had to hunt Magnentius for two years before the latter finally killed himself in Gaul.

The image on which the survival of the empire depended by the fourth century AD: Roman heavy cavalry mowing down the barbarians. From the Arch of Constantine in Rome

Though ruler of a reunited empire, Constantius had to provide for the succession and he was forced to turn to his surviving cousins, Gallus and Julianus. Gallus, tested as a Caesar in the east, proved to be a bloody-minded tyrant and a public menace, and Constantius had to have him executed. Julianus, however, proved to be a model of efficiency in the west. He hurled the Alemanni out of Gaul and soon became, from Constantius' point of view, an alarmingly popular ruler and potential rival. When war with Persia broke out again in AD 360, Constantius tried to clip Julianus' wings by ordering the western army east. The men refused to go and forced Julianus to lead them into another civil war. In a bid to repeat the Mursa campaign of ten years earlier, Constantius was already heading west, when he died — thus making possible a smooth take-over of the empire by Julianus without further troop wastage.

Under Julianus, the mobile army showed its versatility again. In AD 363 he brought the Gallic legions east — this time without trouble — for an attempt to cripple Persia and win a lasting peace on the eastern frontier. He campaigned deep into Mesopotamia, but the plan misfired due to energetic countermeasures taken by the able Persian king, Shapur II. The Persians cut the Mesopotamian canals to create floods and scoured the country bare of supplies. By the time that Julianus was mortally wounded in action (June 363) the Roman army had already been forced to withdraw up the Tigris. The new emperor Jovianus made the so-called 'shameful peace' with Shapur, abandoning key frontier towns and Armenia to Persian control – but the peace extricated the Roman army from the danger of a second Carrhae, and guaranteed the empire's survival for the next fifteen years.

The mobile army perfected by Constantius II and Julianus carried the empire through another relapse into dynastic insecurity. Jovianus died within a year of the 'shameful peace' and the troops elected Valentinian. He returned to Diocletian's decision that the empire could not be ruled by one man. He entrusted his brother Valens with the east and turned his own attention to the strengthening of the west. Valentinian defeated the Franks and Alemanni and then sent a powerful expeditionary force across the Channel to save Britain, which had been all but overwhelmed by attacks from Picts, Scots, and raiders from across the North Sea. The Wall had gone, and both the leading military commanders in the island – the Duke of the Northern Marches and the Count of the Saxon Shore – had been killed in battle. Then, in 368, Valentinian despatched Count Theodosius with a picked mobile force from the western army. The victories of Theodosius were spectacular. He cleared the entire island of raiders, restored the Wall defences in the north, and raided the wild lands beyond, leaving the province in good order before withdrawing to Gaul.

The swift and economical restoration of Roman Britain was one of the brightest military achievements of the later empire, showing the benefits that the new army could bestow in avoiding long and costly campaigns. Speed was the essence of all Roman victories in the middle fourth century – 'Caesar-speed' brought up-to-date. But within seven years of the restoration of Britain a rapid succession of disasters began, with the rulers of east and west failing to achieve full co-ordination of their forces. The first of these defeats occurred in the east, when Valens rashly advanced against the Goths in Thrace with the eastern army alone. Instead of biding his time until his colleague Gratianus (who had succeeded Valentinian in AD 375) could come east with strong cavalry reinforcements, Valens attacked with the troops he had. On 9 August 378 he moved against the Gothic host outside the city of Adrianople. At first the Romans caught the Goths at a severe disadvantage, for the Gothic cavalry had departed on a massed foraging sweep – but they returned at precisely the right moment for a devastating charge against the Roman right flank. The irreplaceable cataphracts and horsed archers were wiped out or scattered. Denuded of cavalry cover, the foot legions died hard, but Adrianople destroyed a vital element in the Roman mobile defences.

Gratianus reacted by appointing Theodosius, restorer of Britain and the leading general of the west, to replace Valens (who had been burned alive when he sought shelter in a cottage, fleeing the rout at Adrianople). Theodosius bought off the Goths by settling them on Roman territory as nominal *federati*, thus sowing the seeds of inevitable trouble in the near future. There was little else he could do. The empire was now to be threatened by the last, most fatal provincial mutiny: the attempt in AD 383 by Magnus Maximus, commander in Britain, to conquer the empire for himself. For five years the fortunes of Maximus prospered, invaluable Roman troops were killed and the span of life left to the western empire was shortened. In 383 Maximus crossed to Gaul, defeating and killing Gratianus at Lugdunum (Lyons). Theodosius bought more time by recognizing Maximus. Four years later Maximus invaded northern Italy and expelled Valentinian II, only to be beaten and killed himself, by Theodosius, at Aquileia in the following year.

Valentinian II was restored as emperor of the west, but he only lasted until 392. He was then overthrown by his secretary Eugenius who became emperor behind the military power wielded by Count Arbogast, a Frankish federate commander. Theodosius finally disposed of this unholy partnership in September 394, defeating and killing Eugenius and Arbogast in the battle of the Frigidus river at the head of the Adriatic. For a year the empire enjoyed united rule again, but the mobile armies which alone made it viable had been destroyed – first at Adrianople, then in the civil wars of Maximus, Arbogast, and Eugenius. The last emperors of the west had no choice but to put their faith in the mass recruitment of barbarian mercenaries.

East and west parted company for the last time in 395, with Honorius ruling the west from Milan, and Arcadius the east from Constantinople. The Vandal leader Stilicho became *magister militum* to Honorius and undertook the defence of the West. In 396–7 Stilicho ejected the Visigothic leader Alaric from the Balkans, not by open battle but by negotiation. This earned a breathing-space in which to break the rebel Gildo in Africa, who had cut off the corn supply to Rome, in 398. In 402, at Pollentia, Stilicho blocked Alaric's invasion of northern Italy, and repeated the performance at Verona in 403. But in 405 Italy was invaded yet again, this time by Radagaisus of the Ostrogoths, with large contingents of Vandals, Alans, and Suevi. This menace was broken by Stilicho at Fiesole and Radagaisus was killed, but the victory only served to divert the barbarian tribes to the west.

The survivors of Radagaisus' invasion joined forces with the Siling Vandals east of the Rhine, and swarmed across the frozen winter in December 406. They flooded westward across Gaul, thus completing the dislocation of the western empire as a defensible unity. With Gaul overrun and Britain left to its own devices, Stilicho might have contrived to save Italy – but he was brought down by a fatal backlash of resentment and distrust at the imperial court. In 408 he was killed on the orders of Honorius, and hopes that Honorius could salvage something from the wreck were ruined by ill-judged massacres of the families of the federated troops which Stilicho had led. As a result the federates deserted to Alaric in a body and the precarious balance which Stilicho had maintained was never restored. Rome fell to Alaric in AD 410, and although a shadow of imperial government was maintained at Ravenna, the western empire never recovered. The last 'emperor of the west', a puppet ruler ironically bearing two symbolic names from the greatness

The empire at its height

By the end of the second century AD the empire had reached its fullest extent, and it was already clear that further conquests were beyond the capacity of the Roman army. Defence of the northern frontiers was now the major concern. The establishment and manning of *limes* – fixed military frontiers designed to slow up barbarian invasions in force, enabling a full concentration of strength to be brought to bear against the invaders – was the most notable preoccupation of

the second century. The most perfect example of a *limes* system to have survived is Hadrian's Wall in northern England (RIGHT) – not built as an impregnable rampart, but as a connected line of surveillance posts to make an undetected breach of the frontier impossible. This picture shows how the Wall made use of a natural escarpments and valleys. BELOW RIGHT: Part of the system which held the Empire together and speeded counterattacks – the Roman road at Wheeldale Moor in Yorkshire

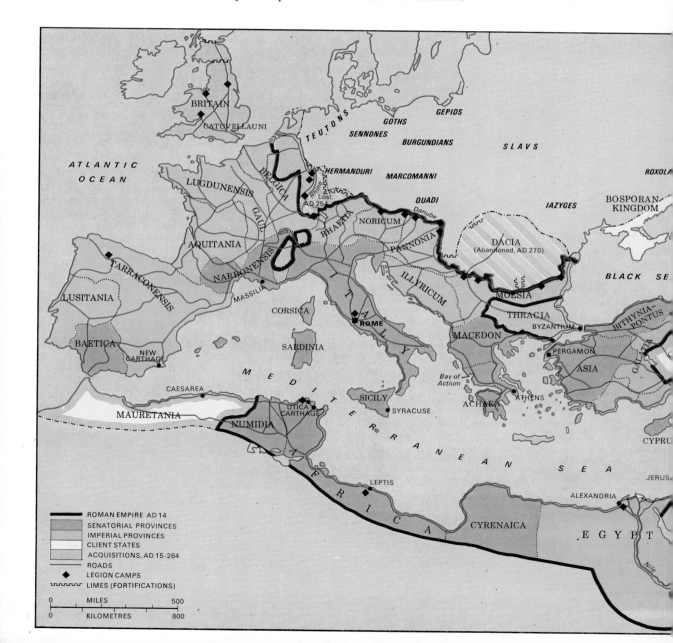

Legend:

- ROMAN EMPIRE AD 14
- SENATORIAL PROVINCES
- IMPERIAL PROVINCES
- CLIENT STATES
- ACQUISITIONS, AD 15–284
- ROADS
- ◆ LEGION CAMPS
- ⌇⌇⌇ LIMES (FORTIFICATIONS)

MILES 0 — 500
KILOMETRES 0 — 800

Military tombstones often yield valuable details of Roman army equipment. This is the monument to Rufus Sita of the Sixth Thracian Cohort (auxiliary cavalry), showing Sita riding down a barbarian

of Rome's past – Romulus Augustulus – was deposed by the Herulian warlord Odoacar, who now ruled in Italy as an independent king. In the east the empire not only survived but flourished, and under Justinian in the sixth century, reconquered Africa and Italy thanks to the military genius of Belisarius, one of the greatest 'Roman' generals of all time. Belisarius and his campaigns, however, fall outside the scope of this book, if only because of the historical conventions which place the age of Justinian in the 'Byzantine' rather than the 'late Roman' era.

Though the later Roman Empire did evolve a new type of army capable of defending the hard-pressed provinces of east and west, there were no margins for untimely defeats or dissensions between east and west, let alone outright civil war or usurpations. Thus the fall of the western empire in the fourth and fifth centuries was to a very large extent self-inflicted, the damage done by the revolt of Maximus being a case in point. Even the fateful defeat of Valens at Adrianople in AD 378 could have been avoided.

The bane of the Roman Empire, as of the later Republic beforehand, was military glory and the political power lying within reach of successful generals. The artful imperial constitution contrived by Augustus and his immediate successors meant that there could never be a fitting divorce between the imperial title and high military command. For over 300 years, Roman 'emperors' were either military commanders playing along with the pretence that their power was no more than an extraordinary magistracy, or nonentities tolerated by the army in the absence of a better man. A naked imperial monarchy, with crown jewels, court protocol, and all the trappings of imperial splendour, would have been far preferable to the uneasiness of the open secret that any tough general with enough loyal troops could make a successful bid for the title. As it happened, Aurelian, Diocletian, and Constantine did institute a formal monarchical style, with the emperor assuming divine status in his lifetime – a belated but useless attempt at stabilization.

Though the empire carried the seeds of its own destruction, the decisive element in the fall of the west was barbarian pressure from the north and east. This in turn was not merely a question of the empire going under to sheer weight of numbers. When Rome fell prey to the barbarians in the fifth century it was because the barbarian rulers had learned too much about Rome – her weaknesses included – either in Roman service or by study and imitation. The new kingdoms that grew up in the 'barbarian west' after the fifth century were not slow to ape Roman tradition, and this did not stop at the outward show of authority. Charlemagne of the Franks did not owe his power merely to reviving the title of Roman Emperor, holy or otherwise, but to the fighting capacity of his horsed troops and the 'Caesar-speed' with which he led them. This does not seem to have been a deliberate attempt at re-creation of Roman methods, but the result of a continuous tradition. The western empire died hard in the fifth century: it was not blown out like a candle-flame.

The origins of the Arthurian legend in Britain is a good example of how Roman tradition was still fighting for life in the sixth century across the Channel. The great chronicle of the invading Anglo-Saxons has a significant story to tell. After detailing the conquest of south-east England down to AD 495, there is a seventy-year gap before the next substantial defeats of the British are recorded. It is to this period that the legends of King Arthur and his 'knights' are traceable. Arthur can thus be 'reconstructed' with perfect credibility as a neo-Roman war leader, commanding an army of armoured cavalry in the late Roman style, and stopping the barbarian tide by a whole generation. Charlemagne, a mere two centuries later, can therefore hardly be considered as a revolutionary innovator.

The defeat of Rome's mobile army

BELOW: The later Roman Empire, showing the enormous pressure on the long nothern frontier from the third century AD. So much could have been accomplished under the Antonine emperors after Trajan's conquest of Dacia: if they had pushed the frontier north from the mouth of the Elbe south east to Dacia, the Rhine-Danube line would have been screened by a wide glacis of occupied German territory and the legions would have had a much shorter northern frontier to defend. But after this prospect faded with the death of Marcus

Aurelius (RIGHT) in 180 AD, the infantry legions and auxiliaries were left with a task beyond their ability. An end to the constant military coups and civil wars, plus a new army of heavy cavalry able to switch between east and west and seal one breach after the other in rapid succession, alone could have guaranteed the survival of the empire. Rome was never to enjoy the former condition but won several victories with her new cavalry until the disaster at Adrianople in 378. After Adrianople Rome had to rely on the uncertain loyalties of the *federati* — barbarian mercenaries recruited in bulk

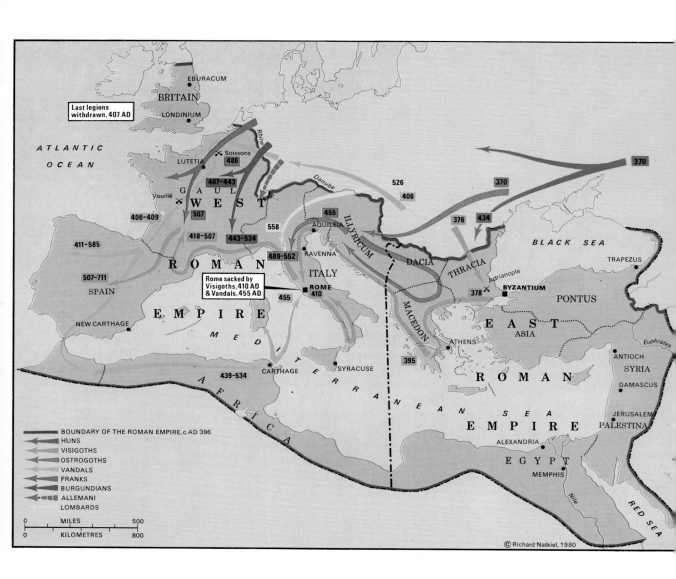

© Richard Natkiel, 1980

LEFT: He might have made the northern frontier permanently safe — statue of Marcus Aurelius in Rome. BELOW: Cavalry of the new army on which the later empire's security depended: light auxiliary (*left*) and heavy armoured cataphract (*right*)

EPILOGUE

The Legacy of Ancient Warfare

It is hard to generalize from the immense variety of warfare in the ancient period, and judge the level reached in the art of war by the fifth century AD. The fundamental lessons had been hammered out by hard experience, and were as true then as they are now, fourteen hundred years later. First and foremost was the truth that survival is impossible when an aggressive neighbour has better weapons and organization than you — the truth the cavemen knew. This has been regularly forgotten and painfully re-established down the ages.

Another enduring lesson, equally prone to be forgotten and rediscovered, was that the condition of military preparedness is never finite. A nation's weapons and military system are only as good as its neighbour's, as the Persians found to their cost when they tackled the Greeks. The much-used phrase 'military machine', though attractive, is a misnomer. Machines cannot evolve, but armies must if they are to avoid defeat by better organized and better equipped enemies who *have* evolved. This the Persians, the Greeks, and above all the Romans certainly discovered the hard way.

Of all the 'forgotten lessons' of war throughout the ancient period and after, one of the strangest must surely be that of the role of the mounted archer. With his ability to blend mobility with hitting-power at will, the mounted archer remains one of the rarest animals in military history. Conventional cavalry armed with spear and sword could be and was trained to perform the most elaborate drills — yet the archer on horseback, first brought to military perfection by the Assyrians, remained one of the simplest, one of the most devastating, yet at the same time one of the least-used 'weapons systems' before the development of the tank.

Five words perhaps enshrine the biggest lesson to be discovered by the ancients in their wars:

SIC VIS PACEM, PARA BELLUM

If you want peace, prepare for war. And, Vegetius might have added, understand it.

A detail from the Arch of
Constantine showing
Roman legionaries
attacking a city

Select Bibliography

GENERAL REFERENCE
Cambridge Ancient History (Cambridge University Press)
An Encyclopedia of World History ed. William L. Langer (Harrap)
The Times Atlas of World History (Times Books)

PRIMARY SOURCES
The Holy Bible (Revised Standard Version)
(All available in Penguin Classics):
Henry Bettinson and A. H. MacDonald, *Livy: Rome and the Mediterranean*
S. A. Handford, *Caesar: The Gallic War*
H. Mattingly, *Tacitus on Britain and Germany*
Jane F. Mitchell, *Caesar: The Civil War*
N. K. Sandars, *The Epic of Gilgamesh*
Aubrey de Sélincourt, *Arrian: The Campaigns of Alexander*; *Herodotus: The Histories*; *Livy: The Early History of Rome*; *Livy: The War with Hannibal*

Ian Scott-Kilvert, *Plutarch: The Age of Alexander*; *Plutarch: Makers of Rome*; *Plutarch: The Rise and Fall of Athens*
Rex Warner, *Plutarch: The Fall of the Roman Republic*; *Thucydides: The Peloponnesian War*; *Xenophon: The Persian Expedition*
G. A. Williamson, *Josephus: The Jewish War*

SECONDARY SOURCES (Troops, weapons, armour)
(Wargames Research Group publications):
Phil Barker, *Armies and enemies of Imperial Rome*; *Armies of the Macedonian and Punic Wars*
Alan Buttery, *Armies and Enemies of Egypt and Assyria*
Peter Connolly, *The Greek Armies* (Macdonald Educational); *The Roman Army* (Macdonald Educational)
Richard Nelson, *Armies of the Greek and Persian Wars*
H. Russell Robinson, *The Armour of Imperial Rome* (Arms & Armour Press)

Acknowledgments

Aerofilms: pp. 226, 227 (bottom).
British Museum: pp. 12, 117, 120–1 (both), 149, 162, 228, 229.
Peter Clayton: pp. 38 (both), 40–1, 49, 100, 165, 170, 181, 192 (both), 204, 207, 213, 221 (middle and right), 230, 244.
Department of the Environment: p. 243 (top).
C. M. Dixon: pp. 9, 232–3 (all), 243 (bottom), 248.
C. M. Dixon/British Museum: pp. 26–7 (all), 28, 31, 35, 91, 92–3.
Giraudon: p. 20 (right).
Sonia Halliday: p. 71.
Sonia Halliday/Archaeological Museum Istanbul: p. 158.
Harissiadis: p. 98.
Michael Holford: p. 146 (top).
Michael Holford/British Museum: pp. 16–7, 23, 59.
MacDonald Educational/Peter Connolly: pp. 142–3 (both), 198–9 (top), 222–3 (all).
Mansell Collection: pp. 15, 42–3 (bottom), 61, 88, 225 (top).

J. G. Moore/British Museum: p. 87.
Photoresources: pp. 6, 42–3 (top), 78–9 (all), 104, 105, 110 (top), 147 (bottom), 151, 178, 197, 225 (bottom right), 237.
Photoresources/British Museum: p. 85.
Radio Times Hulton Picture Library: pp. 22 (top), 32, 32–3, 76, 94–5, 101, 125, 127, 129, 155, 184, 190–1, 205, 208 (left), 225 (bottom left), 235, 239.
Ronald Sheridan: pp. 19, 25 (left), 36, 51, 54, 57, 65 (left), 73, 74, 102, 106–7 (all), 109, 110 (bottom), 112, 114–15, 122 (bottom), 130–1, 136, 138, 139, 147 (top), 156, 172, 174, 179, 187 (both), 188, 208 (right), 210, 216 (both), 247 (top).
Ronald Sheridan/Churchill Museum: p. 221.
Wadsworth Atheneum: p. 123 (right).
Roger Wood: p. 39.

Picture research: Jonathan Moore
Maps and diagrams: Richard Natkiel
Figure artwork: Richard Scollins

Index

Entries in italics refer to illustrations